The Stone Roses

War and Peace

SIMON SPENCE

Photography by
Dennis Morris, Lena Kag[illegible]
and Su[illegible]

VIKING

an imprint of

PENGUIN BOOKS

VIKING

Published by the Penguin Group
Penguin Books Ltd, 80 Strand, London WC2R ORL, England
Penguin Group (USA) Inc., 375 Hudson Street, New York, New York 10014, USA
Penguin Group (Canada), 90 Eglinton Avenue East, Suite 700, Toronto, Ontario, Canada M4P 2Y3
(a division of Pearson Penguin Canada Inc.)
Penguin Ireland, 25 St Stephen's Green, Dublin 2, Ireland (a division of Penguin Books Ltd)
Penguin Group (Australia), 250 Camberwell Road, Camberwell, Victoria 3124, Australia
(a division of Pearson Australia Group Pty Ltd)
Penguin Books India Pvt Ltd, 11 Community Centre, Panchsheel Park, New Delhi – 110 017, India
Penguin Group (NZ), 67 Apollo Drive, Rosedale, Auckland 0632, New Zealand
(a division of Pearson New Zealand Ltd)
Penguin Books (South Africa) (Pty) Ltd, Block D, Rosebank Office Park,
181 Jan Smuts Avenue, Parktown North, Gauteng 2193, South Africa

Penguin Books Ltd, Registered Offices: 80 Strand, London WC2R ORL, England

www.penguin.com

First published 2012
001

Set in 12/14.75pt Dante MT Std
Typeset by Jouve (UK), Milton Keynes
Printed in Great Britain by Clays Ltd, St Ives plc

A CIP catalogue record for this book is available from the British Library

HARDBACK ISBN: 978-0-670-92099-0
TRADE PAPERBACK ISBN: 978-0-670-92181-2

www.greenpenguin.co.uk

ALWAYS LEARNING   **PEARSON**

24.50

The Stone Roses
War and Peace

Based on 400 hours of interviews with over seventy of The Stone Roses'
closest associates, including six former band members, *War and Peace*
is the first major biography of the band that defined a generation.
Originally planned in collaboration with Reni, the reclusive drummer,
this book had been a year in the making when the Roses, against all odds,
announced their re-formation.

It is a remarkable coda to an astonishing story of a band like no other. In
1989 their debut album and the single 'Fools Gold' made them the most
exciting British export since the Sex Pistols. With their incendiary aura
the Roses became figureheads of the 'Madchester' movement.

War and Peace traces the band's genesis, studded with violent gigs and
abandoned recordings, and shaped by their infamous manager, Gareth
Evans. As their jeans grew wider and their songs more anthemic, the
Roses' legendary gigs culminated in the era-defining Spike Island show
in 1990. From this pinnacle the unravelling was spectacular. With the band
refusing to play in America, arrested for vandalizing a record company
and dragged through the High Court, the epic recording of their dark
second album is the stuff of legend. They disbanded in turmoil in 1996.

Since then the Roses myth has grown even bigger. 'I Wanna Be Adored',
'She Bangs the Drums', 'Waterfall', 'This Is the One' and 'I Am the
Resurrection' have become national anthems, and their first
album is widely recognized as one of the best ever made.

But the true story behind their rise and fall – and resurrection – has
never been told. Until now. From the Manchester backwaters
to the worldwide 2012 tour, *War and Peace* lays bare the irresistible
tale of the last of the great bands.

ABOUT THE AUTHOR

Simon Spence collaborated with Rolling Stones manager Andrew Loog Oldham on the acclaimed memoirs *Stoned* and *2Stoned*. He has written for the *NME*, *i-D*, *Dazed & Confused* and the *Independent*. He was at the Stone Roses' legendary Blackpool and Alexandra Palace shows in 1989 and covered their seminal Spike Island show for *The Face*.

To Thalia, Theo and Sylvie

'Revolution is not "showing" life to people, but bringing them to life. A revolutionary organization must always remember that its objective is not getting its adherents to listen to convincing talks by expert leaders, but getting them to speak for themselves, in order to achieve, or at least strive toward, an equal degree of participation.'

Guy Debord, *Situationist International* (1961)

Contents

Contents

Photography

This book includes forty previously unseen photographs from Dennis Morris, Lena Kagg Ferrero and Sue Dean.

Dennis Morris shot to fame as a teenager photographing Bob Marley between 1973 and 1981, before taking iconic shots of John Lydon and the Sex Pistols. In 1985 Martin Hannett, then producing The Stone Roses, tried to convince the band to collaborate with Morris to develop their 'look' – a plan that was abandoned when Morris and John Squire didn't hit it off. But Ian Brown and Reni kept in contact with him. The photographs in this book were taken during informal sessions from 1989 to 1995.

Lena Kagg Ferrero followed the Roses on their 1985 tour of Sweden with Toxin Toy. Her photographs of the Roses had been stored for more than twenty-five years in the loft of her father's house. They are the rarest early shots of the band.

Sue Dean was a well-known face on the Manchester scene in the 1980s, and for a couple of years was the girlfriend of the Roses' manager Gareth Evans. She was the only photographer to capture the Roses consistently throughout their lost years of 1986, 1987 and 1988.

The never-seen-before ephemera from this period was supplied from the archives of Howard Jones, manager of The Stone Roses from 1984 to 1986. Producer John Leckie also supplied private paperwork, as did Jive/Zomba's Steven Howard.

1. Garner, Brown and Couzens on tour bus, Sweden, 1985 © Lena Kagg Ferrero.
2. Squire, Brown, Garner, Reni and Jones on tour bus, Sweden, 1985 © Lena Kagg Ferrero.

3. Couzens and Brown on stage, Sweden, 1985 © Lena Kagg Ferrero.
4. Squire and Garner on stage, Sweden, 1985 © Lena Kagg Ferrero.
5. Couzens, Brown, Squire and Garner on stage, Sweden, 1985 © Lena Kagg Ferrero.
6. Couzens, Brown, Reni and Squire on stage, Sweden, 1985 © Lena Kagg Ferrero.
7. Reni and Brown on stage, Sweden, 1985 © Lena Kagg Ferrero.
8. Thin Line advert for 1985 Swedish tour. Courtesy of Howard Jones.
9. Garner, Reni, Brown and Squire on tour, Sweden, 1985 © Lena Kagg Ferrero.
10. Thin Line press release for 'So Young' / 'Tell Me', 1985, p.1. Courtesy of Howard Jones.
11. Thin Line press release for 'So Young' / 'Tell Me', 1985, p.2. Courtesy of Howard Jones.
12. Thin Line advert, 1985. Courtesy of Howard Jones.
13. Thin Line advert for 'So Young' / 'Tell Me', 1985. Courtesy of Howard Jones.
14. 'So Young' / 'Tell Me' single label detail, 1985. Courtesy of Howard Jones.
15. Ticket for Warehouse 1, 1985. Courtesy of Howard Jones.
16. The Patrol, 1980 © Sue Dean.
17. Squire, Brown and Garner in rehearsal, 1987 © Sue Dean.
18. Brown in rehearsal, 1987 © Sue Dean.
19. Squire, Garner and Brown on stage, 1987 © Sue Dean.
20. Brown on stage, 1986 © Sue Dean.
21. Reni on stage, 1986 © Sue Dean.
22. Reni on stage, 1987 © Sue Dean.
23. Brown and his tattoo, 1988 © Sue Dean.
24. Mani in 1987 © Sue Dean.
25. The Roses at Warehouse 2, 1985 © Sue Dean.
26. Mani, John Leckie and Brown outside the International II, 1988 © Sue Dean.

27. Mani, Gareth Evans and Tim Booth outside the International II, 1988 © Sue Dean.
28. Garner, Squire, Reni and Brown signing the contract, 1987 © Sue Dean.
29. Band contact list. Courtesy of Howard Jones.
30. Mani, Brown, Squire and Reni studio shot, 1989 © Dennis Morris.
31. Reni, Squire, Mani and Brown studio shot, 1989 © Dennis Morris.
32. Fax from John Leckie, p. 1. Courtesy of John Leckie.
33. Fax from John Leckie, p. 2. Courtesy of John Leckie.
34. Fans at Spike Island, 1990 © Dennis Morris.
35. Dressing room at Spike Island, 1990 © Dennis Morris.
36. Crowd shot, Spike Island, 1990 © Dennis Morris.
37. Squire and Brown on stage, Spike Island, 1990 © Dennis Morris.
38. Brown on stage, Spike Island, 1990 © Dennis Morris.
39. Brown on stage, Spike Island, 1990 © Dennis Morris.
40. Squire on stage, Glasgow Green, 1990 © Dennis Morris.
41. Reni on stage, Glasgow Green, 1990 © Dennis Morris.
42. Brown on stage, Spike Island, 1990 © Dennis Morris.
43. Glasgow Green, 1990 © Dennis Morris.
44. Cressa, Brown and Reni on stage, Glasgow Green, 1990 © Dennis Morris.
45. Reni, Mani, Squire and Brown on stairwell, Dennis Morris's studio, 1994 © Dennis Morris.
46. John Leckie's post-resignation fax, p. 1. Courtesy of John Leckie.
47. John Leckie's post-resignation fax, p. 2. Courtesy of John Leckie.
48. Brown in Morris's studio, 1994 © Dennis Morris.
49. Mani in Morris's studio, 1994 © Dennis Morris.
50. Squire in Morris's studio, 1994 © Dennis Morris.
51. Reni in Morris's studio, 1994 © Dennis Morris.
52. The band in Morris's studio, 1994 © Dennis Morris.

Cast

Principal characters in order of appearance

Phil Jones: *concert promoter, Alexandra Palace and Spike Island*

Gareth Evans: *manager of The Stone Roses and owner of the International and International II clubs*

Ian Brown (nickname IBEX): *singer, The Stone Roses*

Matthew Cummins (RIP): *Evans's business partner, co-manager of The Stone Roses and co-owner of the International clubs*

Paul Oakenfold: *DJ at Alexandra Palace and Spike Island*

Dave Haslam: *author; DJ at Blackpool Empress Ballroom, Alexandra Palace and Spike Island*

Dave Booth: *DJ at Blackpool Empress Ballroom and Spike Island*

Reni (Alan Wren): *drummer, The Stone Roses*

Adrian Sherwood: *producer; remixed 'One Love' and support act at Spike Island*

Philip Hall (RIP): *press officer, The Stone Roses, and the band's manager in 1993*

John Squire (often Johnny): *guitarist, The Stone Roses*

Stephen 'Cressa' Cresser: *The Stone Roses' road crew and on-stage vibes*

Mani (Gary Mounfield): *bassist, The Stone Roses*

Peter Hook: *Joy Division and New Order; producer of 'Elephant Stone'*

Steve Lock: *Granada TV producer, filmed Alexandra Palace*

Roddy McKenna: *A&R at Jive/Zomba*

Kevin Cummins: NME *photographer*

Si Wolstencroft: *original drummer in The Stone Roses, 1983–4*

Pete Garner: *original bass player in The Stones Roses, 1983–7*

Andy Couzens: *original guitarist in The Stones Roses, 1983–6*

Pennie Smith: NME *photographer, The Stone Roses' photographer*

Mensi (Thomas Mensforth): *lead singer, Angelic Upstarts*

Cast

Mike Phoenix: *scooterboy and founder of the Twisted Wheel SC club*
Johnny Poland: *scooterboy and style influence*
Johnny Bolland: *scooterboy and manufacturer of the Stone Roses T-shirts*
Kaiser (David Carty): *scooterboy and singer, The Waterfront*
Chris Goodwin: *drummer, The Waterfront*
Michelle 'Mitch' Davitt: *Ian Brown's partner*
Sue Dean: *photographer and girlfriend of Gareth Evans*
Rob Hampson: *scooterboy and bassist in The Stone Roses, 1987*
Geno Washington: *soul sensation and life coach*
John Breakell: *owner of Spirit Studios*
Caroline Reed: *first manager of The Stone Roses, 1984*
Tony Wilson (RIP): *co-founder of Factory Records*
Garry Johnson: Sounds *writer and band champion*
Howard Jones: *manager of The Stones Roses, 1984–6*
Tim Chambers: *co-founder of Thin Line Records*
Martin Hannett (RIP): *producer; co-founder of Thin Line Records*
Steve 'Adge' Atherton: *The Stone Roses' tour manager*
Tony Michaelides: *DJ, Piccadilly Radio, Manchester*
Paula Greenwood: *Piccadilly Radio/Piccadilly Records and PR at the International clubs*
Bob Dickinson: *journalist, Manchester*
Andreas Kemi: The Eye *magazine, Swedish tour promoter*
Toxin Toy (Harald Sickenga, Micke Mürhoff, Anette Svensson and Christian Adelöv): *co-headliners of Swedish tour*
Glen Greenough (RIP): *The Stone Roses' first roadie*
Lena Kagg: *photographer on Swedish tour*
Clive Jackson: *singer with Doctor & The Medics*
Slim (Paul Haley): *The Stone Roses' road crew*
Martin Pendergast ('Little Martin'): *Haçienda DJ and 'Baldrick'*
Al Smith: *'Baldrick' and The Stone Roses' road crew*
Phil Saxe: *source of flared jeans, 1983–4, and manager of the Happy Mondays*
Chris Nagle: *engineer for Martin Hannett*
Dennis Morris: *photographer, artist, stylist and club runner*

xvi

Cast

Helen Plaumer: *John Squire's partner*

Dougie James: *soul singer, club runner and original owner of the International*

Roger Eagle (RIP): *booker at the International*

Stephen Lea: *lawyer, acting for Andy Couzens and The Stone Roses*

Dave Roberts: *A&R at FM Revolver/Heavy Metal Records*

Paul Birch: *owner of FM Revolver/Heavy Metal Records*

Simon Machan ('Big Simon'): *The Stone Roses' road crew, live sound*

Lindsay Reade: *co-manager of The Stone Roses, 1987–8*

Geoff Travis: *founder of Rough Trade Records*

Ian Tilton: Sounds *photographer, The Stone Roses' photographer*

Steven Howard: *managing director of Jive Records and Zomba Music Publishing*

Clive Calder: *founder of Jive/Zomba*

Geoff Howard: *Gareth Evans's lawyer and The Stone Roses' legal representative*

John Leckie: *producer of* The Stone Roses, *'Fools Gold', 'One Love' and* Second Coming

Andrew Lauder: *manager of Silvertone Records*

Lawrence Stewart: *engineer at Coconut Grove Studios*

Paul Schroeder: *producer and engineer on* The Stone Roses, *'Fools Gold', 'One Love' and* Second Coming

Chris Donnelly: *co-founder of Gio-Goi*

Anthony Donnelly: *co-founder of Gio-Goi*

Gareth Davies: *The Stone Roses' radio and TV plugger*

Phil Smith: *The Stone Roses' road crew*

Chris 'The Piss' Griffiths: *The Stone Roses' road crew*

Greg Lewerke: *Gareth Evans's American manager and de facto The Stone Roses' American manager*

Nigel Kerr: *booking agent, The Stone Roses*

Jon Brookes: *drummer, The Charlatans*

Tim Vigon: *creator of* Made of Paper, *the Stone Roses fanzine*

'The Bobs': *Eileen Mulligan, Shirley McGurrin and sisters Colette and Theresa Shryane*

Bruce Mitchell: *founder of Manchester Light & Stage Company*

Geoff Wonfor: *film-maker, videos for Blackpool, 'Fools Gold' and 'I Wanna Be Adored'*

Keith Jobling: *The Bailey Brothers, Factory-affiliated film-makers*

Joe Bloggs: *Bushra Ahmed and Shami Ahmed, Manchester fashion company*

Anthony Boggiano: *manager of Inspiral Carpets*

Barry Weiss: *manager of New York offices of Zomba*

Michael Tedesco: *The Stone Roses' American A&R at Zomba*

Bruce Flohr: *radio plugger at RCA*

Robbie Snow: *product manager at RCA*

Mark Furman: *Jive/Zomba business affairs*

John Fruin (RIP): *Jive/Zomba senior management*

John Kennedy: *The Stone Roses' lawyer*

David Geffen: *owner of Geffen Records*

Eddie Rosenblatt: *president of Geffen Records*

Gary Gersh: *A&R at Geffen Records*

Steve Jenkins: *general manager of Jive Records*

Maurice Oberstein (RIP): *managing director of PolyGram*

Patrick Savage: *The Stone Roses' accountant at OJ Kilkenny*

Simon Crompton: *acid house producer*

Brian Pugsley: *engineer on* Second Coming

Trevor Taylor: *owner of Square One Studios*

Tom Zutaut: *A&R at Geffen Records*

Mark Tolle: *producer on* Second Coming *(Manor Park Studios)*

Al 'Bongo' Shaw: *engineer on* Second Coming *(Manor Park Studios)*

Simon Dawson: *engineer/producer on* Second Coming *(Rockfield Studios)*

Peter Leake: *band manager*

Bill Price: *producer/mixer on* Second Coming

Terri Hall: *press officer, The Stone Roses*

Doug Goldstein: *manager of The Stone Roses, 1994–5*

Bryn Bridenthal: *head of PR at Geffen Records*

Sophie Muller: *video-maker, 'Ten Storey Love Song'*

Robbie Maddix: *drummer, The Stone Roses, 1995–6*

Cast

Susanne Filkins: *A&R at Geffen Records*
Nigel Ipinson-Fleming: *keyboards, The Stone Roses, 1995–6*
Noel Walters: *Ian Brown's bodyguard*
Martell Prince: *The Stone Roses' bodyguard*
Aziz Ibrahim: *guitarist, The Stone Roses, 1996*
John Nuttall: *Reni's manager*
Simon Moran: *promoter; manager of The Stone Roses, 2011–*

Prologue

It was 4 January 1990 and the snow was blowing in off the River Mersey as concert promoter Phil Jones surveyed the Spike Island landscape. Stood beside him, grinning broadly, was The Stone Roses' manager Gareth Evans, who just before Christmas had made an application to the local council to hold a one-off gig on the island. The site seemed massive and a bit surreal to Jones, and he warned Evans it would be a huge undertaking to get the application agreed by the Licensing Authority and the police. But Jones agreed that if it came off it was going to be a totally unique event – which was exactly what the band wanted.

Evans and Jones had searched for weeks for a suitable location to put on such a show, one that would surpass the Roses' night on 18 November at Alexandra Palace in London. While the band had been left under-awed by that gig, the numbers had given Jones confidence. He'd sold 7,500 tickets for Alexandra Palace and estimated he could easily have shifted three times that number. Acid house and rave had opened up a world of possibilities. Through 1989 organizers like Sunrise, Energy and Biology had set up a series of raves in ad hoc countryside locations close to London, with attendances estimated at between 20,000 and 30,000.

No guitar band had pulled off anything close in size or style to these headline-grabbing raves. But the Roses believed they could. Evans and Jones had spent some time fruitlessly scouring the area around the Thames Estuary in Essex. 'You could have done amazing gigs at any of the places we visited but they had nothing there,' Jones recalled. 'Some were just quarries or abandoned caravan parks that were quite near to water.' In the summer the pair had organized a tour of seaside resorts for the Roses, and although it had been ultimately abandoned the idea had culminated in the band's epochal show at the Empress Ballroom in Blackpool. Putting on a gig close to water still dominated their thoughts.

Spike Island was only fourteen miles from Evans's Cheshire farmhouse and less than seven from Warrington, the town where Ian Brown was born. 'Spikey', as it is known locally, is an almond-shaped, man-made island the size of ten football pitches, situated on the north bank of the Mersey Estuary and separated from the industrial town of Widnes by the Sankey Canal. In the late nineteenth century Spike Island had been the birthplace of the British chemical industry and a thriving industrial hub. By the mid-twentieth century the site had degenerated into an eyesore: a toxic wasteland of rusting factories, rail lines, abandoned canal and industrial dockage. Between 1975 and 1982 the island had been reclaimed as green space, but in 1989, despite Halton Borough Council's best efforts, the landscape still bore the dark smears of heavy industry. Vast, foreboding modern factories dotted the horizon, including the mammoth Imperial Chemical Industries (ICI) factory where caustic soda and chlorine were manufactured among huddles of fat chimneys belching out acrid smoke.

For Ian Brown, the location was ideal. 'We wanted to do a gig on an industrial estate or an island. Because [Spike Island] was cut off and had been used for the Widnes Carnival before, it was spot on. Plus we wanted to play in the North-West, and because it was in the middle of Manchester and Liverpool it was perfect.' Crucially for the Roses, it continued their policy of eschewing the traditional rock 'n' roll circuit.

What Evans and Jones had in mind for Spike Island, however, far exceeded the parameters of the local annual festival held there. They were intent on attracting a crowd of 32,500, a figure that roughly equated to half the population of Widnes. The magnitude of what they were proposing would require thorough planning and large-scale construction, including the building of bridges, as the island presently only had one access point. They were also uncertain how the Licensing Authority would react to the idea of Halton Borough Council hosting what would in effect be the country's largest rave to date. The widespread drug use at raves was front-page news, and hastily passed new laws had encouraged increasingly brutal crackdowns on the events, with unedifying TV footage of police, often in full riot gear, clashing with ravers.

The Roses were the British band most closely identified with this insurrection. Since their Blackpool show in August they had been on an unstoppable upward curve. The Alexandra Palace gig in November had coincided with the release of their hit single 'Fools Gold'. After five years of effort, the Roses had arrived at a sound and look that had seen them elected as figureheads of a musical phenomenon dubbed 'Madchester'. It was a scene that posited Manchester as the UK's rave capital and swathed the Roses in an incendiary aura. Brown had fanned these flames with talk of revolution and his desire to see dead, by his own hands if necessary, the Queen, her mother and Prince Charles.

All of this and more had made the Roses the hottest, most notorious band in the world. Expectations for the group – who had declared an interest in playing a gig on the moon – could not have been greater. Yet, as Evans and Jones began to work their considerable charms on the licensing magistrates to allow for the Roses' crowning moment, the band began their spectacular unravelling, which ironically would only further entrench their anti-establishment reputation.

On 30 January 1990 they vandalized the offices of FM Revolver, the label with whom they had recorded their 1987 single 'Sally Cinnamon'. They were arrested the following day and charged with criminal damage, cutting short attempts to record new material. The highly publicized case would drag on until October, with jail time a definite threat. Behind the scenes, as yet unreported, the Roses were also becoming increasingly hostile towards their current record label, Jive/Zomba. Contract renegotiations had begun but the end game was far from certain. Both these situations, coupled with their new-found fame post-'Fools Gold', aggravated an underlying malaise at the heart of the band. They had no new songs.

The announcement of the Spike Island event, advertised as

'Sunset Sunday', served as a welcome distraction from the band's doubts over their creativity, livelihood and liberty. A licence had been granted to allow the show to go ahead on Sunday, 27 May 1990, the day before a bank holiday Monday: 'It was the coaches that did it,' said Jones. The licensing magistrates' main concern hadn't been ravers, drugs or the counterculture sentiment the band oozed, it had simply been how to get all those people in and out of Widnes. 'We said, Your honour, we're going to bus them in,' Jones recalled. Matthew Cummins, Evans's business partner and the often over-looked man in the Roses' management set-up, had come up with the idea to sublet the event to a sole coach contractor. In April, following a single advert in the *NME* listing the towns from where coach trips were available, the event sold out.

With the eyes of 32,500 fans and the world's media soon to be upon them, a series of warm-up dates for Spike Island were seen as essential for the Roses. The band had not played live since Alexandra Palace six months ago. It showed. On 15 May Brown bewildered his band mates at a small venue in Copenhagen by taunting the audience repeatedly with the refrain, 'What're yer doing?' The following night in Lund, Sweden, the Roses arrived on stage an hour late to play to an audience of 700. Brown, again, performed churlishly – like a 'bored, lazy, snotty twat', he later said. The next night in Stockholm, a city dear to the Roses as the base for a band-defining 1985 tour, the 3,000-strong audience saw the band recapture some of their elan and sure-footed magnificence. Post-gig, the tour bus vibrated to the sounds of The Misunderstood, the Stones, The Byrds and The Beatles.

Amid the revelry, there was no escaping the sense the Roses were as frayed at the hems as their famously voluminous jeans. Commenting on the criminal damage case, one of the Roses' road crew was quoted in *Q* as saying, 'It might not be a bad idea to send them down, at least they might go and write some new songs.' The recording and mixing of a new single, 'One Love', intended to co-incide with Spike Island, had already dragged on for months and would not be released until July. After a final warm-up show in Oslo on 19 May, the Roses returned to Manchester for the gig on which all their cards were now stacked.

Over the next six days, in glorious sunshine, Roger Barrett's Star Hire team constructed one of the biggest stages ever built, put up the security fencing, the hospitality areas, and with the aid of the Royal Engineers built the bridges over the Sankey. No expense was spared on the extravagant stage lighting. The involvement of experienced industry events specialists Star Hire had allayed any lingering fears the local council had. On Evans's insistence the facilities expanded to include a VIP area and a helicopter pad, as he intended to chopper in the band. 'Gareth was very flamboyant with the whole thing,' recalled Jones.

The band found themselves with little control over proceedings. Tensions had already surfaced over the pricing of the Spike Island tickets. The Roses had argued with Evans to lower the £14 price, and some tickets had been reduced to £13, but the band had no way of enforcing this. The ticket sales had generated approximately £400,000, the same amount the event was costing to put on, according to Brown, who told the press, 'We're getting nish [nothing].'

There was, however, money to be made – and a lot of it – on merchandising. That was controlled by Evans and Cummins, and it was no secret the pair were wildly unaccountable over this aspect of the Roses' career. The company that produced the Roses T-shirts, New Line Promotions, were under the impression that for every 1,000 T-shirts they made officially, another 500 would be manufactured for unofficial purposes. Until now the band had shrugged off concerns over this. In the run-up to Spike Island, however, the Roses had suggested using an alternative outfit to control the merchandising for the event. Evans had gone against their wishes, and New Line Promotions were now producing thousands upon thousands of the popular Roses T-shirts for Spike Island.

Evans had also negotiated a £100,000 deal with Central Music to film Spike Island. The company planned to screen the show on British Sky Broadcasting and Central TV, and had set up an eight-camera shoot and an outside broadcast vehicle on site. The band were unhappy with this arrangement and, artistically, they were concerned that they may not deliver a great performance. The Roses felt if the show sounded as bad as Alexandra Palace and was broadcast in America, it would dampen the demand growing for them there. Typically, they struggled to make a firm decision on the matter, and left Evans and Central Music hanging in the wind until the day when they insisted they would rather cancel than be filmed.

There was last-minute confusion over the support acts and running order for the event as communications between the band and Evans faltered. The Roses had made it plain they didn't want it to be a Madchester festival. 'The Happy Mondays, that sort of stuff, was definitely out,' Jones recalled. The DJs that had supported the band at Blackpool and Alexandra Palace – Balearic innovator Paul Oakenfold, Haçienda DJ Dave Haslam and Manchester psychedelic favourite Dave Booth – were confirmed. Reni wanted a drum-based support act to feature too, and so the drum orchestra of the 'Lion King of Zimbabwe', Thomas Mapfumo – a Bob Marley figure in his home country and an outspoken critic of Robert Mugabe's government – was booked. Adrian Sherwood's On-U Sound System, featuring former Public Image bassist Jah Wobble and singer Gary Clail, were also set to play.

Evans had been scratching around as late as two weeks before for further entertainment. Barrie K. Sharpe, whose 'The Masterplan' was the hot club record of the moment, turned him down. Pioneering Chicago house DJ Frankie Knuckles was also suggested; he was revered by Manchester tastemakers, and would give the event club credentials. Evans, unfortunately, mistakenly called a different American DJ named Frankie. He booked Frankie Bones, who had played at the massive 1989 Energy event. Bones may have been the 'Godfather of American rave culture' but he lacked the cachet and finesse of Knuckles.

The day before, close to a hundred representatives of the world's press gathered for a press conference at the Piccadilly Hotel in Manchester. The event was stage-managed by the Roses' trusted PR man Philip Hall, who had persuaded them that this was the only way to deal with the massive media interest Spike Island had generated. Evans wanted the Roses to use the conference as a platform to attack the 'anything goes as long as it makes money' chemical industry and to make a stand against pollution. He wanted to speak at the conference himself, but John Squire firmly told Evans it was a no.

Muzzling Evans was easier said than done. He saw the opportunity to make money out of the press conference and asked the BBC and ITV national news crews to pay to attend. Even when it was pointed out to him this was an absurd demand, he would not back down and refused them free access. As a result the event was denied slots on the national news. Those that did find themselves inside the buzzing hotel conference room would never forget it. The press pack was split between those who adored the band and those who were deeply cynical about them. Parisian and Japanese journalists were in the former camp and asked reverential questions. They were interrupted by local stand-up comedian Caroline Aherne. The band knew her but pretended they didn't, playing along with her assertion that she was a journalist. 'I'd like to ask what I think is a really important question as well. What's your favourite colour?' There was tumbleweed silence among the media as the Roses stifled their laughter.

The Roses answered a few more questions politely but dismissed others out of hand, with Brown challenging the press to come up with better lines of enquiry. Already uncomfortable at being there, the band found being worshipped like this embarrassing and their answers grew more flippant and defensive. It appeared to many now that the band was on some sort of colossal wind-up. Frank Owen, reporting for American magazine *Details*, took the bait: 'You're behaving like pigs to these people. It's the whole Manchester sarcasm shit. These people come all this way and you won't answer the questions properly.'

'I think you've got the right stick but the wrong end,' said Brown. A member of the band's crew interjected, 'How do you think the band feel sat up there in complete silence with all you bastards staring at them, asking them fuck all? You come all this way, drink all the free beer and haven't asked shit. You're a bunch of wankers in whatever language you speak.' A journalist from the *NME* passed a spliff onto the small raised stage, and some bloke who was already out of his head hijacked a microphone to protest at the arrest of a pal the night before. Brown encouraged him to speak: 'That's right, you tell them.' Journalists from the *Daily Mail* and *Rolling Stone* were aghast as the bloke went on with his rant. From there, the conference descended into the type of confrontational and chaotic farce that could only serve to enhance the Roses' reputation. Some local chancer took the opportunity to ask Brown about the tickets he'd promised 'our kid'. Reni told him not worry, saying, 'We'll sort you out and your mum.' It was hardly the sort of announcement the media were expecting. Evans rubbed his hands in glee; Hall smiled beatifically; the band trudged off.

The same day the Roses loaded their equipment from their rehearsal space at the International II club, a venue owned by Evans and Cummins, and jumped in the van to go to the soundcheck. Brown strolled around the site, happily chatting to gangs of local kids hanging about. When the police approached to warn the kids they shouldn't be there, Brown grew agitated and had to be dragged away by a crew member. The organization of the event seemed to be slipping away from the band, and this, together with the disappointing press conference and the confusion over merchandising and support acts, added to a sense of foreboding that afternoon that Spike Island might become more Altamont than Woodstock. Hundreds of locals had already signed a petition in an attempt to have the gig cancelled, barges had been driven down the canal to try to knock down access bridges, and the drinks licence had only just been reinstated after having been revoked at short notice.

However, the band's mood eventually lightened. The stage was vast and impressive, raised fifteen feet from the ground. The expensive lighting system hung like a giant mechanical spider above Reni's drum kit, and huge white backdrops on which images of Squire's artwork could be projected framed the band as they soundchecked. Here they were masters of their own destiny. As the band's roadie

Stephen 'Cressa' Cresser grooved behind Squire, the four musicians slowly cooked up a fluid and crystalline sound that seemed to make a mockery of the problems of the past few months, outlining what they were capable of and would now surely deliver.

There was a party that evening in Didsbury, a hip southern suburb of Manchester where the band, bar Mani, lived with their girlfriends in small flats or terraced houses. The party was full of local characters and went on into the small hours. The Roses had always liked to take chances, to see what they could get away with. But they were truly out on a limb with Spike Island. Half of the fun for the band had been in attracting the huge crowd. Now they would have to face it down. They had all dreamed of this moment, but the reality was daunting. Nothing was said, but they were nervous. Despite their outward nonchalance and reassurances from supporters that all they had to do was turn up, the biggest day of their lives would test to the limit the Roses' famous steely resolve.

That morning, the national dailies salvaged what they could from the press conference. The *Daily Star* ran with the headline 'Acid Band Insult PM', quoting Brown as saying, 'Margaret Thatcher should have gone up in the Brighton Bomb,' Mani busied himself handing out free tickets to a stream of visitors to his north Manchester home. 'Then suddenly I realized I didn't have any weed and everyone I phoned up was already at Spike Island.'

On site Phil Jones was battling the first of a succession of alarming problems that day. The security firm booked for the event, Showsec, arrived late and had only sent half the number of men required. It was immediately clear they had misunderstood their brief. They'd been told not to let people with food in, to prevent entrepreneurial activity. They took this to mean *all* food and began confiscating individual sandwiches and soft drinks at the gates. 'It was appalling,' said Jones.

Incidences such as this severely undermined John Squire's enjoyment of the day, a day he would later claim he hated. 'We had lots of rows with management before we went on and we were really angry at the way the show had been managed. It was supposed to be our gig, but the bouncers were taking food and drink off fans as they walked inside, which we didn't want. They were pushing the ticket prices up and we found out they'd employed kids to clean up dirty needles and condoms after the show. It was horrible.'

The crowd was estimated at 40,000. On top of the 32,500 tickets sold, the guest list was close to 5,000, with at least 2,500 more managing to crawl under the site fencing. Evans, Cummins and Jones had not provided for such a huge crowd, and Jones has admitted to a certain naivety in their plans. The on-site food vans and beer tents were quickly identified as inadequate. Jones's biggest concern, however, was the massive tide rolling down the River Mersey, a torrent that swept up huge waves and threatened to flood the island. 'It was a neap spring tide. It was the full moon at the end of May, but none of us had spotted it. You could see this tide coming in and taking land off the island. It was half a mile wide. It was like a disaster movie.' The deputy chief constable of Cheshire Warrington division was stood beside Jones on the stage, and warned him that if the Mersey rose another yard they would have to evacuate the whole area.

There had never been this number of people on Spike Island before. The sun was blazing, the chemicals in the air adding an almost psychedelic Day-glo effect, and although it was only two o'clock in the afternoon, the crowd was already growing unruly. There appeared to be no police presence on the site, which explains why there were only four arrests all day. 'The cops said to me, off the record, We're keeping a very, very low profile but we're here if you need us,' Jones recalled. 'All police leave was cancelled, they were out on the streets in Widnes but they didn't come on site at all.' The smell of hashish and marijuana and the visible effects of Ecstasy were everywhere. There had been no announcement of the running order for the day or even what time the Roses would play. The main entertainment came from watching those without tickets storm the bridges and fencing.

Then, at the sound of a helicopter approaching, all eyes turned to the skies. The helicopter touched down backstage, bringing in journalists from the *NME* and Granada TV. A fraught Jones made it clear to Evans the helicopter could not be used again. The risk of a crowd surge was too great. 'Nothing was really happening to entertain the crowd,' said Jones. 'The tide was still rising and I was worried that if the kids thought it was the band in the helicopter they would stampede.' The band would have to arrive by car. By mid-afternoon the high tide had passed and the only danger now was the growing unrest and tension in the crowd as they waited and waited for the band. The sun was still high in the sky and there was little shelter. It was hot and dusty. People were parched and hungry. In total twenty-seven people were hospitalized but fortunately there were no fatalities.

What was immediately apparent to the Roses as they arrived on site was that the band's T-shirts were everywhere. Close to 30,000 were sold that day, although the band did not get a penny. There was also a huge number of people, as much as 30 per cent of the crowd, wearing what had become known as the 'Reni hat', after the drummer's trademark bucket hat. The Roses were unaware that these were being merchandised too. The band ensconced themselves in the packed but sheltered backstage area, mingling with Bobby Gillespie from Primal Scream, Shaun Ryder of Happy Mondays, Ian McCulloch of Echo & the Bunnymen and trip-hoppers Smith & Mighty, while carefully avoiding the mass media scrum.

Reni, the band member whose dislike and distrust of Evans was most acute, was keen to collar his manager to ask about the sale of the hats. New Order's Peter Hook was stood talking with Evans and Cummins when Reni confronted them. 'Reni was fuming,' said Hook. 'He was shouting about the merchandising stalls selling the hats, What the fuck's going on? Get out there and stop them. Gareth went, Don't worry, I will get out there immediately, I'll get the bastards. When Reni stormed off, Gareth turned round and said, You better take those fucking hats off the stall. It was Gareth selling the hats!'

Out front, as late afternoon turned into early evening the atmosphere was severely flagging. Mapfumo and Sherwood had been and gone virtually unnoticed. The DJs were playing on a tall, scaffolding-clad construction set a third of the way back from the stage on the packed site, where massive speakers and the sound and light desks were also located. Paul Oakenfold's set was cut from two hours to forty minutes to make way for Frankie Bones. 'I didn't say anything because I'd already been paid,' said Oakenfold. 'The Roses made it hard on their fans. You had kids turning up at 2 p.m. expecting the band to be on, and they had to wait until 9 p.m. And they're basically indie kids, so they don't want Frankie Bones playing house.'

Bones's set made what was starting to feel like a long day even longer. 'It didn't go down well,' Dave Haslam said. DJs Haslam, Booth and The Spinmasters revived the atmosphere as the sun began to set. As the Happy Mondays' 'Step On' blared out, a huge cheer went up from the crowd, and people raised themselves to dance. It was a rare sight to see seasoned clubbers rubbing their Michiko Koshino-clad shoulders with fifteen-year-old schoolboys in band T-shirts.

Granada TV producer Steve Lock had flown back to Barton Aerodrome in the helicopter, picked up his car and driven back out to Spike Island for around 8 p.m. As he hurried through the entrance, he heard someone shout his name. It was Evans. He had sent Lock, who was on his own, two tickets and wanted to know if he had the spare ticket with him. 'I've got a guy over here wants to buy one,' he told Lock. 'So he's outside the Stone Roses' biggest ever gig, just before they come on, touting tickets,' Lock recalled.

Despite the efforts of the Manchester DJs there remained an atmosphere of near exhaustion and ill temper among the huge crowd. The band huddled in the Portakabin dressing room, trying to get rid of last-minute nerves. It was 9 p.m. Time. 'I was 100 per cent relaxed,' Brown said when I asked about rumours he'd vomited just before taking the stage. 'If all these people had come to see us, they wanted it. So why should I have been nervous?'

And then they appeared on stage looking resplendent, nonchalant and ready to feed the 40,000; to turn every wrong to right.

★

There is film footage of those opening magical, transformative moments; of Brown intoning, 'The time, the time is now. Do it now, do it now.' Film, however, could not capture the effect the band's arrival had on the mood of the crowd; it was a jaw-dropping biblical reaction, of relief, amazement, worship and unadulterated joy. 'It was like a massive pilgrimage to witness,' said Roddy McKenna, the man who had been instrumental in signing the band to Jive / Zomba. 'It wasn't a gig – it was a statement.' The resurrection of a day that for so long had threatened disaster began; the party was back on. The same camera that captured those opening moments also traced the Roses' immaculate sixteen-song set that followed.

'There'd been a kid there right from the beginning of the stage build who'd been putting his camera everywhere,' said Jones. 'I'd told him he couldn't film anything on the day, but when the Central Music TV filming collapsed I went up to him and said, Right, you can film it all now.' This footage has only recently been traced, although not yet released; when it is, it will render all further description meaningless. Brown has said that the Roses weren't actually playing to the crowd, they were 'just partying with them': 'We were just a very small part of a very big event, because it's the people who make an event, it's not the group. We get off on what they do and they get off on what we do.'

On stage the band enjoyed a clear sound, and the buzz coming off the crowd spurred them on through their set: 'I Wanna Be Adored', 'Elephant Stone', 'She Bangs the Drums', 'Shoot You Down', 'One Love', 'Sally Cinnamon', 'Standing Here', 'Fools Gold', 'Where Angels Play', 'Waterfall', 'Don't Stop', 'Something's Burning', 'Made of Stone', 'Elizabeth My Dear' and 'I Am the Resurrection'. The defining image was of Brown on stage holding a large inflatable world globe, which had bounced its way across the raised hands of the crowd towards the stage, fate providing the perfect symbol.

The wind was now blowing wildly, and out past the hysterical front section of the crowd the band's sound lost much of its potency. Some accused Evans of scrimping on the PA system, but the cause was more elemental. Noise limitations had been enforced, with sound-level meters deployed in eight spots on the site and in Widnes and Runcorn. The wind blew the band's sound far and wide and the volume was louder in Widnes town centre than on site, exceeding the 97 decibels limit. It meant there could be no cranking up of the sound, and the more meandering parts of the Roses' set suffered. There was also a curfew. Although Frankie Bones had promised 'house music all night long', it all had to be wrapped up by 11 p.m.

There was no encore. Squire thought them corny, 'proof rock music had become showbusiness'. Instead, as requested by Brown, Dave Haslam followed the band's set by playing 'Redemption Song' by Bob Marley, and the evening climaxed with a fireworks display. Backstage the elated band was surprised to learn from their crew of the sound difficulties out front, as all they had felt was waves of love from the crowd. As the fans' coaches pulled away, the Roses, their crew and scores of well-wishers headed back to Manchester club the International, also owned by Evans and Cummins, for an after-show party. 'The only drink available was Carlsberg Special Brew,' said *NME* photographer Kevin Cummins. 'It was past its sell-by date and Gareth just wanted to get rid of it.' Brown was huddled over a bottle of Wild Turkey bourbon. Mani felt the band hadn't played well. But there was a sense of relief it was all over.

Reviews for the show, when they came, were mixed – in part because the band's sound had been lost to the elements, but also because the cultural significance of the day was still largely unquantifiable. 'It was the moment when everything that had seemed underground exploded into the mainstream,' said Haslam. 'Spike Island was a full stop, and there was a sense we were entering a new chapter which wasn't going to be as good.' Some journalists found the setting depressing. Bob Stanley of *Melody Maker* described Spike Island as a horrible field surrounded by huge electricity pylons, factories and chemical plants. 'Your hair felt very odd and greasy, like it was totally coated with chemicals from the factories. The best thing about it was being able to say you were there.'

I was, writing about the event for *The Face*. I was nineteen and no doubt being used by editor Sheryl Garratt to try to patch up relations between the band and the magazine following Nick Kent's less than complimentary cover story on them earlier in the year. My article was another cover story for the band, under the headline 'The Third Summer of Love', although the cover shot was a debut for a teenage Kate Moss. I'd like to think it was my piece more than Moss's cute, scrunched-up nose that led to the issue becoming one of the most iconic in *The Face*'s history. Sometimes you have to share the credit. The first Summer of Love – 1988, not 1967 – had happened in clubs. The second, in 1989, was about big raves in open fields. Spike Island was seen as an indication of where the phenomenon was heading for the third: festivals led by bands who fizzed with an energy unseen in rock since punk.

Brown said at the time that the Roses' future plans included London: 'We were a bit disappointed with Alexandra Palace. We want to do a massive venue where no one has played before and where we can come on as late as possible. We want to get away with as much as the British licensing laws will let us.' Rumours, emanating from the ever-opportunistic Evans, quickly spread that the band were planning a secret show for 100,000 outside Buckingham Palace. In truth the glory days were over: the monarchy was safe, a tour of America would soon be cancelled, and plans to record a new album in the summer abandoned. Nullifying court cases, creative collapse and management problems lay ahead.

The last of the great rock 'n' roll bands had already, stubbornly, vaingloriously and quite beautifully reached their peak at Spike Island. It was part of their everlasting mystique that no one could ever really figure them out, their sacrifices and their successes, just how they'd got here and where they were going. Even the band members themselves, over time, seemed to disagree.

I.

The Patrol

It started with John Squire and Ian Brown forming their first band together, The Patrol, during their final year at Altrincham Grammar School for Boys in 1979 when they were both aged sixteen. Initially a three-piece with Squire on guitar, Brown on bass and fellow classmate Si Wolstencroft on drums, The Patrol rehearsed on Thursday nights in the back room of Wolstencroft's parents' house in Hale Ringway, a civil parish close to Manchester airport, situated between the notorious council estates of Wythenshawe and the leafy, well-to-do market town of Altrincham on the south-westerly outskirts of the city.

Wolstencroft, who would go on to play drums in the original Stone Roses line-up, The Smiths and The Fall, had been in the same high-achieving school class as Squire and Brown since the age of eleven. He recalled that despite their rudimentary ability and equipment, including an amplifier Squire's father had made, The Patrol made 'a good noise'. He was closer to Squire than to Brown, having bonded over a shared love for The Clash's 1977 eponymous debut. They had also shared Latin lessons and the distinction of being the first pupils in their year to be caned after being caught drawing graffiti on their school desks: 'We got six with a bamboo cane off the deputy head.'

Brown favoured the Sex Pistols and thought that their 1977 debut *Never Mind the Bollocks, Here's the Sex Pistols* 'was going to change the world'. Although he wasn't fronting The Patrol, who as yet did not have a singer, Brown should have been. He combined a keen interest in politics with a self-confessed 'rebellious streak' and an effervescent personality. He was a born showman, well known for standing in front of the class entertaining everyone with his impersonations of the school's teachers. Brown was also, thanks to his study of karate, not to be messed with. 'I saw him use it on this guy in the chemistry lab,' said Wolstencroft. 'It was pretty impressive. I remember thinking the guy deserved it. Ian gave him a good kung-fu kick to the throat.'

Squire, although less confrontational, was no less defiant of authority. 'I think he was the first kid in the school to play truant,' said Brown. 'And he did that by himself.' He also had a recognized gift for art, which meant that while Brown and Wolstencroft got stuck into football during games lesson, Squire was encouraged and happy to stay indoors painting.

There was a fourth member of The Patrol gang, Pete Garner, who, while not in this band, would play bass with The Stone Roses between 1983 and 1987. Although a year younger and at a different school from the other three, Garner had been close to them, particularly Squire and Brown, since the age of thirteen. He lived in Brooklands, Sale, a five-minute walk away from Squire and Brown, who lived four doors apart on Sylvan Avenue in Timperley, a pleasant village enclave of Altrincham.

Garner shared the elder boys' love of punk, and most days after school the gang of four could be found shooting the breeze at the local hot spot close to Squire and Brown's homes. The allure of girls and cigarettes gave the spot, a bridge over a brook at the top end of Sylvan Avenue, a hallowed appeal. The small stream also signified the boundary between Sale in Manchester and Timperley in Cheshire. 'When I first met Ian he told me he'd seen the Sex Pistols,' said Garner. It was a lie, but an impressive one. Brown further impressed Garner with his copy of the eponymous 1969 album by The Stooges. Squire's admiration for The Clash was self-evident: he played their debut album every day.

For Garner the distinction in the personalities of Brown and Squire was clear. 'Ian was in your face, charming, very confident, full eye contact, people liked hanging around with him and he was always blagging you a bit. With John you had to wrestle stuff out of him, he'd think about what he was going to say before he said it, but he turned out to be creatively brilliant. They were always like that.'

Squire was usually known as John. Other people called him Johnny but never Jonathon. Brown was IBEX, a nickname that is used to this day. It originated from a fad at school where EX was simply added to the initials of your name. 'I knew Ian had done karate,' said Garner. 'I think he was a black belt, but I don't recall it being a big thing in Ian's life when we started hanging out. I suspect as soon as music came in, it went out of the window. We became obsessed with music to the detriment of every other hobby we'd had.' Wolstencroft, Squire, Brown and Garner were all from a similar background. 'Ian and John lived in your bog-standard, post-war semi; pretty much all the houses round there were like that,' said Garner. Or as Brown put it, 'Poor, down to earth.'

Brown, born in February 1963, had lived in Timperley since he was six. His family, including younger brother David, had moved the ten miles east from Warrington in 1969 following the birth of his sister Sharon. His father, George, worked as a joiner and the new house with a garden was something to be proud of. Family always came first for George, who instilled a firm sense of discipline in his eldest son as well as passing on his strong socialist beliefs. He was 'a bit to the left of Arthur Scargill', said Brown.

Culture vulture Garner, a fish out of water at the rough all-boys Burnage High School, recalled being introduced to Ian's mum, Jean: 'The first time I went round to his house, his mum was saying to him, You're not hanging round with him, he's bad news.'

Squire had been born in November 1962 in Broadheath less than a mile away from Sylvan Avenue. His father, Tom, was an electrical engineer working at the vast General Electric Company factory in nearby Trafford Park. Tom's record collection held a sacred place in the life of the house, and included jazz greats such as Charlie Parker, John Coltrane, Dizzy Gillespie and Miles Davis. There was also room for The Beatles, Elvis and Peggy Lee. 'I didn't hear a bad song until I left home,' said Squire. His younger brother, Matt, was best friends with Brown's brother David.

Brown and Squire, legend has it, first met in a sandpit as young children in the fields near their home – and in all likelihood, with their families living so close to each other and the children so similarly matched in age, they did. It's a hazy memory, at best, for both. Until punk brought them together they were not friends. They didn't attend the same primary school, and nor after both passing their II+ did they socialize much at Altrincham Grammar.

'We became friendly at thirteen, fourteen,' Brown said. 'I started chatting to him and I took "God Save the Queen", the first Clash LP and "One Chord Wonders" by The Adverts round to his house. He was into The Beach Boys and The Beatles. We were total opposites. I was very outgoing, the class joker, and he was the loner.'

'Virtually everything we did together was related to music,' Squire said. Before The Clash, The Beach Boys had been Squire's great obsession, initiated by the TV advertising for the *20 Golden Greats* album. It was, however, the Sex Pistols' debut single 'Anarchy in the UK' in 1976 that made him want to pick up the guitar for the first time. 'I think I was fourteen when I heard that and realized how electric guitars could be made to sound. I started pestering my dad for a guitar, got a paper round, started hanging around guitar shops on the way back from school. It was the next Christmas I got the guitar. I'd sit depressed on the windowsill in my bedroom with no amplifier, picking my way through "Three Blind Mice" on one string wondering how long it would take.'

For Squire, Brown, Wolstencroft and Garner, punk was their defining teenage experience and influence. Squire got his mum to take in his grey cotton flares and add zips. Dr Martens shoes became de rigueur, and they were regulars at Discount Records, Manchester's key punk record shop, which had fortuitously for them opened outlets in Sale and Altrincham after establishing its city centre reputation.

Alongside the Sex Pistols and The Clash, another early punk band, Generation X, became a key influence. Squire, particularly, was smitten by the band's eponymous 1978 debut. 'That's where John gets a lot of his sound from,' said Wolstencroft. 'We thought the first Generation X album was a masterpiece.'

'Me and Ian both loved The Damned as well,' said Garner. 'Ian had The Damned's "Stretcher Case/Sick of Being Sick" single, which you got free if you went to a certain Damned gig in London. Ian, being an opportunist, wrote to Stiff Records [home to The Damned and The Adverts] and they sent him one. He was the only person who had it. That single was like the holy grail.'

Brown and Garner also shared a passion for Slaughter & the Dogs, who hailed from nearby Wythenshawe, particularly their 1977 'Cranked Up Really High' single. 'It Won't Sell' by The Panik, released by Manchester independent label Rainy City Records, was another key 7-inch for the pair. 'The guitarist in The Panik went on to be in V2, another Manchester band we really liked,' said Garner. 'You have to bear in mind you've only got so many [punk] records in 1977, so you know every note on everything. As soon as one of us got a single, the first thing you'd do was play it to the others, to turn them on to it.'

From around the age of fourteen, the four schoolboys had also been checking out punk bands playing live. Squire remembered his first gig – The Clash at Manchester Apollo in 1977 – as 'the most exciting thing I'd ever experienced'. Brown also saw The Clash in 1977, and travelled the city to watch Manchester's premier punk bands Buzzcocks, Slaughter & the Dogs and The Fall. He managed to catch Public Image Ltd (PiL), formed by John Lydon after his former band, the Sex Pistols, broke up in 1978, and The Stranglers. Brown and Squire were also both at the famous March 1979 Joy Division gig at Bowdon Vale youth club in Altrincham.

Squire, Brown and Wolstencroft left Altrincham Grammar in the summer of 1979 and enrolled at the Timperley-based South Trafford College to study for A-levels. Brown and Wolstencroft arrived for the first day at college in September, after a summer spent rehearsing The Patrol, in newly acquired, Two Tone-influenced tonic suits. Two Tone was a fresh, young, English take on ska, revolving around bands such as The Specials, The Beat and Madness. The movement was closely linked to the burgeoning mod-revival scene led initially by The Jam and featuring bands such as The Chords and The Purple Hearts. 'Ian, Si and John turned mod,' said Garner, the only one of the gang who didn't, 'which basically meant putting your [upturned for punk] shirt collar down, doing it up to the top button and putting your hair in a side parting. It was like, wait a minute, three weeks ago everybody was a punk!'

At South Trafford College, where Brown took politics and Squire continued to pursue art, they met Andy Couzens, a fellow first-year pupil and the fifth and final original member of The Stone Roses. Couzens played guitar with the Roses for three years from 1983 until 1986. He was originally asked to become the singer with The Patrol after Brown and Wolstencroft saw him have a fight in the college canteen. 'Andy handled himself pretty well. He had a spiky haircut, biker boots and a car, so Ian asked him if he could sing.'

'I said, All right, yeah, why not? Never say no,' said Couzens. 'Ian liked the idea of it: Look at him. He'll be a good singer. It seems ridiculous now.' There were close to 2,500 people at South Trafford College but, even before being approached, Couzens had noticed Brown. 'He was turning up wearing tonic suits. He had a pretty striking look.'

Couzens had 'done punk', loved Joy Division, but since the age of fifteen had been heavily involved with football hooliganism, following both Manchester City and Stockport County 'for the fights, not the football'. Couzens lived in Woodford, a village five miles south of Stockport, and had chosen to study at South Trafford College in an attempt to break away from the hooligan scene. Timperley was almost ten miles from Woodford, a journey he made in an old MG Midget.

For him, joining The Patrol was as much about forging new friendships as being a front man and he began hanging out after college with the gang on the bridge. Garner, now in his final year at Burnage High, gave Couzens a copy of The Panik's 'It Won't Sell' as a welcome. 'The record wasn't that good,' said Couzens, 'but the picture of the band on the sleeve was important. It was a directional picture for The Patrol to go for.' With Garner acting as an ersatz roadie, and Couzens on vocals, The Patrol moved out of Wolstencroft's parents' back room and began rehearsing at the Walton Road scout hut in Sale.

'John was writing the guitar riffs and we were just joining in,' said Wolstencroft. 'Ian wrote one song about Prince Charles. I can't remember what that was called, but it made me laugh.' Brown wrote a song called 'Black Flag', after the famous anarchist symbol. 'Ian would sing that one and play bass,' said Garner. The Patrol also attempted a cover of The Monkees song '(I'm Not Your) Steppin' Stone', which had been part of the Sex Pistols' live repertoire.

Brown and Couzens quickly grew close, travelling together to watch promising Welsh mod-revival band Seventeen, whose fast transformation into The Alarm left a sour taste. 'We realized they were really just doing it for the money,' said Couzens. 'And we didn't like it.'

Wolstencroft, Garner and Squire had no such reservations about the motivations of The Clash. All three bunked off studies to follow the band throughout January and February 1980 on their 16 Tons tour, making gigs in Chester, Wales, Bristol, London and Manchester at the Apollo where The Specials were the support. Squire met *NME* photographer and future Stone Roses collaborator Pennie Smith on the tour. She was famed for her photographs of The Clash, particularly her cover shot for *London Calling*. It was Smith who facilitated the three schoolboys' introduction to The Clash's entourage. 'The Clash treated us really well,' said Garner. 'It was a massive influence.'

Brown also saw first-hand how The Clash treated their fans. The day after the gig at the Apollo, he and Garner acted on the rumour that the band were recording in Manchester. They took a train into the city, intending to go round the studios. It started to rain, and despite their chutzpah they realized that they only actually knew one studio, Pluto on Granby Row. 'We were both soaking wet and we realized how stupid this was,' said Garner. 'As if we're just going to walk up to the studio, they're going to be there and they're going to let us in.'

However, as the pair approached the studio, they were in luck. A car pulled up and Topper Headon, the band's drummer, got out. He took pity on the two bedraggled kids and invited them inside, where

Brown and Garner spent all day watching The Clash record the single 'Bankrobber'. 'They were fantastic,' said Garner. 'Not many bands would do that.' Brown was less star-struck. Observing singer Joe Strummer sat under a grandfather clock, weirdly clicking his fingers in time with it, only served to entrench his opinion that the Sex Pistols were punk's finest band.

Squire was inspired by his experiences on the 16 Tons tour. He wrote The Clash-influenced punk-pop tunes 'Gaol of the Assassins' and 'Too Many Tons' and introduced them to The Patrol's rehearsals. Squire had been working diligently on improving his guitar playing. He'd been to a blues and folk guitar teacher and studied a book called *Lead Guitar* that came with a free flexi-disc of blues-based music. 'That stuff came easy to me. I just liked the sound.' His dad had also rigged up the transformer from Squire's old train set to the record player in his room so he could slow his records down and work out guitar parts at his own pace.

Using wages from part-time jobs, The Patrol recorded both the new Squire tracks at a demo studio in Rusholme, where a pre-Simply Red Mick Hucknall acted as sound engineer. 'Gaol of the Assassins' was surprisingly accomplished. Couzens could carry a tune and the mid-tempo song allowed Squire to show off some fine melodic guitar lines. 'It's like what he would play later on in the Roses,' said Wolstencroft. 'John already had a feel for it, a good rhythm and a good sound.'

A promising dynamic between Squire and Brown was apparent in these early explorations. 'Ian was always brilliant at talking it up,' said Garner. 'If he met somebody he'd convince them within five minutes that the band he was in was the best band ever, whereas John would get down and do the work. You can put a lot of The Patrol's stuff down to John. He was responsible for writing a lot of the lyrics, probably a lot of the music, if not all of it. Together it worked out quite well.' Brown had also handled the harmonies on 'Gaol of the Assassins' and the faster, less intricate 'Too Many Tons', as well as helping write the lyrics.

After recording the demo and producing a limited number of

cassette copies with inserts designed by Squire, The Patrol played a handful of gigs beginning in March 1980. Squire used the college facilities to produce posters and flyers to help publicize the shows, which were mostly organized by Brown, who by now had a scooter to go with his tonic suit and was busy putting his face about south Manchester.

'I was always on the move,' Brown said. 'I had mates all over town, not just from where I was from. I was hanging out with kids everywhere.' Among Brown's new mates was Gaz Smith, the leader of a gang of salty punks from Stretford, home of Manchester United FC, that coalesced around the band Corrosive Youth. This scene also included art students from Cosgrove Hall animation studio who were developing the *Danger Mouse* series, which would become an international hit in 1981. Incongruously among the Mohican haircuts, some Stretford punks had their leather biker jackets adorned with early cartoons of Danger Mouse and his sidekick Penfold.

'They were all right, decent lads,' said Couzens. 'They decided they liked Ian.' People seemed to gravitate towards Brown, agreed Wolstencroft. 'He attracted people with style, no matter who it was or what the style was. He just clicked with people.' The Patrol played youth clubs with Corrosive Youth, including nights at Sale Annexe and Lostock near Stretford. 'It was an excuse for us to all go out somewhere different,' said Couzens. 'I never thought anything of it. We were just doing it.'

For Wolstencroft, the best Patrol gig was at South Trafford College when they supported progressive rockers Scorched Earth. 'It was the first time we were on a stage that was higher than six inches, with monitors and proper equipment. It wasn't packed but there were over a hundred people in the crowd and we were quite good. We had attitude.'

Equally exciting was the band's first gig in Manchester city centre, at the Portland near Piccadilly Gardens. 'It was an old-school late-1970s bar,' said Garner, 'a long room with a little stage at the end.' For Garner, the highlight of all The Patrol's shows came in a village hall in Dunham Massey, an upmarket rural area between Timperley and Lymm. The Patrol included a cover of The Sweet's 'Blockbuster' in their set, and Brown asked Garner to play bass while he sang the song. 'It was the first time I ever played bass. And the only time I played with The Patrol.'

The Patrol also did a cover of the Cockney Rejects' 1979 single 'I'm Not a Fool'. The Rejects (who also included 'Blockbuster' in their live set), alongside the Angelic Upstarts, were leaders of a new energetic street-punk movement dubbed Oi! Brown, Squire and to an extent Garner were hooked on the raw excitement these bands generated. They were direct, avowedly working class and aggressively anti-establishment.

'We all loved the first Rejects album,' said Garner. Both he and Brown were also fans of the Angelic Upstarts' incendiary 1978 single 'The Murder of Liddle Towers', written about amateur boxer Liddle Towers, who died in police cells. Brown saw the Upstarts, celebrated for their left-wing stance, play live between fifteen and twenty times, and even acted as roadie for them. The band's singer, Thomas 'Mensi' Mensforth, a former apprentice miner, became something of a mentor. 'I remember Ian humping gear in at the Mayflower in Belle Vue and another club in Moss Side, a community centre,' said Mensi. 'He jumped in the bus a few times to come to places like Bolton, Oldham and Blackpool.'

Brown also followed the fashion of Oi!, wearing a green MA1 jacket, Levi jeans, and Dr Martens boots with yellow laces, which signified the wearer was anti-racist, or SHARP (Skinheads Against Racial Prejudice). This was important as Oi! nights were plagued by right-wing National Front skinheads who aped the look but whose MA1 jackets were black and bootlaces white. The Upstarts often took what Mensi has called a 'pro-active defensive' stance: 'We would look round the bars for the fascists before the show and we would disrupt them before they had a chance to disrupt it. That's why I wasn't interested in whether my roadies could string a guitar. I wanted to know they could hold their hands up in a row. Although Ian was a little bit skinny, he was a game fucker.'

Wolstencroft and Couzens back that evaluation. 'Ian wouldn't go looking for a fight but he was a fighter,' Wolstencroft recalled. Couzens said Brown was 'not frightened of anything'. Outside the Rotters club in the city centre, a bunch of blokes started having a go. 'Ian stood up to them. He challenged them to hit him and the bloke did.' Brown offered up the other side of his face. 'Ian just kept doing that,' said Couzens. 'Then he said to the guy, You're a prick, you've just made yourself look like a prick, and walked off.'

Under the influence of the proudly patriotic Mensi, the seventeen-year-old Brown had a small Union Jack, with the word 'England' across it, tattooed on his upper arm. 'Later on Ian would be embarrassed by that tattoo,' said Garner. It was difficult to explain and easy to misinterpret. The Upstarts, who had featured on the cover of the *Socialist Worker* newspaper, had introduced an unusually quiet acoustic song called 'England' into their live set. It was written as a tribute to the bravery of the English working classes, whom Mensi reckoned had too often been sent to war on the basis of greed. The song was also part of his arsenal against the rise in popularity of the British Movement and National Front among alienated working-class youth at a time of rising unemployment in the early years of Margaret Thatcher's government. Both neo-Nazi parties had 'tried to hijack aspects of patriotism', said veteran anti-fascist Mensi, who wrote the lyrics in part to 'take the flag back from the people who had hijacked it . . . I was trying to say I can have pride in my country and still have respect for other people. I used to lecture everybody.' Mensi felt he had 'instilled something' in Brown that made him proud.

This new-found fondness for Oi! was not shared by The Patrol's drummer Si Wolstencroft. 'I hated it. The songs were just too quick, with no sort of subtlety to them.' He was the first of the gang to lose interest in The Patrol and college, drifting away from both.

The Patrol blew their one shot of making something of themselves when they missed the chance of playing in front of a potentially influential crowd at the Osbourne Club in Miles Platting, inner-city Manchester. Garner learned one afternoon that

Adam and the Ants were cancelling that evening's gig because their tour bus had broken down. Garner had planned to attend and was on the phone to the venue asking what was on instead. Told they were struggling to find a replacement, he suggested The Patrol. 'I was blagging, telling him they've got a following, they'll pull a good crowd,' said Garner. 'So the guy said, Okay, if you can get them down, I'll put them on.' But Squire could not be located. 'He was sat in a field chilling, hadn't told anyone where he was going, just sat in a field doing what he does.'

Wolstencroft joined a new band called Freak Party, exploring an interest in British jazz funk with bass player Andy Rourke and guitarist Johnny Marr, who had often mixed with The Patrol gang at a pub called the Vine in Sale. Freak Party would become The Smiths, and although Wolstencroft kept in touch with Squire and Brown, their passion for Oi!, and increasingly the scooter scene, saw their paths diverge.

Garner also favoured Marr's musical direction. He'd finished school in the summer of 1980, and after a period on the dole had landed his dream job at Paperchase, the hippest record and poster/magazine shop in Manchester. Marr, whom he knew from primary school, worked in an independent fashion shop called X Clothes nearby in the city centre. 'Ian and John used to come into Paperchase now and again,' he said. 'But we just didn't hang around together any more. They were getting into the scooter thing, listening to the Rejects and the Upstarts, and I'd gone the other way, starting to listen to The Velvet Underground, the New York Dolls and The Stooges. I had long dyed black hair. We were still mates, but we didn't hang around the bridge any more.'

It was Couzens who stayed closest to Brown and Squire, even after he was thrown out of college. 'We basically stopped doing the band and started doing the scooters,' he recalled.

'I never wanted to be in a group,' Brown said. 'I sold my bass and got a scooter with the money – £100.' After leaving college in the summer of 1981, Squire and Brown took a succession of easy-come, easy-go jobs to pay for music, scooters and nights out. 'The first thing I did was scrub pots,' said Brown. The job washing dishes at a hotel lasted about three weeks, after which he worked in an office, on a building site and washed caravans, but was mostly on the dole.

Squire stacked shelves at Tesco. He found work as 'a barman at the local, a labourer and a grease monkey for a roller-shutter maintenance firm'. His dad had tried to get him a job as a forklift truck driver at his GEC factory. 'I hesitated so much the job was taken by someone else. I always think of that as my lucky escape from the mundane.'

Initially the scooter revival had been kick-started by the release of *Quadrophenia* in 1979, and Couzens watched Brown's obsession with scooters grow. He had set him up with a part-time job at his uncle's caravan sales site, and for a time Brown had played the part of the film's lead, Jimmy, riding his scooter to work in his tonic suit. 'It very quickly jumped from that to "scooterboys", who were anything but mods,' said Couzens. 'They were more like Hells Angels or hooligans on scooters. Although John and I got into scooters, it was to a lesser extent than Ian. We continued trying to make music. Ian didn't take any of that seriously and went for the scooter thing hook, line and sinker, up and down the country, on rallies and runs.'

'The Scooterboys were not Mods,' Brown told *Melody Maker*. 'We were a mixture of punks, skins, anyone who had a scooter.' Brown became a well-known face on the scene in 1981. It was a boon year, one that saw the mod look of suits and parkas replaced by the skinhead look of green army combat trousers, MA1 jackets and Dr Martens, scooter clubs springing up all over the country and a fresh wave of national runs taking place.

The first of these was Scarborough Easter weekend 1981, when 10,000 scooterists gathered, followed in July by a run to Keswick in the Lake District that ended in a full-blown, Molotov-cocktail-scarred riot, and resulted in scooter runs being banned from the Lake District for twenty years. Brown was there.

One of Brown's closest scooterboy pals was Mike Phoenix. 'Ian and I met up because on his way to work he used to come down through Sale past our house,' said Phoenix. 'He saw my scooter, stopped and we got chatting.' Phoenix ran a club on Monday nights above the Black Lion pub in Salford called the Twisted Wheel SC, named after Manchester's original Northern Soul venue. Brown became a regular. 'Ian used to sit on the door with me, take the money and watch for the best-looking girls coming in.' The club was rammed with up to 300 people, with another 100 outside in the car park – all dancing to Northern Soul, Motown, ska and 1960s mod music. 'It was magical.'

Brown had a strong and classic look: white Levi Sta-Prest jeans or loose-fit Levi's Red Tab 501s with a twisted seam, Dr Martens boots, Jaytex or Brutus checked shirt and a black Barathea three-button jacket with chrome buttons and an original Twisted Wheel patch sewn on the breast pocket. He was charismatic, spinning stories and telling jokes that would hold the attention of huddles of scooter-boys, and the girls loved him. He had an ability to make easy mates with anybody, even, on one memorable run, a group of Hells Angels. He was unafraid to put forward his opinion on any subject with a cheeky grin. 'But when he lost his rag, he really lost his rag,' said Phoenix. Brown would often tell Phoenix, 'I'm not bothered about being rich but I want to be famous.'

Stockport Crusaders and the Rainy City Cruisers in Salford were the main scooter clubs. Phoenix and Brown knew most of the faces on the scene. The small clique they rode with included members of the Chorlton Trojans scooter club, such as the always ultra-sharply turned-out Johnny Poland, a key influence on Brown's style. The Trojans were renowned for their silver helmets with Mohicans fashioned out of a brush of fox's tail. 'Four or five of us would go everywhere together,' said Phoenix. On the fringe of this gang of characters was Stephen 'Cressa' Cresser, a future member of The Stone Roses' road crew. 'Cressa was a good lad, funny, but he didn't have a scooter,' said Phoenix. 'He used to come along on the back of somebody else's.'

Throughout 1982 and 1983, Brown and his rum and rowdy clique would be regulars at the rallies in Brighton, the Isle of Wight, Morecambe, Great Yarmouth and Weston-super-Mare, as the scooterboys became the scourge of seaside towns. 'You'd go out on your scooter and people would throw things at you and the police would pull you up,' said Couzens. 'You'd get heckled. You couldn't leave your scooter anywhere because it would get smashed up. It felt danger- ous, and that's part of being young. You want to kick against things.'

Brown's gang would go to the Beehive pub in Eccles and fight with the locals, including the lads who'd go on to form the Happy Mondays. 'They'd try and kick our scooters over; we used to fight them every week,' Brown said.

Brown had five or six scooters, including two real head-turners. The first was a Vespa Rally 200, originally dark metallic blue and red, which featured the slogan 'Angels with Dirty Faces' on one side of the rear wheel panel after the 1978 Sham 69 single, and on the other side 'Stormtroopers in Sta Prest', inspired by the track by underground Oi! band The Last Resort. Phoenix, a keen exponent of the art of scooter customization, revamped this scooter for Brown, painting it pink and candy red with a Japanese-style flag on the front and adorning it with a new logo, 'Cranked Up Really High', after a Slaughter & the Dogs track.

There was also a fondly remembered pink and white cut-down Lambretta 'chopper' with 'Sweet and Innocenti' written on the rear panel. Much of the customization was done at Andy Couzens' par- ents' house. Couzens, Brown and Phoenix would take a break from the hassle associated with riding scooters by going for rumbles around Manchester city centre in Couzens' father's white Jaguar. Guided by Phoenix they took the Jag to Clifton Hall in Rotherham, where Couzens and Brown experienced their first Northern Soul 'all- nighter'. 'They'd never come across anything like it,' said Phoenix, 'some dirty old music hall that smelled of stale grease where people were dancing all night.'

John Squire was also noted for his customized scooter and had done the work himself. It was a Lambretta GP 125 in iridescent dark blue, with the petrol tank, the internals and the forks plated in cop- per. The rims were painted and then flicked with paints in the Jackson Pollock-style that would later adorn The Stone Roses' instruments and record sleeves. 'John really was meticulous,' said

Phoenix. 'He had good taste. That scooter would stand up today.' Although not as heavily involved in the scene as Brown, Squire made it to rallies in Skegness and Morecambe. 'John was pretty introverted, quiet, but dry as fuck,' said Phoenix. 'He would stand back and listen to everyone else.' He was also keen to borrow records that were popular at the Twisted Wheel club. 'So he could listen to bass lines,' said Phoenix. 'He was always looking for new stuff and looking to make it his own.'

'Ian was definitely a face on the scene,' said Johnny Bolland, who ran the Stockport Crusaders and would go on to own the company who made the Stone Roses T-shirts. 'He was loud and funny. He had the image and the style. John was just there, one of the crowd.' On the Manchester scooterboy scene, however, the punks and mods who turned skinhead like Brown were far outnumbered by the football hooligans, 'Perry boys', who had taken to two wheels. In fact around the country many of the new scooter clubs often had strong links to football hooligan firms.

Synonymous with this phenomenon in Manchester was a lad called David 'Kaiser' Carty, a well-known face from Moston. Among his crowd was none other than Gary 'Mani' Mounfield, who would go on to replace Pete Garner as the bassist in the Roses. 'Mani stood out, same as Ian,' said Bolland. 'Him and Kaiser were proper Mancs from north Manchester, the rough end of town.'

Mani, who was just a few days older than Squire, said his scooter crowd was made up of 'punks, scallies [Perry boys], pirates, vaga-bonds and ne'er do wells'. They were a rowdy bunch, cruising about and getting 'involved in skulduggery and shenanigans', often clash-ing with the 'smellies' or 'stinkers' in nearby Oldham. 'We'd kick fuck out of anyone with a leather jacket on or with long hair or any-thing like that,' Mani said. They'd been at Scarborough in 1981, and were on many of the big runs such as Great Yarmouth and the Isle of Wight. Mani had a Vespa 90 racer called 'Dirty Jimmy'. Along-side a taste for Motown, Northern Soul and mod-revival acts, they were into the psychobilly scene, a good-time apolitical mix of punk and rockabilly led by King Kurt and The Meteors.

Initially there had been a divide between Kaiser's north Manchester scooterboy crowd and Brown's clique from south Manchester. 'We always used to think the southern Manchester scooterboys were a bit middle class,' Mani said. Slowly that attitude dissolved and the two sets of scooterboys came together, realizing 'we were all into the same scene: dress sharp, have a smart scooter and like good music'. Mani met Squire for the first time in the Northern Soul room at the Pips club and knew him by his nickname, Red John. Squire was a 'real staunch communist', one who always wore a hammer and sickle badge, said Couzens. Mani first encountered Brown under more troubling circumstances. 'We were having problems with this gang of local skinheads,' Mani said. 'The word went out to Ian's south Manchester crew; Mike Phoenix, Johnny Bolland and all their lot.'

'We'd heard about this kid with a swastika on his head, some bonehead who was living near Mani's who was bullying kids and causing trouble in the bars and clubs,' said Brown. 'So Mani's posse came to our posse and asked if we'd go up to deal with this guy. That's how we met. We were policing ourselves in those days. I remember seeing Mani sat down in this council house. I'm thinking, He ain't no fighter.'

'I vividly remember meeting Ian,' Mani said, 'and thinking, That kid looks like Galen off *Planet of the Apes*. He always had that striking simian thing. I liked him from day one because he looked like my favourite telly programme.'

Kaiser would often join Brown's small crew on scooter runs. He was an expert 'jibber', always trying to get something for nothing, be it petrol or steak pie, chips and peas all round for the lads. They called themselves, briefly, the Manchester Globe Scooter Club – largely as a front to sell off hundreds of inch-wide black, red and green patches they claimed were the club's insignia, at 50p each. 'Nobody had any money, we were in a recession,' said Phoenix. 'We were young and just wanted to enjoy ourselves.'

Kaiser and Mani were both part-time members of an irregular Oldham-based band called The Hungry Sox, whose psychobilly and garage rock set was played mainly for laughs. Squire's interest was aroused. He'd tried but failed to keep The Patrol going with Couzens and a succession of new members after Brown and Wolstencroft had lost interest. Now, in October 1982, Squire, Couzens, Mani and Kaiser came together to form a new band, initially calling themselves The Fireside Chaps before changing their name to The Waterfront. They rehearsed at Couzens' parents' house, where a full-size snooker table was often a distraction.

The Waterfront, with Kaiser on vocals, Mani on bass, Squire and Couzens on guitars and Mani's mate Chris Goodwin on drums, recorded a demo tape featuring two songs: 'Normandy (On a Beach)' and 'Where the Wind Blows'. Again Squire's crystalline guitar lines are distinctive, especially on 'Normandy'. The lyrics to the track were written by Kaiser and inspired by a recent trip to France when according to Mani, 'everyone around our way all chipped the train and ferry and went to live in Port Grimaud, just outside St Tropez, for the summer'. Both tracks on the Waterfront demo, which Squire again designed the inserts for, were carefully constructed pop and in part precursors of classic period Stone Roses. Ironically, The Waterfront sounded more 'Roses' than the actual Stone Roses did in their early days, although 'Where the Wind Blows' did feature, remarkably, a whistling solo.

'We spent quite a bit of time on that demo,' said Couzens. 'The first demo with The Patrol we didn't know what we were doing, but that second time we'd got more of a handle on it. John and I talked about The Beach Boys a lot. We were definitely more pop-orientated. We had an idea of what we were trying to do.' They tried to get Brown interested in joining The Waterfront. 'John and I had an idea of having Ian and Kaiser at the front trying to do a counterpoint with one another. That's what we were trying to push, this question-and-answer thing with these two lads at the front singing sweet pop music.'

'We were joint singers for a couple of weeks,' Brown said. 'The Waterfront sounded like [post-punk Scottish band] Orange Juice. I was impressed I knew somebody that could play to that quality.

Since 1978/79 John hadn't done much except play his guitar.' The Waterfront never gigged and came to an abrupt end. 'It was John who said, I'm not doing this any more, and just stopped,' said Couzens. Mani invited Couzens and Brown up to Oldham in an attempt to get something else going. They rehearsed for an afternoon with another member of the Hungry Sox gang, Clint Boon, at his studio the Mill, but nothing came of it.

Squire and Brown appeared to be leaving behind their adolescent obsessions of music and scooters and adopting new, more adult responsibilities as their teenage years faded out. Squire had landed a good job, and Brown was settling into a long-term relationship. The scooter rallies were becoming bigger and bigger, but growing increasingly ugly as racist skinheads, often without scooters, infiltrated the scene. The National Scooter Rallies Association folded in 1986 and the runs came to an end. 'Ian's last rally,' said Phoenix, 'was the Isle of Wight, August 1984. He went down with his girlfriend, Mitch.'

2.

Reni

Brown was bringing in a steady wage working for the Department of Social Security (DSS) in Sale and living in Hulme with his girlfriend Michelle 'Mitch' Davitt, a former Altrincham Girls Grammar School pupil Brown had first met at South Trafford College. At that time Hulme was the poorest, most neglected part of inner-city Manchester. The houses in the area had been demolished and replaced in the 1960s by a brutal, modernist curved row of low-rise flats with deck access above the streets, known as the 'Crescents'. These flats had been award-winning designs, but by the 1980s inherent faults meant they were cold, damp and riddled with cockroaches and other vermin. Crime and drug abuse had become significant and the Crescents were declared 'unfit for purpose' by local authorities. Many of the flats were squatted and the area had acquired a bohemian reputation because of the punks, artists and musicians living there.

Sue Dean, who would go on to be the girlfriend of The Stone Roses' future manager Gareth Evans, lived in the flat below Brown and Mitch on the second floor. She knew Brown and his crowd from Manchester clubs such as Berlin, Legends, Pips, Placemate 7 and Devilles, and had even seen The Patrol at South Trafford College. 'They were rubbish, absolute rubbish,' she said. When Brown moved to Hulme, she followed, and shared her flat with Rob Hampson, a scooterboy and suedehead heavily into Northern Soul. Hampson would briefly become a member of The Stone Roses in 1987.

'Ian had quite a settled life with Mitch,' said Dean. 'She had the proper skinhead look as well. As a couple they were still a bit mad, as anybody who lived in Hulme in that period would be, but to all intents and purposes they were settled down. They were both working. Ian used to drag his scooter up into his flat because it'd get nicked.'

Squire had landed a job as a model maker for the animation company Cosgrove Hall. 'It was my cousin who told me about the job going on the other side of the city, making props and theatrical sets,' he said. 'I thought it sounded like something I could do, so I jumped on my moped and drove over to the workshop while trying to balance a model I'd made of a *Wind in the Willows* riverside house, which was the nearest thing I had to a CV. I got the job, and I loved it.' After Cosgrove Hall's hit with *Danger Mouse*, the company released a seventy-five-minute film of *The Wind in the Willows* in 1983, winning a BAFTA. Squire was employed to work on a subsequent TV series based on the characters in the film.

'By 1983, everyone was drifting off and starting to do jobs,' said Couzens. 'John had a good job. Ian was working at the dole office – behind the counter, where people come in asking for money.' Couzens had learned guitar and missed the old gang. He pestered Brown about forming a new band. In all likelihood the invitation would have fallen on stony ground had Brown not just had a remarkable visitation from soul legend Geno Washington – one that swayed his decision and changed his life.

Fate delivered Washington into Brown's decrepit Hulme flat during a party to celebrate Mitch's twenty-first birthday. In the 1960s Washington had been a mod favourite on London's Soho R&B scene and with The Ram Jam band had scored two of the decade's best-selling albums, both cut live. After a period out of the limelight in the 1970s, when he returned to his native America to study hypnotism and train to be a life coach, his solo career had been given a shot in the arm by Dexys Midnight Runners, who had eulogized him in the song 'Geno', a huge number 1 single in 1980. 'I had a friend who worked at Salford University who was in Geno's road crew and he brought him down,' Brown said.

'We were staying over the night and I didn't just want to go back to the hotel straight away,' said Washington. 'I was signing some autographs and someone was telling me about this party that was going on, would I like to come? I said, Yeah, man. I went and the party was jumping, but I really wanted a joint instead of just drinking the booze. I got talking to a bunch over in the corner, which was Ian Brown and another couple of guys. I kept seeing these girls looking at Ian. They're coming up and talking to him. They all liked him. So I said to him, Looks like you got a lot of action going on. He said, Nah, man, I'm just hanging around. So I said, Hey, look, just to make this shit great, have you got any friends that could bring over some smoke? I'll pay. This friend came over about twenty minutes later. He had some good shit too. So I was on the good foot, I felt like I had had more glide in my stride, I had some loot in my flute.

'So Ian had done this favour for me,' said Washington. 'And when someone is nice to me I try and give them something back if I can. Here's a guy, he's got great personality, got the looks and girls are going crazy over him. I took him away from his friends, over to another corner, and was talking to him seriously. I said, Look, man, you ought to be a pop star, you ought to go into the pop business. I asked him, You sing? He said, No, I don't sing. I asked him, Do you write songs? He said, No, I don't write songs either. Goddamn, I said, Look, when you were in school did you write poetry or some kind of shit like that? He said, Yeah, I wrote a little bit of poetry. I said, Well, listen, because I'm being very serious with you now. If you write poetry, that's only one inch from writing songs, and that's where the pie is in the music business. All you need to do is learn how to sing and write your own goddamn songs and you're going to be cooking with gas, man. He looked at me and said, Really, you think so? I said, I'm telling you the truth, I'm not bullshitting you, I'm trying to help you and tell you a secret that you don't really know that you have. You got the looks, you got the personality and people love you; you're like a goddamn magnet. All you got to do is start writing your poems again and just move the shit to songs. I said, All you have to do is remember when you start off you're going to be shit, but just think you're only warming up. Then the more you do it the more you improve. You got it in your hand, man, do this. Do it for yourself, Ian. He said, Yeah, I'll look into it.'

'Geno was like, You're a star, go do the thing,' Brown recalled. 'I'd never heard of him apart from that "Geno" song. John was asking me to be a singer at the same time and I wasn't interested, but now it was, like, okay.'

After recruiting Brown, Couzens contacted Squire to suggest starting a new group. 'John said the only way he would do it was if Pete Garner came and played bass,' Couzens said.

Squire was still living at home and hanging out with Garner again after interesting him in helping to make an animated film independently at Cosgrove Hall. They spent their Sundays painstakingly putting footage together. 'Just to get five seconds of footage you've got to do hours of work,' said Garner. 'John was doing all the work, moving all the models and stuff.' Garner found the process tedious but was in the right place at the right time: 'John said to me they were getting The Patrol back together and Ian was going to be the singer. And John asked, did I want to play bass? He said he'd teach me.'

The line-up would be Squire and Couzens on guitar, Garner on bass and Brown on vocals. With the addition of Si Wolstencroft, it was basically the old Patrol gang again. After a year and a half of playing with Johnny Marr and Andy Rourke in Freak Party, Wolstencroft had quit the group. In that time they had tried out a number of singers. Marr was even said to have been keen on having Brown front the band at one stage. Finally they had settled on Morrissey, changed their name to The Smiths and made their first demo recordings. 'I just didn't fancy it,' said Wolstencroft. 'I didn't like the cut of Morrissey's jib and the rest is history.' The Smiths replaced Wolstencroft with Mike Joyce, signed to Rough Trade Records and quickly scored two massive hits with 'This Charming Man' and 'What Difference Does It Make?' before releasing their eponymous debut album in February 1984. 'We watched them go from being kids rehearsing, to being on *Top of the Pops*, to being a big and important band,' said Garner. 'So once you've seen your mates on telly, you're like, Fuck, we can do this.'

Initially the old gang rehearsed in the cellar at Couzens' parents' house where they also spent much time playing snooker and watching videos like *Texas Chain Saw Massacre*. There were also run-ins with the police and CB radio enthusiasts as the band cruised the streets, crammed into Couzens' two-seater MG Midget. 'Andy had a CB in his MG and we'd get on it and say, You're all a bunch of dickheads, and they'd try and hunt us down,' said Wolstencroft.

It was in Couzens' cellar where the as yet unnamed band got their early songs together. 'Nowhere Fast' was the first, then came 'All Stitched Up', 'I Can't Take It Anymore', 'Mission Impossible' and 'Tradjic Roundabout'. 'The music was purely John,' said Garner. 'When we started rehearsing, we'd look to John, who'd worked something out at home, and he played that and we'd work that up, play it over and over. The next rehearsal John would have another riff. Ian co-wrote the lyrics, but the creative input for the music was John.'

Brown, as Washington had forewarned, struggled at first. 'We started a few rehearsals and everyone's like, Fuck, we can't put up with that,' he said. 'You'll have to have singing lessons.' He went to see an 'old woman near Victoria Station' called Mrs Rhodes. 'She'd get me there at six o'clock, open the window with everyone coming home from work and have me wailing "After the Gold Rush" [Neil Young] and "Strawberry Fields Forever" [The Beatles] out the window,' he said. It was a challenge. 'She said, If you can't do it, go home. So I thought, Fuck, I'll stick it out. I did three weeks with her.'

Every week names for the band were suggested and rejected until finally Squire came up with The Stone Roses. 'We asked him, What does it mean?' said Garner. 'He said, It doesn't mean anything, it's hard and soft, which is sort of what we are. We went, Yeah that'll do.' It was also the name of a 1959 thriller by Sarah Gainham. 'That was just a mad coincidence,' said Garner. Squire later picked up a copy of the book in a charity shop in Chorlton.

A key early influence on the sound of The Stone Roses was a band called Empire. 'John and I were obsessed with them,' said Garner, who was now running the record department at Paperchase. Empire was Generation X guitarist Bob 'Derwood' Andrews's band and Garner was pushing their *Expensive Sound* album heavily at

Paperchase. Squire was also exploring 1960s psychedelic music, particularly The Misunderstood: Cherry Red Records had released a compilation of their work in 1982 called *Before the Dream Faded*. 'John turned me on to The Misunderstood and I used to love that record as well,' said Garner.

The band listened to The New York Dolls too, following the output of the group's charismatic guitarist Johnny Thunders, as well as the debut 1967 Pink Floyd album, *The Piper at the Gates of Dawn*; Love's 1967 album, *Forever Changes*; and another of Garner's favourites, MC5. Couzens said they listened to The Beatles' *Revolver* 'a lot', while Squire said he 'spent a lot of time with "Red House"', a track from Hendrix's *Are You Experienced*. 'A lot of the licks [on that track] made it on to Roses records later.'

The Stone Roses may have had high hopes, but with Garner and Brown still learning their roles they were more just mates having a laugh. So when the opportunity arose for Wolstencroft to join a real band in January 1984, he jumped at it. The Colourfield were the new act of former Specials and Fun Boy Three front man Terry Hall. Wolstencroft passed the audition and for a while The Stone Roses continued to rehearse without a drummer. Various people came down to Couzens' cellar to try out, including Chris Goodwin. 'There's a few drummers out there who could say, I was in the Roses for one rehearsal,' said Garner. None of them stuck around for much longer. 'We couldn't find anybody,' said Garner. 'So either John or Ian wrote a "drummer wanted" ad and put it up in A1, the music store on Oxford Road. I'm assuming they might have put down influences to indicate what kind of band we were. I don't remember if they put down Generation X, The Clash and Empire, but we were into those bands.'

Alan 'Reni' Wren had just turned twenty when he saw the ad in May 1984. He lived in Gorton, a rough part of inner-city Manchester, and was a self-confessed 'stinker', or 'smelly', into the New Wave of British Heavy Metal scene. A live-wire jobbing drummer with an eye on the big time, he was playing with a number of local rock bands, such as The Dealers and Tora Tora. He had landed in the latter band after his friend Simon Wright left the group to join rock legends AC/DC in 1983. Ian Paice of Deep Purple was a key influence on Reni's drumming style, and he listed the bands UFO, AC/DC, Thin Lizzy and Van Halen as favourites. He was, as Brown said, a 'proper rocker' who used to go to the annual Monsters of Rock festival at Donnington Park. He was also in a vocal harmony group and a fine singer.

Reni was born in April 1964, the second of six siblings. He held down a day job as a signwriter, having studied graphic design at college, although he said he never completed the course, 'kicked out' for missing classes. Reni had displayed freakish abilities on drums as a child, playing on the kit set up in the pub his mum and dad ran in Denton.

Instead of writing down the number on the ad, Reni took it off the wall and stuck it in his pocket so nobody else would see it. 'I bet he thought, Who the fuck is Empire?' said Couzens. 'The number in the advert was my house, and to this day I think he said his name was René, with the French accent.' Reni didn't have his own transport, so Brown and Couzens went to pick him up from his home for the initial audition. 'He was from the other side of the tracks,' said Couzens. 'He had a Rottweiler called Bella the size of a big bloke.'

Couzens and Brown loaded up Reni's drums and the three drove to Decibel studios in Ancoats, where The Smiths had rehearsed. 'They brought him in and we were working on something,' said Garner, who recorded all the band's rehearsals so they could listen back and sift out all the good bits to keep. 'We said, The song goes like this – thinking he'd listen for five minutes and then join in. Within ten seconds he was in and the band sounded better than it had ever sounded.'

'He changed us overnight,' said Couzens. 'No Reni, no Roses. It would have faltered like all the other things John and Ian and I had done. John was a punk guitarist when we met Reni, but Reni could play anything. He had a musical talent none of us had.'

'When I went to the audition I thought they made a horrible racket,' said Reni. 'But I was struck by their commitment. The whole group was such an oddball collection of long-hairs, scruffs and smoothies I just had to join.'

According to Garner, 'We never said, Shall we have him in the band. He was basically in the band, why would you not have him? He was easily the most talented musician of us all, way beyond everybody, including John. We were all pissing about a bit. He was a serious drummer who could have joined any band. He'd played with some quite big local bands from his area and done proper gigs. We all felt pretty lucky he'd joined us. Rehearsing got more enjoyable because he could play any style of music. That's when it got serious, from the moment Reni turned up.'

And, said Garner, Reni fitted into the gang straight away. 'It was bizarre. He was into a totally different type of music, he came from a totally different part of Manchester, but instantly I loved him.' Reni didn't think The Stone Roses were in any way musically brilliant, they weren't, but he thought they had something even if he wasn't quite sure what it was. He was also keen to broaden his horizons, and happy for the gang to introduce him to their haunts and influences. It was not a one-way dialogue: Reni turned the circumspect band on to AC/DC.

The Stone Roses continued rehearsing at Decibel for a few weeks before moving to nearby rehearsal rooms at Out of the Blue on Blossom Street, where for a time they shared a room with Easterhouse, who were signed to Rough Trade and being tipped as the next Smiths. When some of Easterhouse's gear went missing the Roses were kicked out and moved to Spirit on Tariff Street, close to Piccadilly Station. John Breakell, who owned the basement set-up, would become a key benefactor. Since opening in 1981 Spirit had been home to The Smiths, Simply Red, Carmel and the Happy Mondays. It cost £6.50 for an eight-hour day, but Breakell would often let the Roses rehearse for nothing. 'They'd say, I'll give you £2, John, I'll give you £3 next week,' he said. 'But it never materialized.'

The Roses recorded their first demo at Spirit in an overnight session on the newly installed Brenell eight-track. The studio was basic. 'Half the mics didn't work, the faders were all crackly,' said Breakell.

The sound of the toilet flushing often interfered with recordings, and 'the wiring was so shit, when you put the hairdryer on in the toilet it put the eight-track machine on'. Having borrowed the keys from the cleaner, the Roses invited themselves into the studio to record four songs: 'Nowhere Fast', 'Mission Impossible', 'Misery Dictionary' and 'Tradjic Roundabout'. The band played the producer of the demo, Tim Oliver, a Slaughter & the Dogs track as an indication of the sound they hoped for. 'We were looking for something with a bit of attitude,' Couzens said. 'That's what we were getting at, the attitude.'

The first Breakell knew of the recording was when he got a frantic phone call from his secretary the next morning saying the band wouldn't let her in and asking if she should call the police. 'I realized it was The Stone Roses, so I said, Leave 'em, and I took the phone off the hook and went back to sleep,' he said. He was also in for a surprise when he discovered Reni and Squire had painted the live room overnight. 'It wasn't the Pollock style,' he said. 'It was a bit mad. Reni was an amazing character.'

The four songs the Roses recorded would become mainstays in their early repertoire. 'There were a few other early songs such as "Coming of Age" that lasted a month and we didn't continue with,' said Garner. 'Misery Dictionary', which the Roses would retitle 'So Young', was written as a reaction to The Smiths. 'We were all young and enjoying ourselves and our mates were in a band that were known for misery, shyness and depression,' Garner said. 'It didn't seem right to us.' The band also changed the title of 'Nowhere Fast' to 'Just a Little Bit', after realizing The Smiths also had a song called 'Nowhere Fast'.

The Roses limited the demo to a hundred copies. 'For an eight-track, it's the best demo that's ever been done – definitely,' Brown said. He was proud of his lyrics to 'Tradjic Roundabout', which name-checked Martin Luther King. 'They had some kind of passion. It's like being hit by a ton of bricks, but there's always a tune.' Squire would concur. 'Wild sounds with attractive melodies,' he said of the band's early output. 'We chose the name The Stone Roses because it reflects the contradiction.'

Couzens and Brown were the most proactive members, often driving down to London for the dual purpose of a night out and to hustle the demo tape. It was on one of these trips that the pair met Caroline Reed, who would become The Stone Roses' first manager. Reed already managed the Rhyl-based Clash-influenced Mercenary Skank, and offered the Roses their first gig supporting the band at an anti-heroin benefit at the Moonlight Club in West Hampstead in October 1984. Brown had seen an ad Reed placed in *Sounds* for 'bands wanted', sent the Spirit demo off to her, and told her they were big on the Manchester scene. 'She didn't know it was our first gig,' he said.

The Roses rehearsed hard in Spirit for their debut, adding new songs to their set, including a cover of Nazz's 'Open My Eyes' (Nazz had been Todd Rundgren's 1960s breakthrough act). There were new originals, such as 'Heart on the Staves', written according to Garner because 'the tortured artist, false emotion thing annoyed us', and 'Tell Me'. With its 'You can't tell me anything' lyric, it was 'Rage Against the Machine before you were allowed to swear'. Another original was 'Getting Plenty'. 'Not about sex,' said Garner. 'I don't think there's a single song the band has done that's cheesy, singing about chicks like that. That would have been wrong.' And there was 'Fall', a barbed song written about the Factory Records/Haçienda scene. 'All of us felt the Factory thing was a bit pretentious,' said Garner. Factory, famed for Joy Division and run by Tony Wilson, dominated the city – especially now New Order were firmly established. The Haçienda, said Garner, was 'generally empty with an awful sound and freezing cold'.

'We were very anti-Factory, anti-Haçienda,' said Couzens. 'James Anderton, the Greater Manchester police chief, had shut everything down apart from this one place that monopolized everything, the Haçienda, and it was a dump. John and I were members really early on, but it was the only place to go. So it became a resentful thing, this big shining light in this sea of shit. Manchester was a horrible, dirty, scruffy place.'

The band was so determined to impress at their debut gig they even rehearsed stage moves. 'We were all young, energetic lads so we'd enjoy ourselves,' said Couzens. 'Leading up to London we were all excited.'

The Roses were an instant hit in London. They soundchecked by playing 'Open My Eyes', and on the strength of that Caroline Reed offered to manage them. There was also a surprise guest that night: The Who's Pete Townshend. He was equally impressed. 'We didn't know when we set out to do our first gig that we were going to be supporting Pete Townshend,' said Garner. 'That was pretty surreal. I believe the previous gig Townshend had done was some massive stadium on The Who's farewell tour.'

'We came off stage and Townshend was, like, You look really good up on stage and your drummer's great,' said Brown. 'Then he said, as an end of the night thing, I want to play a couple of tunes, and he asked Reni, Do you want to do it? Reni's like, Yeah! He ended up playing three or four The Who tunes with Townshend.'

'One of them Reni didn't know,' said Garner. 'I was on the side of the stage and Reni mouthed to me, How does it go? . . . What an experience. But I was thinking, Shit, man, our secret weapon is out of the bag. My worst fear had come true. Reni was going to get poached – oh fuck, he's going to join The Who now. First gig and we've lost him.'

Squire shared the same fear. 'We were told he'd said he really wanted to use Reni on his next LP. We were like, Shit, Reni's going to leave. Townshend's nicking Reni.'

'At that time Reni was awe-inspiring,' said Couzens. 'To play with him made us sound phenomenal; he was just this force. Just to watch him play was inspirational. That's what got Pete Townshend that night. He was inspired by what he'd seen.'

'We were buzzing on the way back to Manchester,' said Garner. 'Can you imagine? We came back thinking, Fucking hell, we've made it.'

Caroline Reed organized for the Roses to support Mercenary Skank at Exeter Labour Club and the Kensington Ad Lib club in November. The two bands were not a natural fit. The Ad Lib gig was reviewed in *Sounds*. Mercenary Skank were praised but the Roses panned, described as 'one-paced and blustering' and 'loud-mouthed and careless'.

'The review and the next few gigs were the comedown, back to earth,' said Garner. 'Playing in front of two men and a dog and no one's really interested.' The review had been especially disappointing because *Sounds* was the weekly music paper Garner and Brown preferred over rivals *NME* and *Melody Maker*. Brown particularly 'knew what journalists did what at *Sounds*', said Garner, and he targeted Garry Johnson as the man there most likely to give the Roses a leg-up.

Johnson was respected as the poet of Oi!, his poems 'Dead End Yobs' and 'The New Face of Rock 'n' Roll' having been included on the seminal 1981 compilation *Strength Thru Oi!* Johnson, like Brown, had the gift of the gab and had blagged the job on *Sounds*, where he spent three years 'travelling the UK, staying in five-star hotels all expenses paid, taking lorry loads of speed and meeting heroes like David Bowie, Rod Stewart and Debbie Harry'.

Johnson listened to the Roses demo tape Brown had sent him. 'You didn't have to be Mystic Meg to predict they were going to be massive,' he said. Johnson had family in Manchester and organized a trip to the city to interview the band. He spent a 'wild weekend' with the Roses, and the resulting piece featured in *Sounds* with a mention of the band's name on the cover. 'Garry tipped us as being a big thing for 1985 and we were a tiny band who'd done one demo tape and a few gigs,' said Garner. 'He was a champion of the cause.'

Johnson wrote in *Sounds* that, 'with their tense and galactic brand of starkly atmospheric sound The Stone Roses are a breath of fresh air'. He took the demo around every major record label in London and was 'turned down by every single one . . . I did all their publicity,' he said. 'They stayed at my flat in London, living off Marmite on toast and McDonald's milk shakes.' Brown and Reni even appeared on stage at the Cockney Pride pub in Piccadilly Circus with Johnson's mate and Oi! legend Frankie Flame. The Jam's Bruce Foxton offered to produce the Roses in the studio and there was talk of Buster Bloodvessel of Bad Manners being an early fan. 'Things were going nice and starting to happen,' Johnson said, 'and then I blew it and went on a massive bender.'

'Garry was always taking speed, constantly,' said Couzens. Speed was also popular with the band, but not to the extent Johnson snorted it. The Roses weren't big drinkers either. Couzens was tee-total and Brown avoided beer altogether. Johnson took the band to a Bruce Foxton gig and introduced him to them. Whether Foxton's offer of producing the Roses was serious or not, Squire was not keen. 'We'd been big Jam fans but it was mainly me and Ian,' said Garner. 'John was never really having it. Garry had organized some photographer to take a photo of us with Bruce Foxton, but John refused.'

Before going AWOL Johnson did manage to get a few more column inches for the Roses with a bogus story about Garner beating up the lead singer of teen pop act Kajagoogoo at a showbiz party. There were two more nights with Mercenary Skank for the Roses in January 1985, both in London, at the Fulham Greyhound and at the Marquee, where there was a microphone-throwing incident that saw them banned. Brown complained that the venue didn't like the way he would 'leap around' on stage, preferring bands 'to be nice and safe'.

Relations with manager Caroline Reed became strained, said Couzens. 'She was going out with one of Mercenary Skank and she was all over them. We were like a by-product of a bad problem.' Couzens kicked her door in one night and Reed gave up answering the phone to them. But the Roses already had a new manager lined up.

Howard Jones had been a Factory Records director and the manager of the Haçienda since its opening night in 1982 but had severed his ties with the club and label. Now, at the age of thirty-two, Jones was putting together his own record label called Thin Line with Tim Chambers of the Factory Records video arm, IKON, and famed Joy Division and New Order producer Martin Hannett. All three were keen to prove themselves outside of the Factory family, particularly Hannett, who had become estranged from Tony Wilson due to arguments about money invested in the Haçienda.

The Roses had been introduced to Jones through Steve 'Adge' Atherton, keyboard player with the recently defunct band Third Law, who was now working in a loose capacity at their Spirit rehearsal rooms. It was the first of many key interventions by Adge that would result in him becoming the band's tour manager – a title that ill reflected his prominent role.

'Adge knew everybody and everything,' said Jones. 'He rang me and said, Look we've got a great band rehearsing, come and check them out.' Jones saw it as an audition and had used Spirit in that capacity before as he sought out acts for his new label. He would normally set the band up in the live recording room and watch from the control room, separated from the band by a glass partition. The Roses demanded Jones and Chambers go into their rehearsal room. 'Right from the bat they wanted control of the situation.'

It was 15 November 1984 and they played four songs at 'excruciating levels'. 'I couldn't hear anything that was going on musically but there was something about them,' said Jones. Reni was 'out of this world . . . The way he played, his facial expressions, his finishing, how he'd kill a cymbal once he'd hit it, he'd got total natural technique. Johnny [Squire] was behind his fringe, Pete and Andy were bouncing off one another and Ian was right in your face. They already truly believed they were the greatest band in the world.'

Most bands would have jumped at the chance to work with Thin Line, but 'we weren't a normal band,' said Couzens. 'We weren't into that cap-doffing attitude you get with a lot of bands. We were really genuinely, unbelievably arrogant. Ian was perfect for it because he drew people in anyway. We were like, We don't need your help. If you want to help, great – well done, pal; now fuck off. It was like that. Don't expect any thanks.'

Jones would use Tim Chambers, who was closer in age to the band, as his conduit in attempting to assert influence over the Roses – having found his initial suggestion that Garner cut his hair strongly rebuffed. 'They were very much a gang and a little bit suspicious of Howard because they felt he wasn't one of them,' said Chambers. 'So my role was a foot in both camps.' Chambers clicked with Brown and Squire over a shared interest in the aesthetic and politic of punk and the concept of Situationism.

Brown was reading Guy Debord, the French Marxist theorist, and *The Anarchists* by James Joll; he also had photocopies of Jamie Reid's *Suburban Press* magazine. 'These were the things we were thinking about,' he said. 'I loved the slogans like, "Use the medium, don't let it use you" and, "No two situations are the same". That's the one we always used in the Roses – it really meant something to us.' Chambers loaned the band his collection of punk fanzines, which included *Sniffing Glue, London's Burning* and San Francisco's *Search and Destroy.* 'They were not trying to ape punk,' he said, 'but they had a thirst for knowing about stuff, they wanted an informed emotion. They were sucking up all these influences looking for their vision. Ian was always writing lyrics or notes or memos to himself.'

The band were serious about rehearsals, unnervingly focused and instinctive in their approach. Arguments were commonplace as they aspired to turn their rock bombast into a white light sound. They were now more often than not to be found rehearsing at the Lock-Up in Chorlton, south Manchester, another facility owned by Spirit's John Breakell, where The Smiths also rehearsed. Brown and his girlfriend Mitch had moved to a flat in Chorlton, and Squire, whose Cosgrove Hall workplace was in the area, lived with them there for a while. Brown and Mitch would move flats regularly, always staying around south Manchester, and often sharing with Squire.

Jones also lived in Chorlton, and the new Roses manager often blagged the band free rehearsal time at the Lock-Up on flimsy excuses. 'I love Howard and he was instrumental in those days in pushing the Roses along, but he was just full of shit,' Breakell said. In the Lock-Up new songs were added to the Roses set, including 'I Wanna Be Adored'. ' "I Wanna Be Adored" just felt like the mellow one,' said Garner. 'I discussed it with Ian, because he said to me, I need to write some more lyrics, there's only four lines in it. I said, No, no, that's why it's so good. Less is more. John wrote the bass line that runs right through it, and the rest of it is ethereal. It was unusual in the set; most of our songs were fast and quite angsty, and that had quite a groove to it.'

It was at the Lock-Up that Jones introduced the band to Martin Hannett, the real ace in his plans for Thin Line. Although they had fallen out, Tony Wilson said Hannett was a 'genius', and the record producer was revered for his work with Joy Division and New Order. Hannett was looking for the next U2. He'd produced their 1980 single '11 o'Clock Tick Tock' and seen them progress to the verge of world recognition. 'Martin was saying to me there are bands in the indie market that could be as big as U2,' said Jones, who felt the Roses' style at present was closer to The Cult.

'When Howard brought Martin down,' said Garner, 'we were like, Oh Martin who produced Slaughter & the Dogs, rather than, Oh it's the Joy Division producer. Ian and I were asking him about Slaughter, we'd heard all these great stories. He was a bit taken aback because everyone wanted to talk to him about Joy Division apart from us.'

Hannett didn't just like the Roses, he loved them: their attitude and sound immediately clicked. News that Hannett had agreed to work with the band spread fast. 'Manchester was a village in those days with just a small group of people who did things, so you inevitably bumped into each other,' said Chambers. 'Tony Wilson said everyone he knew had left to go and join the Roses. There was a joke that at Thin Line we were forming Renegade Records.'

'They were trying to set up an alternative Factory,' said Couzens. On this principle the influential Wilson hated the Roses. Chambers described it as 'tribal': 'If you're one of us you hear The Stone Roses as the future, if you're one of them you hear it as a tuneless heavy metal racket. The Roses were a force, which meant you either loved them or you didn't, they polarized opinion. I'm not sure it was specifically Factory Records they were against, it was more upsetting the current power-base: what is black must be white, what is yes must be no, that inarticulate rebellion against established order.'

3.

Sweden

Since early 1984 Tony Michaelides had hosted an alternative Sunday-night music show called *The Last Radio Programme* on Manchester Piccadilly, the biggest radio station outside London. Over a beer in the Haçienda the Roses' new manager Jones called in a favour from him, who he knew from his time at Factory Records. 'Howard was a hustler,' said Michaelides. Jones sent Garner over to Piccadilly to drop off the Roses' original demo tape the following Sunday.

'It was only fifteen or twenty minutes before the show started and the tape was a quarter-inch reel-to-reel,' said Michaelides. 'I took it into an editing suite and listened to it with the young girls, Paula [Greenwood] and Ro [Newton], who were my helpers. It had an immediate impact on us, so we played "Misery Dictionary" straight away on air. It had an element of discordant chaos, punk in a way, but it wasn't completely at odds with the Paisley Underground thing I was pushing.' The response was instant, with listeners calling in to praise the track.

Michaelides played 'Misery Dictionary' and the other three tracks on the Roses demo consistently on his show through late 1984. He had asked Jones about the possibility of Brown and Squire coming on the show to play an acoustic set, but Jones wanted it to be the whole band. The Roses went into the Piccadilly live studio – more accustomed to hosting orchestras than rock bands – to record a live session on 12 January 1985. The songs were 'Heart on the Staves', 'I Wanna Be Adored' and 'Tell Me'. An early soundcheck had to be abandoned after Reni's drumming interfered with the station's smooth afternoon soul show. 'So we had to soundcheck the band an hour before we went on air,' said Michaelides. 'It was punk radio, total mania, everything in the spirit of the moment. There was a little bit of an interview after the session, but they were not really great interviewees. They're not really the sort of band you'd sit down and interview.'

'Piccadilly did not know what on earth was happening to them,' said Jones. 'They thought they were getting a local band and they got a band on fire.' Spirit's Steve Adge was in the studio with the band and, Garner said, 'threw a chair at us, just to add to the tension' halfway through the live broadcast.

The relationship with Piccadilly Radio continued when the Roses played their sixth gig at a *Last Radio Programme* showcase at Dingwalls in London on 8 February. 'There wasn't a huge turnout but we'd brought forty or fifty people in a coach down from Manchester,' said Michaelides. 'The Roses were the headliners. Ian got right out in the audience and he was going up to people and singing in their faces.'

There were London journalists at the show, including Jon Wilde, who in 1989 would write a scathing *Melody Maker* cover story about the band. 'I was talking to him about the Roses and getting excited, but he didn't think that much of them at all,' said Paula Greenwood. 'And they were definitely doing things that became part of what they became later on. It was raw but you could hear the potential. The set was pretty short, about twenty minutes max, inspired by the Sex Pistols. Best to keep the audience wanting more. What I was into more than anything was the energy. They were exciting for teenagers like me who'd missed punk. Ian used to come off the stage and be quite menacing.'

'I was aggressive on stage,' Brown said. 'I was always walking around the crowd singing in people's faces, high kicking, or kissing someone's girl, winding someone up. I sang to the girls to get the lads wound up. Everywhere we went I used to get on that. And it worked – people remembered us.'

'He's got balls of steel; that's why you want him as your singer,' said Garner. 'He'd go out into the crowd and pick someone's drink up in front of them and say cheers, not in a threatening way but in that Ian way, and he got away with it. It was just bravado.'

Following Dingwalls the Roses came to a decision over what

songs to record for their debut single on Thin Line. Jones corralled the Roses into the twenty-four-track Yellow II studio owned by Peter Tattersall – over the road from his more famous Strawberry Studios in Stockport – to record 'So Young' and 'Tell Me', with Martin Hannett producing.

'Martin had got an abscess on his tooth, so he wasn't in a great mood and he drank copious amounts of Guinness and was rubbing raw cocaine onto his gum,' said Jones. 'He said it was to deaden the pain but I'm sure as much went up his nose. He adored the Roses. He liked rawness.' Hannett had his own image to keep up, and that was, said Jones, of 'a grumpy, miserable bastard that you only spoke to when spoken to. He liked that authoritarian studio thing because otherwise the whole band would have tried to interfere in the recording.' The Roses did to a certain degree, until Hannett, who always kept a revolver on his desk, threatened to shoot them. 'It was all Phil Spector homage – there were no bullets in the gun,' said Jones. 'Can you believe how lucky they were? They were in a fantastic studio as an unsigned, unknown band, with Martin Hannett – but they didn't see it that way. That's the arrogance level of them.'

While recording the original demo at Spirit, the Roses had just counted to four and performed the songs live with limited overdubs. This first single session was more arduous as Hannett recorded each instrument separately. Hearing themselves in perfect clarity was an eye-opener and led to rows in the studio. 'It never came to blows,' said Couzens, 'but you couldn't really tell John anything. That's where a lot of the arguments used to come from. If Ian, or I, would say anything about anything, he used to go mad. One of the biggest arguments we had was over whether we should have "The" in front of "Stone Roses". Fucking ridiculous. Petty but very intense.'

'We argued violently for that one; it had to be The,' said Garner. 'When it was released, "So Young" just said Stone Roses and I had a fit at Howard because that was wrong. On the back of the sleeve he spelt rhythm wrong; how amateur. We tended to get animated and upset about things that seem ridiculous now.'

'Too much enthusiasm and not enough thought went into that record,' Brown said of the single. 'They weren't really songs, just a sound. It's a good noise. We played the original version [of 'So Young'] in the car. Martin's first remix was the most extreme thing I've ever heard. We went for a drive and Reni's nose exploded, blood everywhere – there was so much treble on the record that his nose went with the frequency. We should have gone with that version. It was pre-Mary Chain and full of feedback. It was beautiful. But we went with the safer mix.'

'So Young'/'Tell Me' would not be released until August 1985, giving Jones plenty of time for hype. He had already issued a lavish press release to publicize the fact the recording 'with the enigmatic' Hannett was taking place. In it he promised three mixes of the single 'Hurt', 'Hard' and 'Heat', and bragged of 'further info' coming soon in the music press. The mixes would never materialize.

Bob Dickinson was the first local journalist to interview the Roses for an article that would appear in *City Life* (Manchester's *Time Out* equivalent) on 29 March. Again it was a favour pulled in by Jones, who had supplied Dickinson with the band's original demo tape. 'The sheer attack the band packed into that demo was amazing,' said Dickinson. 'The guitar sound was so intense. It was very un-Manchester. There was a mini-wave of jingly-jangly bands such as The Railway Children, The Waltones and The Man from Delmonte getting written about. I got the impression that the Roses had heard a lot of British stuff from the 1960s.'

Dickinson asked Squire about this musical reference point. The guitarist said he was more interested in Slash Records, the seminal late 70s/early 80s LA punk record label that was home to bands such as The Germs and The BoDeans. 'We don't want to be clothes horse puppets,' said Squire. 'If there's another group like us, we haven't heard of one.' 'We're five people who all want to be a front man,' said Brown. Asked about the current music scene, Squire said, 'There's nothing exciting enough to make you want to buy it or play it. There was nothing exciting us at all, so the best thing was for us to do it ourselves.' The killer quote in the Dickinson piece came from Reni. 'We don't want to be another up and coming band of the 80s,' he said. 'We want to be *the* band of the 80s.' Later, Reni said, 'The respect and musical integrity of Echo & the Bunnymen with the Wham! bank account would be ideal.'

Dickinson wrote that the Roses were 'dramatically different from all other bands' and coined the term 'Deviant Merseybeat' to describe the band's sound. 'I wanted to say they were a bit more 60s "freakbeat" but they rejected that idea,' he said. The label more often hung around the Roses' neck in this period was 'goth'. This was largely as a result of the photograph by Kevin Cummins used to accompany Dickinson's article. Garner wore a ruffle shirt, Squire a bandana and Brown had his hair slicked back. 'We definitely weren't goths,' said Brown. The photo was taken in Didsbury's Marie Louise Gardens. Cummins worked for the *NME* and was famed for his shots of Joy Division and The Smiths.

To Cummins the band 'felt a little bit like outsiders, because Manchester was so dominated by Factory and the Haçienda'. This first photo shoot with the band was also supposed to be used by the *NME*. 'When we did that session, just because of the way they looked, I wanted to do them in a more pastoral setting. I wanted it to be more hippyish – that was the feel of the shot.'

The photograph was intended to accompany a full-page feature in the *NME* written by Ro Newton. The teenager went to the Roses' next gig at Preston Clouds on 29 March intending to inter-view the band, but was left appalled. 'Nightmare,' said Garner, wincing at the memory. 'We hadn't played in Manchester so anyone who was on the scene who knew us travelled to Preston to see it. There was a big contingent of kids who went to this venue in Pres-ton every week, so as soon as we started playing it was just waiting for a spark.'

The Roses provided the spark. They opened their early shows by playing a discordant racket to grab the crowd's attention before starting up the first song. It was an idea taken from the Sex Pistols. 'We were also having equipment problems,' said Couzens. 'The gear was fucked up, so you can't stand there in silence – there's nothing worse. Reni called it rumble tunes, just drums and a bit of noisy guitar. The gear breaking and a droning rhythmic racket: it sets people off – it can, anyway.'

'There was a proper fight,' said Garner. 'It all kicked off.' Before abandoning the stage, the Roses played a cover of 'Love Missile F1-11' by Sigue Sigue Sputnik. 'Just a total piss-take. We sort of liked it because it was a bit naff. It was a disaster, so John started playing the riff and we joined in, laughing, just to try and make light of the situation.'

'It was a full-scale riot,' said Jones. 'A lot of drinking went on, then a load of amphetamine seemed to appear. I was standing next to Ro and I had to grab her under the arms and pull her out of the audience so she didn't get trampled in the mayhem. She was pretty shaken up.'

A horrified Newton interviewed the band backstage. 'Ian wasn't condoning it, but he wasn't agreeing with her that it was outrageous and horrible,' said Garner. 'He was playing devil's advocate and she took umbrage. She hated us. She thought we were celebrating it, whereas if you were going out in Manchester, that happened all the time. I thought afterwards, We've upset the wrong person there.'

There was also a 'drunk guy in the dressing room mouthing off' during the interview, said Jones. Having repeatedly asked him to shut up, Jones finally got someone to drag him out. 'As he's getting dragged out he said, Do you know who I am? I said, I don't give a shit. It was Mani.'

The interview never appeared, but Newton penned a live review for the *NME* that slaughtered the band. Ever the opportunist, Jones took out an ad in the *NME* and quoted the opening paragraph: 'Imagine the sound of fingernails scraping down a blackboard, amplified to an intolerable degree. The Stone Roses are tuning up. The angst-ridden vocal penetrates the plethora of deranged drumming and screaming feedback. The effect is impelling.' The review itself went on to say that 'it is a disgrace, they're thugs, hooligans, there's nothing good about the band,' said Jones. 'But I stopped it there, because obviously that opening paragraph sounds really interesting. I put Ro Newton's name under it and she went berserk.'

A gig in Oldham was cancelled for fear of a repeat of the Preston riot, before the Roses headed to Sweden for a band-defining tour starting on 10 April. During a break in the band's activities, Brown had gone hitching around Europe with Mitch, and in Berlin met the Swede Andreas Kemi, who ran a magazine called *The Eye*. Brown had done his usual shtick of talking up the Roses. 'I told him we were a big group in Manchester,' Brown said. 'He set up about eight or nine shows.'

Kemi was enthused by the Roses' original demo and planned a joint tour for the Roses with Swedish group Toxin Toy. After exchanging letters with the Roses, Kemi even fronted the money for the ferry over. Before setting off, Jones told the band they'd need £50 each spending money and Reni sold his motorbike to raise the cash.

They travelled over to Stockholm in a big Chevrolet truck. Couzens had replaced his MG Midget with a 1950s black Chevrolet, and sacrificed that beauty to pay for the truck. It was a vast improvement on the transit van the band had used, which had no seats in the rear, forcing them to perch on their equipment. As well as the band and Jones, former New Order roadie Glen Greenough was along for the ride. He was a big drinker and blew his dole cheque in the casino on the ferry going over to Sweden. In fact the whole band blew almost all their money on the ferry as they celebrated Reni's twenty-first birthday.

Toxin Toy – Harald Sickenga, Micke Mürhoff, Anette Svensson and Christian Adelöv – had formed in October 1984 and were equally excited by the prospect of the tour. Kemi was predicting that the Roses were going to be huge. He had appointed himself Toxin Toy's manager and spent a month organizing the tour, making hundreds of calls, sending out demos, photos and press releases, in an effort to book gigs and get publicity. Kemi and Toxin Toy had also arranged a big tour bus with space for backline equipment and the PA system, a driver, a sound engineer, a photographer and even someone who would fix sandwiches and food. The impressive amount of gear weighed two tons, with 2 x 3,000 watts for sound and 24,000 watts for the lighting.

The carefree Roses were unaware of much that had been organized. Their only plan was to meet Kemi in Stockholm. 'If this guy hadn't turned up at the train station in Sweden we'd have been fucked,' said Garner. 'We didn't know where we were going really, we had no real itinerary,' said Couzens. 'It was just like, We're going to Stockholm, and we said we'd be there on this date and we just jumped in the back of this Chevy truck and threw what gear we could in it.'

Toxin Toy's studio was in a shabby industrial area just below Karolinska Sjukhuset, where a murdered prostitute had been found a month earlier chopped up in a black garbage bag. Kemi had arranged for the Roses party to stay in a grim, ghetto-like area in Lidingö. 'We felt bad that the guys in The Stone Roses had to stay in that hellish area,' said Sickenga. The Roses saw it through different eyes. 'Toxin Toy saved our arses,' said Garner. 'We'd have been skint and deported after a week without them.'

'Sweden made us as a band,' Garner said. 'It was totally different from doing a gig every few weeks; we became a proper band in Sweden.' He described it as the Roses' 'Hamburg moment', referring to the period The Beatles spent honing their sound at the Star Club in Hamburg pre-fame. 'It was absolutely brilliant,' he said, 'not a bad memory. We were five kids in a foreign country, doing gigs, it was our gang; it was fantastic.' 'We came together as a unit,' said Couzens. 'It became a natural thing. We just got up and did it and the music was there and everything else was on top of it.'

The nights in Sweden varied wildly, from trendy clubs in Stockholm to huge sports halls and tiny village gigs around the country, and rarely passed without incident. At one, while Brown was in the crowd trying to provoke a reaction, a guy pulled a gun on him. 'Ian just walked up and put the barrel in his mouth, and gesticulated, Come on then, come on then,' said Couzens. 'For us at that time, it was normal. That type of incident didn't faze us at all. I can't believe we carried on playing. I think we were halfway though "I Wanna Be Adored".'

'That could have been the end of the story, couldn't it?' said Jones. 'When the Kaiser Chiefs sing "I Predict a Riot", it's going to be a very pleasant riot where everybody has a nice time. When the Stone Roses sing "I Predict a Riot", things get set on fire, smashed and burned. There was that incredible energy attached to this band. That did give way to the musicality, but the energy was still in the individuals. That presence was still there.'

Another memorable gig took place at the small but cool Rock-borgen club in Borås. The police turned up in riot gear and arrested half of the audience, claiming many in the crowd were minors. 'The police wanted to search the bus – they suspected we had under-aged girls high on drugs in there, which was not true,' said Sickenga. At Studion, a big rock club in Stockholm popular with acts from the US and Europe, the stage walls were mirrored, and during 'I Wanna Be Adored' Brown ran straight into one of the mirrors and smashed it. 'We never understood if he did it on purpose, or if he just didn't see it,' said Sickenga.

'Something happened every night,' said Jones. 'One night the PA caught fire; Ian pushed the PA off the stage at another gig and we didn't get paid. We were booked into this one place that was like a small house. The stage had a fireplace and Reni had a piss in it and we all left without playing. We were literally doing a gig a day, otherwise we didn't eat. We were getting loads of Swedish reviews but it was more about how mad we were and how all the gigs ended in a riot. The reviews were saying we were good, exciting and charismatic.'

'It was great,' said Brown. 'We got in the daily papers.' In one Swedish interview, Brown explained much of the band's method: 'We all write all the music, it's a joint effort,' he said. 'We just get in a room and play along and bash it out and at the end of the night we've got a decent song. I write all the lyrics. Our inspiration is from people who we've seen and respect and they ended up copping out.

Our inspiration is the fact there's no decent live music for anyone to go and see. That's all we're trying to do, make people enjoy it and enjoy it ourselves. Musically, we like a lot of 1960s music, 1960s psychedelic stuff, we like a lot of early punk stuff. So we try and combine the melody of the 60s stuff with the energy of the punk stuff. We're not a punk band and we're not a 1960s band, we're just a 1980s band.'

Driving the tour bus was a character dubbed 'the Last of the Vikings', who kept a well-used aluminium baseball bat and a crowbar to hand. Running low on fuel on an overnight drive between gigs, he used these tools to attack a self-service petrol pump that had swallowed his money. 'When he was done, we got all our banknotes back and all that was left of the pump was the pipe with hose,' said Sickenga. 'Then he said, Okay, go on and fill up, there's an alarm on the pump, we have fifteen minutes before the cops get here.'

The photographer on the tour was an old friend of Sickenga's called Lena Kagg. A selection of her photographs from the tour can be found in this book. One of them would also be used on the back cover of the Roses' 1987 single 'Sally Cinnamon'. 'It's a photo of Johnny [Squire] jumping off the roof of the bus,' said Jones. 'There was a riot going on, so to get into the venue we had to climb out of the skylight of the bus and jump onto the side of the building.'

After the opening shows there was a nine-day gap until a final clutch of dates that would climax at Lidingö Stadium on 30 April. The band were largely surviving by eating the food provided at gigs, and on the road they often stayed at fans' houses, but at the Stockholm flat the band were growing desperate. 'We didn't want them to starve to death on their first tour out of the UK,' said Sickenga. Toxin Toy's drummer Adelöv worked as a manager for a grocery store outside of Stockholm. 'I don't know what possessed him,' said Jones. 'He let us go into the supermarket after it was closed, in the middle of the night, and stock up on food. It was like supermarket sweep: we just ran around the supermarket filling baskets up.'

Jones began to work the phones, trying to organize more gigs for the band to fill their days off. He successfully scored a handful of further slots, including supporting Australian indie rock band The Go-Betweens. There was still much downtime and the atmosphere in the flat became strained. The band could be vicious towards each other, but most of the tension was released on Jones. 'Every night was a new prank they thought was hilarious,' said Jones. 'They'd unscrew my bed or fill my boots with jelly. Eventually I made them find me somewhere else to live.'

Out of all the band members, Jones found he had most in common with Squire, and would sometimes spend time with him on days off in Stockholm at a Picasso exhibition or admiring Henry Moore sculptures. Jones also observed the strong relationship between Squire and Brown. 'They had an understanding that was very intuitive,' he said. 'They didn't speak that much. The way they communicated was just eye contact. If Ian was doing right, John would do nothing. If Ian was doing something wrong, John would just give him a look and Ian would stop saying whatever he was saying. They were almost like twins. That came from a real closeness.'

For Squire, the tour of Sweden showed him the Roses 'really could happen . . . Before then I wasn't sure if we could make it. Something happened to me in Sweden. I can clearly remember the day. I was walking back to the flat we were staying at – under a concrete underpass with loads of graffiti. It was a bright sunny day and it was next to the water. I just felt that this was too good not to do full time. It just felt so right, there was no way I could pass up the opportunity of seeing where it could go. I still had a job at Cosgrove Hall. I'd taken a holiday to go to Sweden but I decided that this was it. I couldn't go back.'

4.

So Young

Post-Sweden there was a new sense of commitment as the rest of the band followed Squire and quit their day jobs to sign on the dole and concentrate fully on the band. 'John was giving up a fantastic, creative job he really loved,' said Garner. 'And he was on good money, so it was a big thing for him. When he did that, that made us all feel, Wow, we're serious now, we've become a proper band.'

The Roses' first gig back in England was a low-key affair at a newly opened club in Manchester. The International, on Anson Road in Longsight, had hosted American Paisley Underground bands such as The Long Ryders and Los Lobos. It was owned by future Stone Roses managers Gareth Evans and Matthew Cummins. Special guests for the Friday night on 10 May 1985 were It's Immaterial; admission was £2. Among the crowd were two girls from Sweden who had made the journey over to see them play. 'I thought we'd never see any of these people again,' said Garner. 'We'd become the kind of band you'd travel across countries to see play,' said Jones. 'Those girls knew the Roses were going to be huge.'

That night Jones told the band they would have to sack Reni if the drummer's 'disruptive' behaviour didn't change. Jones had organized for MTV to interview Brown and Squire at the show, but while they waited backstage for the crew to arrive, Reni had gone to the front of the venue and hijacked the interview. 'Reni just did the interview on his own,' said Jones. Jones was furious, having already discussed with the band that Squire and Brown would handle the media. He was serious about ousting Reni. 'Ian said to me, Are you fucking stupid?' said Jones. 'He said, It's not happening. You're going to have to manage him better. It's your problem, not mine.'

'He couldn't even get me to cut my hair, never mind getting someone sacked out of the band,' said Garner. 'As far as we were concerned, if Howard got us gigs and put our records out and things were moving forward, then we were happy.' But Couzens said the band did come perilously close to sacking Reni. 'Myself, John and Ian were driving over to Reni's one night to sack him. And it was only as we were ten or fifteen minutes away from Reni's house we thought, What the fuck are we doing?'

Hannett had by now mixed 'So Young' and 'Tell Me' at Strawberry Studios, and Jones busied himself preparing the release of the Roses' debut Thin Line single, organizing the artwork and arranging manufacturing and distribution. He used many of his connections from Factory Records. The Cartel, an organization who distributed Factory in the UK, would do the same for Thin Line, and Jones was also talking to Rough Trade about distribution in Europe. During this process Jones sought to clarify which names to put down for the songwriting credits. 'I said, You've got to talk it out yourselves,' he recalled. 'Then Ian and John came to see me on their own, which is always an ominous sign, and said we're going to do Squire and Brown like Lennon and McCartney, but we'll sort out everything else with the band.'

The decision did not go down well. After a tongue-in-cheek 'secret' gig at the Gallery, a hip venue in town, where the Roses played under the name of The Boned Noses, Reni and Couzens both left the band and there followed a six-week stand-off. 'Put yourself in mine, Reni's and Pete's shoes,' said Couzens. 'You've got your first record coming out and it's the most exciting thing. Then you get confronted with John and Ian and your manager saying this is how it's going to be: it's not, as we've all discussed, "The Stone Roses" as songwriters, it's going to be "Squire/Brown". We all used to say it would be "The Stone Roses, no egos". No egos among us, just one big ego to the outside world. We were all into the Sex Pistols and the way they always credited the songs was: Jones, Matlock, Cook, Rotten. We had discussed all this. It wasn't going to be our surnames like the Pistols, but it was just going to be "The Stone Roses". That was the breaking of the bond right there. It became them and the rest of the band.'

'These issues come out and destroy bands,' said Garner. 'That's pretty much what happened. We had a rehearsal one day and there was an almighty kick-off. Andy and Reni quit and it was left with us three in the room, John, Ian and myself. I said to them, I think you're really out of order because all along everyone's said we're all in this together, we're all brothers. It soured everything and destroyed the idea of us as a single unit.'

Couzens blamed Jones, who he felt was trying to take control of the band by divide and rule, and had misled Brown and Squire over how publishing worked. Nonetheless, he felt Brown and Squire had turned their backs on the contributions he and Reni had made. 'Squire/Brown didn't reflect the way we worked or had ever worked,' he said. 'As I've said, no Reni, no Roses. From a musical point of view, Reni's a genius, inspirational in everything he does. And in the rehearsal room when we were working on stuff his ideas were brilliant. John and I always worked really well together. Sometimes just the two of us sat down to work songs out. It was an instinctive thing between the two guitars.'

The residual resentment over the songwriting credits never completely went away, yet Couzens and Reni were finally persuaded to rejoin. 'Reni and I had put so much work in up to this point, it was our lives, so you don't want to walk away. But I did feel quite hurt by what went on.' Then Reni acted the grown-up. 'As things started getting more political it was Reni who sat back and started saying to people, Hang on a minute, we're all in this together, aren't we?' said Jones.

Before 'So Young' was released the Roses were back together for a gig on 4 July, with Doctor & The Medics in London at the Fulham Greyhound. The band didn't get paid for the show after Reni walked into the manager's office and pissed in his bin. Clive Jackson, the singer with Doctor & The Medics, said the Roses and their crew turned up for the gig in Couzens' Chevrolet truck as a force to be reckoned with. 'I remember the Roses' lighting technician [Green-ough] produced a great big sheath knife and started to cut a tin to put over the lights to create shadows,' he said. 'I could see how ser-ious they were. Ian was confrontational on stage. It's just that pose he had: I'm hard enough to take the entire crowd on. It was great to watch. There was an aura about the whole party – a sense that this is going somewhere.'

'Being in the bubble I didn't stop to think of how we appeared,' said Garner. 'We never went out to be intimidating, but because of the nature of the posse around us perhaps we did appear that way.'

The band's road crew would become integral to the legend of the Roses. Greenough operated the lights and Adge was the general 'Mr Fixer'. Even now, playing a series of one-offs when they didn't need a tour manager, it was obvious this would be Adge's domain. Alongside these two was Slim, a former New Order roadie who shared a flat with Greenough. His real name was Paul Haley and he would form the backbone of the crew for the next three years.

Slim was particularly impressed by Reni. 'He was the first thing that opened my eyes to the band,' he said. 'When I saw him drum-ming in the band, I was like, Jesus, you've got a drummer here; the way he played it and changed it, did a bit of jazz, went into the reg-gae thing; his whole performance. Reni was a star, an entertainer in his own right.' Even during soundchecks Reni would leave people with their mouths agape. 'At these early gigs it was always Reni people would talk about afterwards, saying, Where did you find that drummer?' said Garner.

Steve Adge organized the Roses' next show on Saturday, 20 July 1985 and it would go down in folklore. The ticket read 'Warehouse 1 – The Flower Show' and advised '11 p.m. till very late'. Admission was again £2. It was not the first Roses gig in their hometown of Man-chester, but it felt, said Garner, like the 'first proper one'. Adge had hired a disused British Railways arch near Piccadilly Station, on Fair-field Street. He told the authorities he was organizing a video shoot with a band miming to an audience. It was the first warehouse party in Manchester. The Roses' crew helped to crudely whitewash the walls and build the staging. Bruce Mitchell from Manchester Light & Stage supplied the lights and PA. There was not enough power, so the ever-resourceful Greenough risked life and limb plumbing straight into a streetlight outside.

'It seemed like an ace idea: rather than play the International on a damp Wednesday night, hire a venue that isn't a venue, invite everyone you know, we can go on any time we want,' said Garner. 'We soundchecked and went back to Ian's and then went back at midnight, so we didn't have a clue whether there was going to be five people there or fifty.' Although the exact location of the party was not revealed until the day, the first 'Flower Show' attracted well over the 200 people Adge had expected. He had timed the show to start late and had people handing out fliers outside nightclubs, so there was a mass influx from places like the Haçienda.

The crowd was a bewildering mix of youth tribes. Among the punks, goths, Perry boys and skinheads, stand-out faces included Mani, Stephen 'Cressa' Cresser, Johnny Marr and Andy Rourke of The Smiths. Adge's Hyde contingent mixed with people from Liverpool and the Swedish girls, who had been staying at Couzens' parents' house. There were no portable loos, bar, planning application, licence, or health and safety, just a little van making frequent trips back and forth between the venue and Spirit to replenish the cash-and-carry beer supplies.

'The situation got a little crazy because they miscalculated as to how everyone would react,' said Brown. 'We went on stage just as the tension was about to explode and we managed to defuse the bomb with our set but it was touch and go for a while.' The Roses went on at 1.30 a.m. and played their short set with an overwhelming energy, anger and excitement that left Reni close to collapse. 'After the gig he had what was tantamount to a fit,' said Jones. 'We had to hold him down in the van. It was incredible, he was dehydrated and so hyped, he literally was shaking.'

The party ended around 5 a.m. Adge lost over £200, but planned to organize similar shows on a monthly basis, each housed in a different location. For the Roses, the Flower Show continued to build the buzz leading up to the release of their debut single. 'It was where we got our following,' Brown said. It had been a huge success, allowing Jones to brag of the band's policy of 'playing secret dates as and when they feel'.

Manchester was well served with independent publications such as *Pulp*, *Muze* and *City Life*, and, with the release of 'So Young' / 'Tell Me' imminent on 17 August, they were broadly supportive of the Roses – as was Tony Michaelides at Piccadilly Radio. Paula Greenwood interviewed the band for *Muze*. She was still working for Michaelides but was also now working at Manchester's main independent record store, Piccadilly Records. She had been impressed by the warehouse show. 'They created this whole thing around them that they were different from any other band in Manchester,' said Greenwood. 'They had that attitude that they were going to be massive and there was no doubt about it. Ian in particular was incredibly confident about their music and future success.'

Squire had created the single's cover art, a colourful collage structure made up of an assortment of broken glass and electronic innards. Inspired by the Sex Pistols' sleeves, abstract expressionism and New York art, he wanted the cover art to be as dynamic as the music. 'I knew exactly how it should look,' he said. 'If people know what you're doing, what you think, what you sound like, then you should give them all of it yourself. You shouldn't have other people doing your sleeves and telling you how your videos should be, dressing you. It should be you. It should be complete.'

To support the release of the single, the Roses played two shows: at the Marquee in London and in Manchester at the Haçienda. On both dates they played with psychedelic revival band Playn Jayn. The Marquee was a venue they'd been banned from earlier in the year but 'they didn't realize the second time it was us again,' said Garner. The Roses' thirst for attention, specifically another incident involving Brown and the venue's equipment, led to them being banned again. 'How many bands can say they got banned from the Marquee twice?' said Garner.

Martin Hannett took control of the band's live sound at the Haçienda on Thursday 15 August. Alongside the Haçienda regulars and the Roses' small following there were many among the crowd eager to see if the band could deliver on the hype. Among them were pop band the Thompson Twins, who retreated to the base-ment bar as Hannett pumped the volume up to ear-splitting levels. 'We used to finish with "Tell Me" pretty much all the time and that was Ian's cue to jump in the crowd,' said Garner. 'He was in the crowd and there were a lot of people dancing and getting off on it.' That night at least three major label A&R men attempted to beat down the Roses' dressing-room door; none was successful.

Thin Line had pressed up 1,200 copies of 'So Young'/'Tell Me'. Jones used 200 for promotion and the rest immediately sold out. Piccadilly Records sold 500 copies and many of the other 500 were snapped up in London by fans of Hannett's work. Thin Line had splashed out on music press ads and *Sounds* gave the release a prom-inent push. John Peel played it on his Radio 1 show and the single had climbed to number 2 in the *Melody Maker* indie singles charts by September. But it was in Manchester where the single was the biggest hit, played in clubs including Cloud Nine, the Polytechnic Friday night disco and the Ritz, the city's popular indie club where DJ John Gannon was a friend of the band.

The Roses were not entirely satisfied with their debut. They were happy to have a record out, but the tracks had been in their set for almost a year now and they felt musically they had already out-grown them. 'I never wanted to hear "So Young" again,' said Garner. 'I didn't really like the vocal on it and there was no groove to it. It was pieces stuck together.' Brown was delighted with the buzz the single created in Manchester, in the clubs and record shops, but said it was 'dreadful angst-ridden rock . . . It wasn't good enough; ser-iously, it was shit. We hated that record the day we heard it.' For Reni, 'it was alright at the time . . . We were all fresh faced kids. It was the first time we'd ever been in a studio and that's how we were; it was powerful and raw. All our gigs were powerful and raw. All our rehearsals were powerful and raw.'

By coincidence, or some said deliberately, Factory released the debut record by the Happy Mondays (an EP called *Forty Five* but more commonly referred to as *Delightful*) on the same day as 'So Young' / 'Tell Me'. It was the beginning of what would become a long symbiotic relationship between the two bands. Initially it was the Mondays – already being promoted by Factory as 'the Happy Hooligans' – who exerted the greater influence. Inspired, Squire would soon invest in a wah-wah pedal that would affect the Roses' sound dramatically. 'The Mondays had a massive impact on the Roses,' said Garner. 'If you listen to the stuff the Roses were doing before the Mondays arrived, I think you can hear us change.' There were many incongruent links between the two bands, but it was Stephen 'Cressa' Cresser who'd be the main bridge between the two groups.

Cressa was now a regular face at Roses' rehearsals, but as the Roses gigged sporadically, playing fewer than twenty-five times between now and the end of 1987, he also followed the Mondays, becoming a regular member of their crew. Cressa had been mates with Squire and Brown since their scooter days and had introduced the Roses to the Love album *Forever Changes* and other 1960s psychedelic rock acts. Alongside Cressa's taste for psych rock, he mined deep into the American Paisley Underground scene (name-checking bands such as The Three O'Clock and Plan 9). On the contemporary British music scene, both Cressa and Squire rated The Jesus and Mary Chain.

'They were a big influence, they really opened my eyes,' said Squire of the Mary Chain. 'They were like a reconnection with the music I'd initially got into. I could hear The Beach Boys in those chord changes and melodies. I could hear The Shangri-Las and The Ronettes and it made melodies – pop melodies – relevant again. After listening to the Mary Chain I found I could start to write proper songs. We had no pop sensibility in our music until I heard the Mary Chain; they showed me there was a way of combining what I loved about punk rock and what I loved about The Beach Boys.'

The Mary Chain's drummer, Bobby Gillespie, also fronted Primal Scream, whose debut 1985 single 'All Fall Down' had also made an impression on Cressa and Squire, who had seen the band play at the Haçienda. Cressa spent a lot of time at Howard Jones's flat, digging through his records. 'He'd be listening to Steve Miller, Todd Rundgren and The Byrds, and a lot of that stuff started to influence Johnny [Squire],' Jones said. 'They wore out my copy of *Forever Changes*.'

Cressa was a regular at the Haçienda (the No Funk night on Tuesdays was a particular favourite), where he formed part of a small, stand-out clique that included 'Little Martin' Pendergast and Al Smith, who would also become a key part of the Roses' crew. Along with Mike Pickering, Little Martin was an influential DJ at the Haçienda, and in August 1985 he hosted a night there called 'The Summer of Love'. 'Kaftans not compulsory,' read the flyer. Acid, 1960s psychedelic rock, plus modern electro and disco, made for an alluring and pioneering night, three years ahead of the 1988 acid house/Ecstasy-inspired 'Summer of Love' in London clubs. Cressa, Little Martin and Smith were also ahead of the curve in sporting flared jeans. 'Big ridiculous flares,' said Garner. 'It turned everybody's heads.' The Roses would become intrinsically linked to flared jeans during their 1989 heyday, but the genesis of the idea can be traced back to this period.

The real pioneer of this mid-1980s flares revival was Phil Saxe, the manager of the Happy Mondays. With his brother, he ran a stall called Gangway on the market in the Arndale Centre in the city centre. Prompted by a request for flares from a gang of teenage girls in 1983, Saxe had sourced dead stock from firms like Levi's and Wranglers. The Happy Mondays had been the first lads to pick up on the look, coupling 25-inch flares with paisley or flowery shirts and little goatee beards. Cressa had run with the idea.

The style-conscious Squire paid particular attention to these developments. It was precision stuff: 18-inch Wrangler cords quickly became desirable, and the 25-inch flares passé – although this did not deter Cressa, who said flares represented 'a philosophy'. Squire wore baggies bought from the Saxe brother's new shop called Somewear In Manchester, which had opened in the Arndale in 1985. 'They became the next big thing,' said Saxe. 'They were 16-inch bottoms but a bit baggy on the leg. They were the opposite of flares and the Mondays led the way with that as well.'

5.

Hannett

Martin Hannett was a producer of immense vision and talent, with a repertoire of technological inventions in his arsenal. But his idiosyncrasies in the studio, ballooning weight and non-too-discreet drug addiction were having repercussions as he walked the fine line between genius and madness.

The Roses recorded and mixed what was expected to be their debut album for Thin Line with Hannett at Strawberry Studios in Stockport during six sessions starting on 27 August 1985 and concluding on 1 September. The sessions started at 9 p.m. and would run until 9 a.m. when the BBC Philharmonic would arrive to begin their day's recording. Hannett was not the easiest producer to work with at the best of times, but the Roses would experience a legend in near meltdown. 'We caught Martin at the wrong time,' Brown said. 'He was a lovely, real nice man, but out to lunch. He was a good laugh but hard to work with.'

It was difficult to understand for instance why he became obsessed with the way Pete Garner played the bass with a pick. Hannett spent an inordinate amount of time attaching a tiny little microphone to the bassist's thumb to record just the sound of his plectrum hitting the strings. 'He spent hours and hours doing that and then mixed it into one of the tracks,' said Garner. 'We sat back listening to the track and I said, Martin, I don't know what you did with that thumb microphone but I can't hear it. He said, Yeah but you know it's there.'

Hannett also insisted on cutting a hole in the roof of the studio to give him access into an attic room that he said had a 'certain sound' he wanted to capture. He had Slim, who was helping the band with their gear, hump up Reni's drums, the required microphones and leads, and recorded Reni in the attic. Hannett continued to do so even as the noise leaked out over nearby houses and the police were called. Later, in the film *24 Hour Party People* (2002), Hannett would be fictionalized recording the Happy Mondays' drummer on a roof. In the studio with the Roses was the real source of the story.

Hannett, whose productions of Joy Division were noted for the strength of their drum sound, spent much time securing the ambience he required to make the most of Reni's contributions, which would dominate the album. He also had a peculiar way of recording the band's guitarists. Hannett had Squire and Couzens endlessly play their parts, often hundreds of times. When they were exhausted he'd say, 'Right, I'll put the tape on now,' leaving the guitarists incredulous. 'Have you not been recording?' they would ask. 'No,' Hannett would smile, 'I was letting you get warmed up.'

'Martin's technique was to destroy you completely with relentless retakes,' said Couzens. 'His idea was that when he finally put the tape on the only thing that would come out of you would be honest.' To an extent it worked and amid the walls of noise Hannett created with the Roses' twin guitars, Squire showed off his growing technique on trademark solos and lead riffs. Many of Hannett's disconcerting actions were all, perversely, down to his deep love of the Roses. He truly believed the album would be one of his greatest works. He told the band one track they were recording, 'Trust a Fox', frightened him with its aggression and intensity like no other band he'd ever recorded. Driven relentlessly by Reni with a harsh guitar sound and intermittent feedback, Brown's vocals bit hard on the line, 'I'll cut your face up as soon as say hello'. 'Trust a Fox' was indeed the band at their most feral and potent in this unrefined stage of their career.

Couzens was tasked with picking up Hannett every night and delivering him to the studio. This often involved delays, as Hannett insisted on stopping off at various dealers' houses to collect cocaine and heroin. Once at the studio, the producer would invariably get the munchies and start making cheese on toast. 'We probably wouldn't start recording until midnight,' said Couzens. 'Martin was massively overweight, sweating profusely, and taking far too many drugs.'

Hannett's long-standing engineer was Chris Nagle, a diabetic who had to inject himself with insulin and reacted badly to extremes of temperature. Hannett would insist on having the air-conditioning on in the studio to make conditions freezing cold. 'Chris was up and down, up and down with his sugar levels,' said Couzens. 'They were as bad as each other; both off their nuts.' Nagle's relationship with Hannett was strained and the two men would often disagree over versions of the songs the Roses were recording, adding another layer of tension to the bewildering atmosphere. Often Nagle would walk out.

During one vocal take, by the time Brown had finished the song, Hannett had nodded off at the mixing desk. 'He didn't just gradually fall asleep,' said Couzens. 'You'd be halfway through a take and he'd collapse on the desk and that would be it.' One time in the vocal booth Brown could get no answer from Hannett or Nagle. 'I walked into the control room and there was no one in there,' he said. 'So I woke Martin up and said, Martin, where's Chris? And he said, He's gone to the pub for a pint.' It was the vocals that Hannett seemed to pay least attention to, recording them quickly with few retakes. 'Martin always used to say, What do you want me to do? That's what he sounds like,' said Couzens. Reni did not contribute his honeyed vocals to the mix and hadn't yet sung with the band – or even told them he could.

According to manager Jones, Hannett was never happy with the vocals on the album, apart from 'I Wanna Be Adored', 'which he said he got bang on'. On 'I Wanna Be Adored' Hannett also created a guitar sound for Squire that allowed the song's classic riff to snake majestically out of the speakers. Essentially the atmospherics and dynamics of the song were those that would finally appear on the album *The Stone Roses* in 1989. Brown's vocals were thin in parts on Hannett's version, and there was also a noticeably odd dislocation between the drums and the rest of the band. These twin problems, the latter perhaps intentional on Hannett's part, were also evident on another classic on the album, a new song called 'Here It Comes'. Nonetheless, the stridently melodic song hinted at the sound the band would go on to develop and would be better captured at Spirit for the B-side to the band's 1987 single, 'Sally Cinnamon'. Hannett's version of 'Here It Comes' remains a definitive moment, catching the band perfectly between punk pupation and their metamorphosis.

The Roses were recording pretty much all the material in their repertoire for the album, and Hannett added clever guitar effects and gave some of his magical 'space' – a glacial clarity and unfathomable intensity – to their earliest, punk material. 'Getting Plenty', 'Tradjic Roundabout', 'Mission Impossible', 'Just a Little Bit', 'Heart on the Staves' and 'Fall' all brimmed with aggression, intensity and spite. Brown's vocals were confident, joyous and tough on these familiar songs, matching the assault of Reni's drumming. Lyrically and sonically these early songs seemed to reflect the atmosphere of Friday-night Manchester: violent, unforgiving and dangerous. Hannett managed to hold the band back from metaphorically pushing a broken bottle in the listener's face, with a hand that marked him out as Britain's best record producer of all time.

'Working with Martin was a nightmare but enjoyable as well, exciting and odd . . . You see those films of people in the studio with Phil Spector. It was like that but worse,' said Couzens. Inevitably, amid the craziness, the Roses turned on one another, especially through the mind-warping nights. Squire, for instance, decided Garner's bass lines were not good enough and insisted on playing them himself. The band also had little respect for their plush surroundings. Strawberry was the North-West's premier 24-track studio, but the band abused the free phone, microwave and pool table.

Having recorded ten songs, the Roses emerged blinking into the morning light as the BBC Philharmonic trooped past them. Hannett was not quite finished with them. 'We did all the songs we had, even the ones we'd sort of dropped from the set,' said Garner. 'And then Martin put us on the spot to do a new song.' He didn't lock them in a room to do it – as the other pre-eminent British producer Andrew Loog Oldham had done when forcing Mick Jagger and Keith Richards to write their first original material for The Rolling Stones – but Hannett acted with a similar certainty and belief. The band had something more in them. He wanted it. The Roses delivered 'This Is the One'. Virtually note for note, word for word, it was the version that would appear on the band's eponymous 1989 album.

Hannett had finally caught the butterfly, and he pinned 'This Is the One' down at Strawberry. Couzens would always maintain the opening melody on the song was his, this being the period shortly after Brown and Squire had made their land grab on the songwriting. As an indication of the group's abilities and promise, just a year after Reni joined, 'This Is the One' was a breakthrough they'd made together – thanks to Hannett. 'Martin taught us how to arrange our songs and pull our melodies out,' said Brown.

The album was to be titled *Garage Flower* after Brown's lyric 'I am the garage flower' on 'Tell Me'. The Roses were left shell-shocked by the experience of recording it. 'It was six nights of hell,' said Couzens. 'Martin was giving me what I always thought was speed and it was speedballs, which is a very different thing, coke and smack, and I was snorting it. I had no idea.'

Listening back to the Hannett album the band began to have doubts over what they had recorded. 'We weren't really in control,' Brown said. 'We hadn't rehearsed through. It was like five excited kids running into a studio and trying to play louder than each other. We jumped at it [the chance to work with Hannett], but we shouldn't have.'

After the recording, Hannett flew to Stockholm to set up Thin Line Sweden with Andreas Kemi at *The Eye* magazine. Hannett wrote off Kemi's car as soon as he'd left the airport and then disappeared for two weeks. Jones pressed ahead with his plans for the Roses, which now included releasing two more singles, 'I Wanna Be Adored', and then 'This Is the One', before *Garage Flower*. 'Ian wasn't very happy with "Adored", but John had done the artwork for the cover,' said Jones. It was another patch-up of bits and pieces, collaged and painted; and Squire completed the cover of 'This Is the One' in a similar way.

With the album complete, Jones was keen for the Roses to work on their image. Hannett suggested they collaborate with renowned photographer and stylist Dennis Morris, who'd risen to prominence as a teenager photographing Bob Marley. Morris was also associated with the Sex Pistols and had created the logo for Public Image Ltd, as well as designing covers for Bob Marley and Marianne Faithfull. It seemed a perfect fit, and Hannett invited Morris to a band rehearsal. 'I think Martin brought me in to have a look at it to confirm his feelings for it,' said Morris. 'Martin was *really* into the band, he found something in them and if he'd continued working with them he would have taken them to where they wanted to go.'

Morris offered the Roses their next gig at the Embassy Club in London on 11 September. He ran a regular night called Grace Under Pressure, putting on bands and exhibitions and attracting a crowd of people, including Boy George. The night the Roses played was billed as 'a celebration of Rebel Rock the year it all began, 1977', with a Morris photograph of Sid Vicious on the flyer, and the strapline 'looking into the future with Stone Roses'. 'They played and everybody hated them, said they were shit,' said Morris. 'I said, No, no, they're going to really happen. They said, You're crazy, man.'

Hannett's idea was that Morris would put together a cohesive image for the Roses that would help them achieve recognition in fashion-conscious London circles. 'We always knew to be a truly great band you've got to look like a band,' said Garner. The Roses may have acknowledged the importance of the idea, but Squire was not happy to hand over control to Morris. 'There was just a clash of personalities,' said Morris. 'I think John felt a bit threatened by me getting involved. I wasn't interested in taking over; I just liked the band. I really got on with Ian, Reni and Pete, but Squire had a problem with me. So I just pulled away and thought, That's fine, I'm cool with it.'

Morris would, however, retain an informal relationship with the band. 'When they were in London we used to hang out, have a few beers, go and have some Jamaican food,' he said. Sometimes the Roses would go back to Morris's studio. This bond and these meetings would result in Morris building a vast catalogue of images of the band throughout their career. These shots have never been published, until this book.

After the Embassy Club, there were no Roses gigs for six long weeks. It was in this period that the band's relationship with Thin Line disintegrated. The Roses were initially unhappy with Jones's plans to expand the label. Hannett was also recording The Railway Children and The Man from Delmonte for Thin Line, and Tim Chambers had brought a band called Gifted to the label. All three bands were generating strong press interest. 'The Roses thought they could be fourth on this label's roster, not first, which would have been unbearable for them,' said Jones. 'So they started making demands.' One was that Jones abandon his ambitions for Thin Line. 'I said that wasn't why I left Factory. I wanted to do something myself. The label was more interesting to me than the band and that really upset Ian.'

The issue was complicated by the fact that the Roses didn't have a contract with either Thin Line or Jones, and everything had been done on handshakes. Jones knew that by paying for the recordings of both the Roses' single and album it meant the label owned the rights to them. The band was suspicious that Jones was somehow trying to rip them off. It was not just the sound of the album the band was unsure about, it was the business aspects relating to it. They wanted a proper contract.

A further concern for the Roses was Jones's frequent alteration of his plans for them, as Thin Line's fortunes wavered. 'One week we might be doing a second single somewhere, the next week it was forgotten about and Howard would be talking about something else happening, a new strategy or idea,' said Garner. Jones was now staring at a bill of £11,000 for the recording of the Roses' album. Strawberry Studios was encountering financial difficulties, and owner Peter Tattersall had readjusted his opinion on the amount of free time Hannett was owed in the studio. It was money Thin Line didn't have. Andy Couzens had already loaned Jones £1,200 to pay for Chris Nagle's bill as engineer. The cost of releasing the album independently would be beyond Thin Line's budget. As an alternative, Jones suggested trying to get a major label interested, licensing the recording to them for release. 'Howard took the album to Rough Trade, who were a big deal,' said Couzens. 'Scott Piering, the promotions guy, was dead honest. He listened and said, Yeah, I like "I Wanna Be Adored" and "This Is the One", but the rest of it is shit.'

'We didn't entirely take this talk of Howard shopping the album to the majors seriously,' said Garner. 'We didn't really want it to come out, certainly not on Thin Line. If we had put that album out then, we'd have wasted "I Wanna Be Adored" and "This Is the One". It would have just come out and sold to a few people in Manchester and been forgotten about.' Brown said progression comes from hate, and he hated the album. After it was recorded, the band rehearsed at the Lock-Up with a renewed sense of vigour. 'This Is the One' was not the only new song the band had come up with that suggested a future away from their raw beginnings.

They invited Jones to rehearsals to check out a new song that had a 'different vibe'. It was 'She Bangs the Drums'. They had lacked the confidence to record the song for the album, but it was one that they knew was another step away from the band Hannett had captured. Jones was blown away by it, suggesting it could be another single. 'John was playing the bass line to "She Bangs the Drums" in rehearsals before he played guitar on it,' said Garner. 'We worked on getting the bass line sounding really good, then I took over and he wrote the guitar.'

It was the start of the Roses' most fertile period, as Squire and Brown began to work as a partnership. 'We were terrible at the start,' Brown said. 'We couldn't even write a melody line, the sound was just rubbish. We were loud, noisy, tuneless, big-mouthed, brash and bratty. We had the energy but we didn't have the melodies. So [after recording the album] we concentrated on learning how to write and shape them. We'd work out our earlier songs in rehearsals then I'd come up with the words. But then John and I sat down with an acoustic guitar and wrote the songs and the vocal tunes together. Made it more musical. John and I went to Italy to write. We slept rough – we took an acoustic guitar and sleeping bags.'

In this period, late 1985, Brown and Squire also came up with 'Sally Cinnamon', 'All Across the Sands', 'The Hardest Thing in the World', 'Sugar Spun Sister' and 'Where Angels Play'. Neither of them worked, and they lived in each other's pockets. Time, space and the newly discovered effects of marijuana resulted in more reflective, carefully thought-out material. Lyrically, Brown and Squire were drawing on their experience of life, situations with friends and the things they wanted. In this batch of more considered songs, it's easy to see the influence of their Swedish experiences. Behind the hallucinogenic suggestions and softer colours in the songs, there remained a vicious streak to the lyrics.

'We were coming up with songs that were more sophisticated than those we'd recorded for the album,' said Garner. What made them sound even better was the fact that the Roses had also discovered that not only did they have the best drummer in Manchester, he could sing sweet harmonies. 'When Reni started singing at the Lock-Up, it was like, Wow, he can actually sing,' said Garner. 'The secret weapon has another level.'

It was also now clear that Squire and Brown, as well as pairing off to write the songs, were making the key decisions. They both had a burning intensity to be the best. If you didn't match up to that, you got dropped. Thin Line didn't. Ultimately, despite its impressive personnel, it was an ill-financed indie label. There was not time for sentiment. 'They delivered a final ultimatum and insisted I fold Thin Line to concentrate on managing them or they'd cease to cooperate with placing the album,' said Jones. 'Martin said, Leave it, let's move on to The Man from Delmonte, and when the Roses get big we can sell the album.'

On 26 October the Roses travelled to London to play at the Riverside club, picking up a promising review in *Melody Maker*. This was the start of the new Roses, 'an unholy tryst of Smiths whimsy, Jam punch and US psychedelia', according to the review. It concluded presciently, 'At last an energy that is directed not dissipated, a band who actually know what they are doing'. The Roses followed this with a gig at Manchester University on 2 November. Squire had taken on board Morris's ideas about creating an identity and image. Assisted by his new girlfriend Helen Plaumer (who worked as a costume assistant at Cosgrove Hall), he had made matching shirts for all five members. The striped shirts, in both black and white and red and white, were influenced by ones he'd seen on The Beach Boys. 'Ian was worried they were a bit Morrissey-ish,' said Jones. 'People had already compared him to Morrissey and he didn't like it.'

The band's final gig of 1985 was on 30 November – another Manchester warehouse show organized by Steve Adge, this time at railway arch 99 on Temperance Street. Advertised as 'Warehouse 3 . . . Take Two, What a good year for the Roses (the Video Shoot)', the show had the same set-up as the earlier Flower Show warehouse gig – 11 p.m. till late, £2 on the door – but it was freezing cold and only fifty people turned up. There was also a power cut, as some kids who had earlier tried to hustle Adge for cash had unhooked the generator and made off with it. It was a low point. Factory Records had stolen The Railway Children from the financially bankrupt Thin Line, and they were being tipped for stardom. The Roses, in stark contrast, were going nowhere.

Those who had heard tapes of the Roses' album scoffed at it, and it was suggested the new shirts and more melodic songs were an effort to fit in with the prevailing indie scene. Brown was not having that. 'That's just stupid people talking rubbish,' he said. 'We've just got a lot better. If people expect The Stone Roses to stand still they're following the wrong band. We'll always move on and if record companies can't see the quality then that's just tough. I know these people are stupid but they'll have to catch up with us. They will in the end, because they will have to be in on the action. And we will be massive.'

At the under-attended warehouse night it was easy to see why a consensus was building that, after the initial flourish of hype, the Roses were never going to make it. It was not just the power cut.

Brown had adopted a psychobilly cut, shaved at the sides with a long centre section died blonde to either flop forward or quiff up; Squire had lost the bandana and hid behind his floppy fringe; Garner was in psychedelic trousers with his long dyed black hair; Couzens had a clean-cut, hard, rockabilly look; and there was Reni, in shorts with his shirt off, showboating as if he was on stage in Las Vegas. They didn't look right and when they played live they tended to trample all over the delicacy of their new songs, unable yet to shake off the punk aggression.

Yet the band's irrepressible sense of destiny, determination and belief remained undimmed. Manchester needed to wake up to The Stone Roses. The city did. Brown and Reni covered the place with graffiti proclaiming 'The Stone Roses' overnight. 'Me and Reni decided we'd been ignored for long enough,' Brown said. 'So we sprayed everywhere. Reni was spraying the front of the library and there was a copper stood just around the corner – but the copper couldn't see him!'

The graffiti stunt was a spectacular success in one respect, as it put the band on the front cover of the *Manchester Evening News* and got them television exposure on the regional ITV network Granada. But the disinterest in the band was replaced by disgust. 'That caused us a lot of problems,' Brown said. 'The Manchester music press blacked us out, they pretended that we didn't exist because they thought that we were the barbers of all Manchester architecture.'

'I had the police at my door saying, If you don't tell us who did it we'll arrest you,' said Jones. 'I said, I can't stop fans doing it.' Reni was unrepentant. 'As far as I'm concerned all the spraying did was brighten up the town's architecture which was rather dull and grey,' he said. 'It was our town and we'd do what the fuck we want there,' said an equally belligerent Couzens. 'If you weren't on Factory you weren't anybody. The graffiti thing was very much a statement: you will take notice.'

After the graffiti the Roses struggled to get booked in their hometown. They wouldn't play live again for three months. They tried and failed to get a slot at the new and influential Boardwalk club that had hosted Sonic Youth and Primal Scream. 'They said, We're not having you lot in here,' said Couzens.

'That's when Ian and Andy went to see Gareth Evans at the International,' said Garner. 'Any opportunity was an opportunity, and we went to see what Gareth had to say – to see if he could do anything for us. I felt like we were cheating on Howard by going to check out what this other guy could offer us.' Jones knew Evans well, and claimed to have set up the initial meeting to introduce the Roses to the man who would become their new manager.

'We went to interview Gareth and thought he was a nutter,' said Couzens. 'But the key was he ran the International, so we could get gigs and it was free rehearsal space. We thought we could use him.'

'I think we'd been in the room two minutes,' said Brown, 'and Gareth said, This is what I do, and he dropped his trousers and he had got these underpants with an apple on the side. "Pommes" they were called, and he was dealing in them.'

'He was trying to impress us, saying he could sell anything to anyone, anywhere, anytime,' said Squire. 'He had a whole box of them in the corner. But he insisted on taking off his trousers and trying to sell us the underpants he was wearing.'

'We thought he was crazy, but funny,' said Brown. 'We got on well with him. We thought he was Al Capone, and he thought he was Al Capone too. But we wanted that kind of guy, a Frank DiLeo [the cigar-chomping, suspected-Mafioso, one-time manager of Michael Jackson]. We wanted our manager to be as well known as us. All the great groups had famous managers, so we needed a guy like that. We clicked straight away.'

Squat and charismatic, with a wicked sense of humour, Evans made no secret of his various schemes. He did not exude trustworthy qualities. Nonetheless, Evans offered the band unlimited free rehearsal space at the International and free drinks and entrance to all the gigs he was putting on there. Despite never having managed a band before, his attitude chimed with Brown. 'He didn't have any fear and that appealed to us,' Brown said. 'He didn't believe anyone was out of reach.'

Evans was in his mid-thirties. He had grown up in Wales and moved to Manchester in the 1960s in his early teens. In that decade he would claim to have been one of Manchester's top mods, running the city's prominent Jigsaw club and rubbing shoulders with Eric Clapton, Elton John and Keith Moon. He'd run a chain of hairdressing shops called Gareth and Colin Crimpers in the 1970s before he launched a salon design company, moved into sports retailing and finally ended up dealing gold bullion. From there he'd acquired, with his business partner Matthew Cummins, the International. The club had overtaken the Haçienda to become the key live venue in Manchester, and Evans and Cummins now owned a second, bigger venue – the International II.

The Roses wanted a manager in the classic mould, and they had found one. Jackson had DiLeo, the Stones had Andrew Loog Oldham, the Pistols had Malcolm McLaren – and The Stone Roses would have Gareth Evans. Incredibly, given the competition, history would judge Evans as the most astonishing band manager of the lot.

It was impossible for the Roses to truly know what they were getting into. His given name was not Gareth Evans, for a start. It was Ian Bromley. The name change was rumoured to be the result of a teenage brush with the law. The bond between Evans and Cummins was ultra-tight. Evans's first wife, with whom he had a son who had Down's syndrome, was Cummins's sister. They were deliberately running the 'Pommes' underwear factory into the ground. The story was that there had been a government scheme offering businesses a certain amount of money, tens of thousands, if the company could raise a certain amount of capital. The underpants were a ruse to secure the government money, which, once deposited in the pair's bank account, was withdrawn immediately.

Dougie James was someone who could testify to Evans and

Cummins's business charms. Soul singer James was introduced to the pair in 1984 while planning to buy a hotel called the Andalusia on Palatine Road. 'A friend of mine said, I've got two guys who'd be useful to you, they deal in finance,' said James. Evans was dating a girl called Paige, whose father was a gold dealer and ran a jewellery shop in Manchester. It was Paige's father who had enabled Evans's entrée into the speculative world of gold dealing. 'At the first meeting Gareth brought £50,000 in a plastic bag and stuck it on the bar and said, That's what I'm dealing in,' said James. 'It really wasn't his, it belonged to the gold dealer.'

Nonetheless, James agreed that Evans and Cummins should get involved in the deal, not just to buy the Andalusia but also a club that was going out of business called Genevieve's. They bought both and renamed the club the International. James, who had experience promoting at Manchester's influential punk club Rafters, hired legendary promoter Roger Eagle to book acts for the new club, and his shrewd policy had seen the International become an instant success. In the first two months the club made £22,000 profit. It was only when it came to divvying up the money that James discovered that Evans and Cummins had, in taking care of the paperwork for the club, put the International in just their own names, effectively excluding James from the club's ownership. James would spend the next five years battling Evans and Cummins in court over this issue, ultimately successfully.

The International and International II had gone on to become huge successes, regularly hosting up to twenty-five bands a month. Evans was obsessed with putting up posters for the venues and kept rolls of them and a bucket of paste and brushes in his beat-up MG Montego, always looking for an opportunity to slap up a few. Manchester had the largest conglomerate of students in Western Europe, many attracted by The Smiths and New Order, and Evans also shrewdly targeted this audience. There was an element of chaos to his method, but he got things done, his club was happening and there was a phenomenal energy surrounding him and the International clubs.

Yet, despite his success, Evans remained an outsider on the trendy Manchester scene, which was ruled by the Haçienda and Factory and more lately the Boardwalk. He didn't like Tony Wilson, thought he was a 'toff' and up himself. When the Roses came knocking on his door, Evans was as eager as the band to tear down that established order.

6.

Gareth

Evans and Cummins drew up a management contract for the Roses as the band began their new regime of daily rehearsals in the basement of International II. It was an old dancehall on Plymouth Grove, a few hundred metres from the International, where 2,000 punters could be crammed in. It had a huge basement with a labyrinth of rooms. Amid the beer cellars and dressing rooms, the Roses turned one room into their new home.

Andy Couzens' father Colin had paid for a lawyer to look out for his son's band, and Evans was fuming when Couzens informed him that he wanted the lawyer to look over the contract. 'Gareth didn't want that sort of advice around,' said Couzens. 'He said to me, What is it with you? You come with a lawyer attached?' Evans wanted Couzens out of the band. 'He even offered me £10,000 to leave the band. Ian said, Take the ten grand and we'll split it and you can join again tomorrow. Gareth even accused me of being an undercover drugs officer.' Evans attempted to intimidate Couzens by parking his car outside the guitarist's parents' house and waiting there. 'I used to come out of my drive and he'd be there. I'd drive off and he'd follow me. I don't know why. Proper nutter.'

Evans had been quick to spot where the power base was in the band and was busy treating Squire and Brown like superstars, showering them with gifts and meals. 'Gareth would split the band,' said Couzens. 'You'd get John and Ian and then Reni and me, with Pete sat on the fence somewhere in the middle. He always had a wad of money in an elastic band and he would drop it in front of you thinking you'd be impressed.' Couzens never was.

He was not the only one to warn the band about the contract Evans and Cummins wanted them to sign. Chief roadie Slim advised them to see a lawyer. Even his own staff didn't entirely trust Evans.

Paula Greenwood, now handling press and promotions at the International, also told Brown to get legal advice. Despite his best efforts, and mainly due to Couzens' belligerence, nothing was officially signed to make Evans and Cummins the new managers of The Stone Roses when, on 5 March 1986, the band played their first dates of the year. After supporting The Chiefs of Relief at Warwick University and returning to the same venue three weeks later to support goth outfit Love and Rockets, the band played at Manchester University on 10 May, where they again wore their matching striped shirts. Brown's hair was newly shorn, with bleached highlights, and, as well as being hugged by two girls invading the stage, he was back out singing among the crowd, trying to provoke a reaction.

On 31 May the band travelled to Ireland to play McGonagle's in Dublin. The club was packed out with a heavy metal crowd, and as soon as the Roses started to play a riot broke out. 'We turned up in our little Beach Boys shirts with our little psychedelic pop songs, got one song in and it was clear they didn't like us,' said Garner. 'It started getting a bit antagonistic and John went into the riff for "Smoke on the Water". The place just erupted. They obviously realized we were taking the piss and there was a deluge of beer glasses and bottles thrown at the stage. We had to get off. They wanted to kill us.'

This would be Couzens' last gig with the band. He decided to fly back from Ireland while the rest of them travelled on the ferry. The Roses were so broke on the journey back to Manchester, Steve Adge convinced a café owner to let him use the facilities to cook a meal for them all in exchange for doing the washing up. 'Andy flying back didn't go down well at all,' said Garner. 'That's what killed it for Andy.' Evans seized the opportunity and attacked Couzens relentlessly over the incident. 'He became really angry and nasty and put his head to my head and threatened me,' said Couzens. His stance on the management contract had already ostracized him from the rest of the band, who were coming to the conclusion that the benefits of signing with Evans and Cummins outweighed the pitfalls.

'It solved a lot of problems at once,' Squire said. 'People immediately thought we were mad but we got in there and started rehearsing. It never struck us this was a bad move.' The band knew the management contract was outrageous. Evans and Cummins were after 33 per cent cut of gross profit and wanted the band to sign for a period of ten years. 'We didn't really care,' said Garner. 'What we wanted from Gareth we were getting, and it was obvious to all of us what he was asking for was ridiculous. We even suggested to him to make it more ridiculous. We all knew if this all goes tits up, anybody with a brain could see we'd just been exploited. Plus, it was like we've got nothing at the moment, so he'll be getting a percentage of nothing. I was happy to sign it just so we had a rehearsal space.'

On 29 June 1986 there was a summit meeting between the band, Evans, Cummins, lawyer Stephen Lea and Howard Jones at the Eighth Day café in Manchester. 'Gareth said to Howard, Look, the band want to work with me, they want to do it my way, there's no room for you, go away,' said Lea. 'Then he was like, Now let's go back to my office and discuss where we're going to go from here.' In the office at International II, Evans settled into the only chair, behind his desk, while the Roses and Lea sat on the floor. He started talking about the route he wanted to take from now on. Couzens lasted five minutes, got up, said that it wasn't for him, he wasn't interested, and walked out. Lea lasted a few more minutes. It was obvious Evans wasn't going to listen to anything he said. 'Andy was waiting downstairs in his car,' said Lea. 'His attitude was, Well, fuck that for a game of soldiers, I'm out of here. I was immensely disappointed that the others all seemed to be sitting there and going along with it.'

Couzens left The Stone Roses that day. Although upset, he would be one of the first to acknowledge that the Roses looked and sounded better without him. He felt that Squire had been angling to get him out for some time, an assertion that was backed by Brown. 'John didn't want to play with him. John was getting better and coming out with these lovely lines and Andy would come in with these big, chuggy rhythm guitar parts and cover it up. So John came to me and said he didn't think he could play with him any more.' Brown did express regret at having 'used' former manager Howard Jones. 'Took him to the cleaners really. I'm not too proud of that, but a lot of it was his fault.'

The Roses played five dates during the summer of 1986 as a four-piece before retiring from live performance for almost six months. In part this was down to the fact that along with Couzens went the band's tour vehicle, but also Reni had injured his hand putting his fist through a pane of glass in a door at his parents' house. He still has the scar. Although he couldn't hold a drumstick, Reni soldiered on, making the band tape one to his hand and playing like that. The shows were at the Leeds Warehouse, the Three Crowns Club in London, Manchester Ritz, Liverpool Mardi Gras (where Cressa brought Happy Monday Paul Ryder to watch the band) and Barrow (where they all took to the sea late at night until Garner pointed out their close proximity to Sellafield nuclear power station).

Garner had finally heeded Jones's advice and cut his hair to shoulder length, Squire wore leather trousers, while Brown alternated between shaving his head back to its natural dark colour and then bleaching it in a Tintin style. Squire had also made the band a matching set of harlequin shirts to wear. Sue Dean, who was now Gareth Evans's girlfriend, was a keen photographer and captured the band live and in rehearsal during this transitional period in photographs seen for the first time in this book.

Dean, who already knew Brown, had started seeing Evans before he got involved with the Roses. She was a few years younger than the band and part of a tight-knit gang of girls who seemed to know everybody on the Manchester scene. Her best friend was Sarah Dalton, who would go on to marry Bernard Sumner of New Order. Dean had first met and impressed Evans after blagging her way into the International, and he'd suggested a job for her on the door of the club, thinking she would make sure everyone knew the International for being somewhere that Manchester music people got treated well. Dean hadn't taken him entirely seriously, but soon met him again while hanging out at Howard Jones's flat. Evans had pulled his familiar trick of dropping a wedge of money on the floor to try to impress her. 'If you looked at it closely it wasn't all money, it was newspaper, and money wrapped around the outside,' she said. Dean picked it up and threw it back at him.

Evans didn't need sleep. 'He'd do the club until two or three in the morning and at six in the morning he'd be up and out, saying, Life's too short, we've got to do this, we've got to do that,' said Dean. 'He'd go out at 6 a.m. and do things and then be back at the international for 12 for the load-in for the next band. That was every day.' He appeared to live his life in a permanent state of disarray. He would take band merchandise from the International and wear a different band T-shirt every day, thinking it made him 'down with the kids'.

When the International's chief booker Roger Eagle had doubts about the Roses, Evans responded by sidelining him and putting Cummins in charge of that side of the club. Cummins had a vast record collection and proved shrewd at spotting new and upcoming bands. Evans himself had a unique way of judging bands. 'Gareth worshipped his son Mark and would take him to a lot of the sound-checks and introduce a lot of the bands to him,' said Dean. 'If they weren't nice to Mark you didn't go back to the International, doesn't matter how big you got, you did not get another gig there.'

Despite his chutzpah and enthusiasm, Evans was unsure of how the music business worked. He had a habit of turning every conversation towards the Roses, often asking all and sundry what they thought of the band and professing he really had no idea if they were any good or not. Although this may have just been a clever ruse, he certainly wouldn't discuss the ins and outs of music publishing with the band, like previous manager Jones. Evans never seemed to have a clue how that worked, no matter how many times he asked people to explain it to him.

Top of the list, as far as Evans was concerned, was to get a new record out. The International ran local band nights every Monday, and these events would often be buzzing with A&R men. Evans would offer up free drinks and try to push the Roses. Until he realized how much money it would cost, Evans had planned on forming his own label for the Roses, International Records, taking an office above the estate agents opposite the International. Although Couzens was out, the band had still not signed the management deal and Evans was keen to impress them with some swift action. He'd heard rumours that the Happy Mondays' manager Phil Saxe was interested in signing the Roses to Factory, and Howard Jones was bragging that he had got interest in the Hannett-produced Roses album from A&M Records. If either Factory or A&M offered the band a deal, it would spell the end for Evans's dream.

The Roses themselves, although all still signing on the dole, maintained a beguiling swagger and confidence that they were going to be huge. As far as they were concerned, it was a done deal. With little other distraction, they worked hard on honing their new sound, rehearsing five days a week at International II, often stepping out of the basement and onto the main stage. In the band's early set list there had always been two guitars fighting for space; with Couzens gone, there was more room for the songs to breathe. 'John could play nice melodic stuff,' said Garner. 'We could hear ourselves properly. We had Reni singing. As upsetting as it was with Andy, after he'd gone the sound changed quite drastically.'

The band dynamic also altered once Couzens had left. As a five-piece, there had always been two camps within the Roses: Squire and Brown in one, and Reni and Couzens in the other (Reni had moved into Couzens' parents' house), with Garner playing the diplomatic Henry Kissenger role. 'After Andy left, it was like a unit again,' said Garner.

Brown and Squire, both now in steady relationships, were still sharing a flat and deeply committed to the band, more new songs spilling out of their partnership. Brown had started listening to Prince Far I and 'War on the Bullshit' by Osiris, alongside band staples such as The Beatles, Pink Floyd, Hendrix and Love. To add to the list of classic songs they had already written, they added 'Waterfall', 'Going Down', 'Mersey Paradise' and 'Elephant Stone'. The set list was now shorn of all their aggressive early material and packed with definitive masterpieces.

'Me and John would plan all the time,' Brown said. 'The band was all we talked about. We lived together so we had nothing but time on our hands to get things right. When we were writing songs, we'd spend two or three days sometimes just to get one word – because a word needs to roll right. We were so deeply into it. "Waterfall" was the first time we went, Wow this is it.' Squire worked on the band as if it was a job, not a hobby, and applied himself with single-mindedness and persistence that bordered on the obsessive. 'We got together with the deliberate intention of composing classic songs,' he said. The band, he felt, was 'original, commercial and inspirational' all at the same time.

All they needed was a deal, and Evans was determined he would be the one to strike it. Howard Jones discovered Evans had succeeded on 19 September 1986. On that day, David Rose, the MD of A&M Records, visited Manchester with a cheque for £30,000 and a contract for the Roses to sign to A&M. Evans was aware that Jones had been negotiating with A&M, using the Roses' Hannett album as bait, and had been hastily, desperately, organizing an alternative. He was worried that if the band signed to A&M they would get rid of him. In the afternoon, with the band unaware of the offer Jones and Rose were hours away from presenting, he had the Roses sign a contract with FM Revolver.

'I got to the International and showed the A&M contract to Ian, and his face was a picture,' said Jones. 'He said, We've signed. That was the moment where I knew it had all gone a bit pear-shaped. I've got an album, I've got a band I know is going to be brilliant, and they're now signed to a Birmingham heavy metal label and Gareth doesn't know what the hell he's doing.' There was talk of the possibility of cancelling the deal with FM Revolver, but it would involve lawyers and be protracted. It was too late.

FM Revolver was actually based in Wolverhampton, but Jones was correct in his main assertion: it was a subsidiary of a company called Heavy Metal Records. How Evans had come to strike a deal was down to his relationship with Dave Roberts, who acted as an A&R man for the label. Roberts had got the infamous Macc Lads a deal with FM Revolver, and Evans knew him primarily through his work as a journalist for *Sounds*.

'Gareth rang me at home one day and said, I'm managing this amazing band, The Stone Roses, they're selling out the International, big following here,' said Roberts. 'He gave me this big speech and then asked about the label and distribution. I think Gareth got us confused with Revolver Records, which was based in Bristol, and part of that whole Cartel distribution network [which included Rough Trade, Red Rhino, Backs, Fast Forward, Nine Mile, Probe and Revolver]. He got FM Revolver mixed up with Revolver.'

What had swung it for Roberts was hearing a demo of 'Sally Cinnamon' that the band had cut at Spirit studios in Manchester. Spirit owner John Breakell said Evans had supplied cases of beer to lubricate the recording session: 'Did Gareth give me any money for recording? Probably not.'

Roberts thought the demo was amazing, and suggested to FM Revolver boss Paul Birch that they should be branching out. John Squire was as shocked as Howard Jones when he travelled down to Wolverhampton to meet his new prospective boss. Sat in the reception area, Squire could see Birch at his office desk. He had a bouffant poodle hairdo, dyed blond, and skin-tight spandex trousers. 'I'm not going in fucking there with him,' Squire said.

Squire was reassured he would not have to deal with Birch – who kept his real passion for Northern Soul fairly well disguised – and it was Roberts who would handle the relationship between the band and the label. Roberts organized for the eight-track Spirit demo recording of 'Sally Cinnamon', plus, from the same session, a new version of 'Here It Comes' and the first cut of 'All Across the Sands' (one of the most underrated songs in the Roses' repertoire) to be remastered in Macclesfield at Cottage Studios. 'We didn't really have budgets to go recording stuff, and I thought the demos were great in their own right,' said Roberts. 'We took the demo and tried to brighten it up a bit with the band, and that became the "Sally Cinnamon" single. I think they were pretty desperate to get a record out. We just paid for those tracks to be remixed, that was the token advance, probably a few hundred quid.'

Squire designed the cover for the single, with a photograph of an old-fashioned bubblegum machine taken by his brother Matt, and Roberts organized a photo shoot for promotional purposes. This took place at the run-down Belle Vue greyhound-racing stadium and saw both Squire and Brown in Mary Chain-influenced leather trousers. Squire's striped jumper and Reni's outdoor jacket had started to more closely resemble the band's breakthrough style, although Brown's hair was still closely cropped.

However, Brown's musical tastes were now radically shifting. In the contract with FM Revolver there was an option to record an album, and Brown discussed this with Roberts. 'We were talking about what kind of producers they would want to do the album,' said Roberts. 'Ian said we should be using some kind of dance producer. He said, We're not an indie band, we should be a dance band and we should be trying to bring in those kinds of elements. I was surprised because I pretty much perceived them as an indie guitar band. But Ian had that vision.'

Before the single was released, label boss Birch insisted on seeing the band live. Evans made sure the show, the Roses' first in six months, at the International on Friday, 30 January 1987 was packed. It was their perfect set-up: all their gear was already there and they were familiar with the club's PA system, lights and crew. Evans may have signed them to the wrong Revolver – and dumbfounded the band during soundcheck by asking that the vital monitors be removed because they looked 'untidy' – but he was an expert at promotion.

The band was amazed by the turnout of over a thousand people. The Roses' core following was closer to fifty, all of whom Evans had put on the guest list. That day Evans had everyone connected with his clubs – the DJs, bar staff, and even Brigitte in the kitchens – on the streets giving away free tickets. Friday and Saturday nights at the International were club nights, and Evans would make his money at the bar. Birch left impressed. 'Sally Cinnamon' was scheduled for release at the end of February 1987.

Mancunion, the Manchester University Students' Union newspaper, was also at the International and interviewed the band for an article that ran under the headline 'The Coming of the New Stone Age?' Brown was asked his thoughts on the scene: 'A lot of people say it's really good on the indie scene but I don't think it is,' he said. 'They all seem to be doing the same thing, a lot of twee-type things. A lot of people on the indie scene say they're not interested in commercial success. That's rubbish – everyone in the music business is in it to make money. The only difference between the indie scene and the national scene is that they don't sell as many records. It's the same set up with agents and backers just on a smaller scale. It's all about pulling in bribes and favours. It is a sick business, the only way to do it is to make enough money to get out of it.'

The release of 'Sally Cinnamon' was delayed as Birch and Roberts created a new 'indie' imprint to house the Roses. FM Revolver/Heavy Metal Records product was distributed by BMG, a major record label. To qualify for the indie charts, which Birch and Roberts were aiming for with 'Sally Cinnamon', the rule was no distribution by a major record label. They formed the Black imprint to house the Roses' single and struck up a deal for independent distribution with the Cartel to get round that problem.

To help promote the single – which was coming out on 12-inch vinyl only – Evans arranged to pay for the 10,000 print-run of *Buzzin'*, a free, A3-sized, music newspaper originating from Stockport, in exchange for putting the Roses on the cover. Brown would appear on it alone, wearing a beret. The photograph and the other shots of the band used to illustrate the three-page spread were taken at an Italian restaurant in Rusholme, an evening Evans had orchestrated. During the proceedings he proudly presented the band with the management contract to sign. 'He had a photographer there taking photos of us eating food and signing the contract,' said Garner.

'The angle on these photographs is spaghetti, so don't eat it all at

once,' Evans instructed the band. As Evans had wanted, the contract was for ten years and guaranteed him and his partner Matthew
Cummins a 33.3 per cent share of the band's gross earnings. Evans
had got an angle on everything, and although Garner said he had no
idea what Cummins actually did, the argument was that, as there
were two managers and everything was split equally, then 33.3 per
cent represented two sixths.

The band sought no competent advice before signing the contract and didn't take it seriously. They drank red wine and were still
laughing away the onerous nature of the contract, even suggesting
Evans double the length of the terms. Managers taking a figure of
25 per cent was not unheard of, so although Evans and Cummins
were clearly over the line, they were not that far over it. Plus, paperwork meant nothing to the Roses, and they felt they could walk
away from the deal in the future. It was a situation everyone was
happy with. Evans and Cummins were reassured and the Roses
were loved. Both parties felt they had got one over on the other.
'When you've got nothing and someone's offering you something,
yeah, I'll sign it and worry about it later,' said Garner.

In the *Buzzin'* cover feature, the Roses praised their new manager, defining the relationship they had with him as, 'upfront, no
bullshit'. The band were asked about the year and a half that had
passed since their debut single, 'So Young', had packed every dance
floor in the city's clubs. 'We blew it,' said Reni. 'No, what happened
was: we did a few gigs, poorly attended gigs, released a single that
really sold quite poorly and everybody thought there was a hype on
because we came from nowhere but when you think about it, where
were we in the first place, we had nothing with "So Young", we only
sold a few thousand copies.'

'As far as I'm concerned, we put out "So Young" and the next
thing we wanted people to hear was "Sally Cinnamon",' said Brown.
'There was nothing we really wanted to put out in between those
two songs.' Were they bothered that people may have thought them
washed up in the interim? 'It doesn't bother us at all,' said Squire.
They were also asked about the radical new sound ('softer, vocals

more restrained, mellow acoustic edge', as *Buzzin'* described it) of 'Sally Cinnamon'. 'We learned how to write,' said Brown. 'I also think it's because we produced "Sally Cinnamon" ourselves. We've got a record coming out that sounds the way we want it to. Anyone who hears it and thinks we've mellowed out should come and see us live, because live we're just as hard as we always were.'

Looming large in the article was Evans, driving the band and interviewer round the city in his Jeep. '"So Young" is now going on the Black Market for £4.50,' he bragged. 'And they've just played "Sally" at Legends and the place went wild. That was just an upfront tape copy; there had been no promotion behind the single or anything and the dance floor was packed; it was good, and still this band is going to make it, still this band has got a huge following in Manchester.' *Buzzin'* described Evans as a man with 'firebombs on the end of his tongue'.

The response to the release of 'Sally Cinnamon' in May 1987, however, was muted. 'It was weird,' said Garner. 'It's almost like it was all over but we knew we were actually becoming a really good band, just nobody else knew. I don't even think "Sally Cinnamon" was representative of where we were at musically. It was a bit throwaway. The new stuff we were doing was a lot better than that. People knew us in Manchester but outside we weren't really getting any press, we'd only played these odd places, we'd never done a proper tour in England.'

'Nothing happened with "Sally Cinnamon",' said Dave Roberts. 'Piccadilly Records in Manchester sold the bulk of them but nowhere else cared. We didn't get any radio play, didn't get any reviews. We didn't have budgets for a PR or pluggers, we generally did everything ourselves. I tried to plug the *NME* with it. No one came back even acknowledging it, let alone saying they didn't like it. No one cared.'

Evans handed over cash and instructed all the staff at the International clubs to go out to every record shop in Manchester and buy the record – about four or five times. Having seen that FM Revolver had failed to get the record in the city centre Virgin shop, he paid the store a visit and persuaded them to stock it. He managed to get another local record shop to devote an entire front window to the single. Tony Michaelides at Piccadilly Radio gave it his full backing, and within weeks it became his show's most-requested track. Evans also engineered a spread in the *Manchester Evening News* and a small feature in *Cut* magazine where he distressed the journalist by throwing a can of Special Brew through a window during the photo shoot.

Even so, 'Sally Cinnamon' only just managed to scrape into the lower end of the indie charts in June, thanks largely to sales in Manchester. The Happy Mondays, by contrast, were being talked of as 'the band of 1987' with their John Cale-produced debut album *Squirrel and G-Man Twenty Four Hour Party People Plastic Face Carnt Smile (White Out)* and singles 'Freaky Dancin'', 'Tart Tart' and '24 Hour Party People'.

The Roses played a meagre ten shows in 1987, four of them at the International club. 'The gigs they were doing at the International were always strange,' said Dave Roberts. 'I went to see them in Liverpool after "Sally Cinnamon" came out and there were about six people in the crowd. Five of them I'd invited. It was all pretty low-key apart from in Manchester when they played the International every month to a thousand people. But the band's attitude never wavered. That gig in Liverpool, Ian was still a total star. He was quite confrontational live but in a good way. He was in your face, moving around, just an amazing charismatic front man.'

When the Roses played the International on 26 June, sharing the bill with The Waltones, they finally picked up some favourable national press. The show was reviewed for the *NME* by Dave Haslam, who would prove to be a useful ally. As well as writing for the *NME*, Haslam ran popular Manchester magazine *Debris* and was a DJ at the Haçienda. 'Sally Cinnamon' was a big record at Haslam's regular Tuesday Temperance club night. In his *NME* review he picked out Reni and Brown for particular praise, predicting a bright future for the band.

Dave Roberts, who had heard the band rehearsing at International II, was also now convinced of their potential. The deal FM

Revolver had struck was for two singles and an album, and Roberts tentatively booked studio time at Cottage Studios. Contractually the Roses were due a small advance for this second single. This, plus the cost of recording, represented an investment Paul Birch felt was a risk after the poor sales of 'Sally Cinnamon'. 'Paul wasn't sure about the band and nothing was resolved,' said Roberts. 'We didn't really make a decision about the second single. We didn't say, No, we're not doing it, and the band didn't force our hand.'

'We thought they were wankers,' said Brown. 'We phoned up and said we don't recognize the contract.' By releasing 'Sally Cinnamon', however, FM Revolver had given the band a platform from which they could progress. Evans had got the bit between his teeth and was now hoping to sign the band to a new label and a more lucrative contract. The bubblegum pop sound of 'Sally Cinnamon' had finally shaken off 'the albatross', as Brown called it, of 'So Young'. It was the start of a new beginning for the Roses. But for bassist Garner it was the beginning of the end.

7.

Mani

Pete Garner had been a close friend of Brown and Squire since he was thirteen. He was now twenty-three and deeply unhappy. Much had happened in the intervening ten years, not least the fact the band he had joined in 1983 was now on the verge of achieving something magnificent, with the bulk of their classic songs and their definitive sound all but complete. But while Reni, Squire and Brown had developed into world-beaters, his playing was in stasis and his confidence had begun to ebb away.

'The problem I had was I was in a band with arguably *the* drummer of his generation, *the* front man of his generation and *the* guitarist of his generation and little old me on bass. Everybody had moved up three levels and I'd moved up one level. I felt like I was letting the side down.'

Garner had always had the most exquisite taste in music and was frustrated that his skills on bass couldn't match the sound he wanted to achieve. His creative contribution to the band, he felt, was negligible. He'd come up with the bass part for 'All Across the Sands', but more often Squire would write the bass lines for him. 'Most of the songs were done by Ian and John. They'd write stuff at home or go somewhere to write and bring it in. But obviously no one was writing the drums, so Reni's creative input is there. He's doing the harmonies, he's making all the songs sound better. If he was pissed off things were being brought into the room complete, he was still enhancing them. I didn't feel like I was doing that.'

He also found dealing with Evans difficult. 'Every week there would be a new crisis. It ground me down. There was so much shit going on behind the scenes. I felt the pressure piling on. I loved being in the band but I didn't love everything that went with it.' His frustration and doubt built up. The Roses were at the age where men share laughter rather than their problems. The band were aware Garner was struggling to keep up with them musically, but not how depressed it was making him. Garner was having some sort of breakdown.

The Roses would often meet in his city centre flat before rehearsals. One weekend, he'd been thinking. On Monday, 'Ian, John and Reni came round and I said, I've got to talk to you,' he recalled. He told them, 'I don't think I can do it. I don't want to do it any more.' And then he told them he wanted to leave, why, and how he felt. 'It was fucking hard,' he said. 'I was really upset about it but I felt much better once I'd spoken my mind and got it all out.'

The band didn't try to stop him and openly discussed with Garner who his replacement should be. Rob Hampson was the first to put his name forward for consideration. He was the Northern Soul-obsessed, suedehead scooterboy who had lived in the flat below Brown in Hulme in 1983. He was also a friend of the tour manager Steve Adge and had been to many of the Roses' shows. The problem was Hampson had never played bass before. Nonetheless, Squire, Brown and Reni told him if he could learn the songs he was in. Garner even offered to teach him.

Hampson had not made sufficient progress to take the stage with the band for the three live dates Evans had organized for the Roses in July and August 1987. Instead they asked Garner to play. He agreed on the proviso Evans book no more dates. 'It felt really weird, like going on a date with an ex-girlfriend. I didn't really want to do them but I didn't really want to drop them in the shit either.'

In July the Roses played Sheffield's Take Two club. The band they were sharing the bill with had draped a Confederate flag across an amplifier. Brown took offence, demanding what he called the 'flag of slavery' be removed. The next date was at Liverpool Planet X where they played to no more than thirty people, followed in August by a slot at the Liverpool Sefton Park Earthbeat Festival. 'We played on a hill that had a moat-style pond around it, and the audience sat on the next hill,' said Garner. Brown tried to get closer to the audience, diving into the moat. After this final show with Garner,

Brown – sporting a blond spiky flat-top to go with his Lydonesque stage stares – had to pull apart roadie Slim and manager Evans. Slim had enquired about wages he and soundman Simon Machan were owed. Evans had started shouting and Slim had gone for him.

Garner was glad to escape the chaos. The only thing that annoyed him was a response Brown gave to a question about why Garner had left. Brown thought it funny to imitate the Sex Pistols, who said they sacked their original bassist Glen Matlock because he liked The Beatles. Brown said the Roses had sacked Garner because he didn't like The Beatles. 'This appeared in the press,' said Garner. 'The first band I got into as a kid was The Beatles. I was obsessed with them. So I was furious, really upset.'

Rob Hampson appeared in one photo session with the Roses and was cast aside. Up stepped Mani, who knew Brown and Squire from the scooterboy scene in the early 1980s, and had played in The Waterfront with Squire and Couzens. He had also followed many of the early Roses gigs and was familiar with Cressa and the rest of the crowd. He would claim to have never played in any other bands before joining the Roses, and had just been 'in my bedroom pogo-ing about with my tennis racket'. In fact, he'd played in not just The Waterfront but popped up briefly in bands such as The Hungry Sox, T'Mill and the Inspiral Carpets in a scene that centred on Clint Boon in Oldham. None of the bands had amounted to much at that time, and he'd had a few jobs, including one in an abattoir. Boon was now playing keyboards with the Inspiral Carpets and they were on the rise.

Boon had come across Squire and Brown at the Boardwalk and they told him they were looking for a bass player. The next day Boon bumped into Mani's brother, Gregg, who told Mani. 'I got hold of Squire's number and called him up,' said Mani. 'I said, The job's mine. They were sick of auditioning bassists and John sounded relieved. We should have come to you first, he said.'

'I always knew I was the main man for the Roses,' said Mani. He was a few weeks from turning twenty-five and gave up his day job to join. As a bass player he modelled his style on James Jameson, the uncredited bassist on most Motown Records hits in the 1960s and

1970s; Paul Simonon of The Clash; and Peter Hook of Joy Division and New Order. Mani said he always felt he 'was playing catch up when it came to John and Reni' but, as had happened when Reni joined, there was no discussion. He was in. Evans had no say and would always have trouble working out the band's new member. The persona of a north Manchester scally was completely alien to him.

'Andy Couzens had gone and now we were starting to shape songs,' said Brown. 'When Mani joined in 1987 it made us more musical. John and Reni had improved. I'd improved. But Mani was the final piece of the jigsaw and everyone around us knew it.'

'We'd rearranged the songs over and over until we sounded like nobody else,' said Reni. 'Mani was crucial. He upgraded our potential. He was my perfect rhythm partner and great company. I got tighter on the drums and the bass lines got funkier.' Mani called Squire a 'Beatles head' and said the guitarist turned him on to Hendrix, while Reni introduced him to Funkadelic, Sly Stone and Miles Davis. 'Northern Soul was doubly important to all of us,' Mani said. 'You can hear it in the music.'

Mani's impact and influence would go beyond the musical. He was still a Perry boy, with a classic long-flicked fringe, and his personality was infectious. He'd got the style and the cheek. He looked at the band's image and told them, 'You've got to look like proper scallies.' Not only did the Roses begin to sound better after Mani joined, they started to look better too.

His first gig with the Roses has often been documented as 13 November 1987 at the International, three months after Garner's last gig with the band, and the final Roses show of the year. The bassist, however, recalled debuting at the Birmingham Hummingbird to a small crowd. 'The next night we played to 1,000 people at the International, then we went to Cardiff or Hull and played to about five people.' This disparity in audience had not gone unnoticed in trendy Manchester circles, and it was becoming a joke that the Roses were being spoon-fed a crowd by Evans.

★

Mani was the right man in the right place at the right time. The night at the International would lead to the band being offered a deal by Rough Trade Records. Evans had shrewdly employed Lindsay Reade, the former wife of Tony Wilson, to help him manage the band, and it was she who had got the country's premier indie label interested. Reade knew the music business, was sharp and well connected. She'd been invited to watch the band rehearse in the basement of International II and, despite her initial doubts, was won over when they played her a set that included most of the songs that would end up on their classic 1989 album.

Reade was also impressed by Evans's charisma and cunning. 'He was hell-bent on this band. Tony [Wilson] was a very driven man, but Gareth took the biscuit. He was a visionary in the sense he knew how successful they were going to be.' Evans offered her 10 per cent of his and Cummins's cut of the Roses and she moved into his office opposite the International. The office had only one phone, but Evans played games in there as if it was a major outfit. 'He'd be on the phone and ask people to hold, keep his hand on the receiver, and then go back to them after a few minutes to say he'd been on the other phone to the MD of EMI or whatever. It was showmanship,' she said. 'He would tell lies when there was no advantage to doing it. He just enjoyed it.'

Reade had taken a Stone Roses demo down to London to A&R people she knew, including a contact at Phonogram. Geoff Travis, the boss of Rough Trade Records, liked it enough to commit to a visit to Manchester to see them live. Rough Trade seemed the perfect home for The Stone Roses. The label's most iconic band was The Smiths, who before splitting up had released four hugely successful albums with the label. It was at the centre of the UK's largest independent distribution network, the Cartel. Travis had a long history in the business and also ran Blanco Y Negro, home to The Jesus and Mary Chain.

Travis arrived at the Roses' International gig with Rough Trade's other leading business figures, Jeannette Lee and Peter Walmsley, and they were all deeply impressed. 'It was jam-packed and it was just sensational from the minute they played their first note,' Travis said. 'We turned to Lindsay after about ten seconds and said, We want to sign this band.' Reade went backstage, after the show, to tell the band the good news. 'You'd think they'd be over the moon,' she said. 'But this lot, it was like a damp squib. No reaction. Particularly John Squire, he looked like he just didn't give a shit. I thought, Don't you realize, this is your big moment – you've got the deal.'

The Roses took the train to London to meet with Travis. They met him at a pub opposite Euston station and spent a couple of hours sounding him out. 'We talked about dance music, about Love, and about music we liked,' said Travis. 'Everyone was animated and it seemed to be a good conversation.' Travis reiterated his desire to sign the band and felt they had come to a good understanding. He was so eager to get things moving that, before contracts were issued, he offered to pay for the band to make their next single. The Roses told Travis that they wanted to record 'Elephant Stone' and that they had already secured the services of New Order bassist Peter Hook as producer. Travis agreed.

It was Evans who had talked Hook into the job, after prompting from the band. 'We had rated New Order's dance tunes,' said Brown. 'When "Elephant Stone" was ready to record, we started to look for a good producer for a dance record and then we hit on his name.' The song's distinctive wah-wah-driven guitar riff had been inspired by the Happy Mondays, while Brown said the track was an ideal showcase for the talents of Reni. 'We wanted people to hear what he could do,' he said.

Hook had visited the International, and been supplied with free drinks all night by Evans, as his band mate Bernard Sumner advised him would be the case. He was not prepared, however, for Evans to next turn up at his house unannounced to ask him to produce the Roses. 'I don't know how he found out where I lived.' Evans gave him a copy of 'Sally Cinnamon' and told Hook the band wanted their next single to 'sound better than this'. New Order were four albums into their astonishing career, having just released *Brotherhood*, their third UK Top 10 album. Hook had heard about the Roses,

1. On the tour bus, Sweden, 1985 (*from left:* Pete Garner, Ian Brown, Andy Couzens).
'Not every gig ended in a riot but more often than not it did. You couldn't take us anywhere. We were animals' Andy Couzens

2. On the tour bus, Sweden, 1985 (*from left:* John Squire, Brown, Garner, Reni, Howard Jones).

'We were getting in people's houses and going in their kitchens and cooking ourselves food. It became the cool thing to do to have us come round to your house and have us eat you out of house and home' Howard Jones

3. On stage, Sweden, 1985
(*from left*: Couzens, Brown).

'We came on at one gig and
there was a kid leaning on the
stage. Andy kicked him in
the face as the opening salvo'
Pete Garner

4. On stage, Sweden, 1985 (Squire with painted guitar, Garner).

'John might have worn the bandana for four weeks and then he moved on.
I wore some pretty ridiculous things . . . there was a lot of stuff we'd do
once and then never do again' Pete Garner

5. On stage, Sweden, 1985 (*from left*: Couzens, Brown, Squire, Garner).

'A yob Morrissey, a mob orator with yodelling vocal'
Sounds, describing Brown, December 1984

6. On stage, Sweden, 1985 (*from left*: Couzens, Brown, Reni, Squire).

'The Smiths were doing really well and there was a lot of jingly-jangly twee type
bands around, completely the opposite of what the Roses were doing – maybe that's
why people didn't quite warm to them' Paula Greenwood

7. On stage, Sweden, 1985 (*from left*: Reni, Brown).

'Ian, in those days, was a much more physical performer.
He was almost Jagger-esque in his movements about the stage'
Howard Jones

8. Thin Line advert for the
1985 Swedish tour.

'The tour had minimal resources
and we lived day by day. It was true
rock 'n' roll. We learned a hell of a
lot and had a hell of a good time'
Harald Sickenga, Toxin Toy

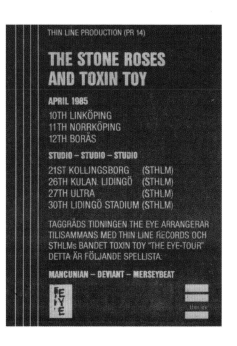

THIN LINE PRODUCTION (PR 14)

THE STONE ROSES
AND TOXIN TOY

APRIL 1985
10TH LINKÖPING
11TH NORRKÖPING
12TH BORÅS

STUDIO – STUDIO – STUDIO
21ST KOLLINGSBORG   (STHLM)
26TH KULAN. LIDINGÖ   (STHLM)
27TH ULTRA   (STHLM)
30TH LIDINGÖ STADIUM   (STHLM)

TAGGRÅDS TIDNINGEN THE EYE ARRANGERAR
TILISAMMANS MED THIN LINE RECORDS OCH
STHLMs BANDET TOXIN TOY "THE EYE-TOUR"
DETTA ÄR FÖLJANDE SPELLISTA:

MANCUNIAN – DEVIANT – MERSEYBEAT

9. On tour, Sweden, 1985 (*from left:* Garner, Reni, Brown, Squire).

'If you asked Ian or John or Reni; they said from day one, we're going to be the
best band in the world, we're going to be the biggest band in the world, and
they were unashamed about it' Slim

.thin line

THIN LINE PRODUCTION

TELEPHONE: 061-860 6470

PRESS RELEASE 1st AUG 85

"...with their tense and galactic brand of starkly atmospheric sound,
the STONE ROSES are a breath of fresh air"
   Gary Johnson "Sounds"

"...imagine the sound of fingernails scraping down a blackboard,
amplified to an intolerable degree, the STONE ROSES are tuning up.
The effect is impelling"
   Ro Newton "Melody Maker"

"...STONE ROSES are something dramatically different from all
other bands"
   Bob Dickenson "City Life"

STONE ROSES formed in late'84, and after a series of London shows
at venues such as the Greyhound, the Marquee, Kensington Ad-Lib, they
were signed to THIN LINE PRODUCTIONS.
   In early'85 following a highly successful tour of Sweden and Norway
THIN LINE enlisted the services of producer MARTIN HANNETT (who
has since become a director of THIN LINE PRODUCTIONS), the result of
this union is the STONE ROSES debut single -
   "SO YOUNG / TELL ME"
   Recorded at Yellow 2 / Strawberry Studios, Stockport the 12" 45 rpm
single was cut at CBS, and will be pressed at EMI. Distribution by the
CARTEL.
   STONE ROSES have since embarked on a series of both highly
publicised and yet "secret" live dates, such as the acclaimed "Flower
Show" Wharehouse Party - the very first in Manchester. This follows
both STONE ROSES and THIN LINE policy of making music not only
available in a record format, but also in the live arena.
   STONE ROSES are - IAN vocals , JOHNNY guitar , ANDY guitar ,
PETE bass , RENI drums .
   STONE ROSES Crew are - Simon sound engineer , Glen lighting ,
Slim backstage.   EXECUTIVES: H. MARSHALL-JONES, T. CHAMBERS, M. HANNETT

·thin line

THIN LINE PRODUCTION

TELEPHONE: 061-860 6470

PRESS RELEASE 1st AUG 85

Ex FACTORY and IKON hands TIM CHAMBERS , MARTIN HANNETT and HOWARD MARSHALL - JONES are brought back together as the board of THIN LINE , an Audio and Video Production Company.

THIN LINE signed a CARTEL distribution deal recently and their first release "SO YOUNG / TELL ME" by the STONE ROSES , a Manchester five piece will be in the shops around 19th AUG. Initially available in a 12" 45 rpm format , it has a dealer price of £1.70p , inclusive of VAT , and comes in a highly original four colour sleeve.

Say's MARTIN HANNETT ("Father of post - modern neo Gothic dance music") " I never stopped making masters - I just neglected to place them".

THIN LINE will plaster various ornaments onto utterly magnificent restaurant wallpaper.

To coincide with the release of the single the STONE ROSES will play a few live dates -
SAT   10th AUG The MARQUEE
THURS 15th AUG The HACIENDA
SAT   24th AUG The MARQUEE

The STONE ROSES will also continue their policy of playing secret dates as and when they feel...

EXECUTIVES: H. MARSHALL-JONES, T. CHAMBERS, M. HANNETT

10. and 11. Thin Line press release for 'So Young' / 'Tell Me' single, 1985.

'Independence in music for me meant the freedom of expression. Independent for Ian and John's generation was independent of the big companies taking all the money when they could take it for themselves' Howard Jones

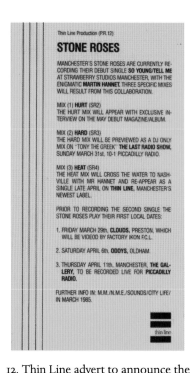

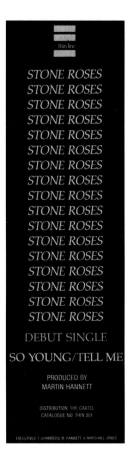

12. Thin Line advert to announce the Roses recording their debut single, 1985.

'The Roses reminded me of early Joy Division in the way they felt they had to kick doors down to be recognized'
Kevin Cummins

13. Thin Line advert for 'So Young' / 'Tell Me', 1985.

'The Roses put on a front of being completely new and better than anyone else' Bob Dickinson

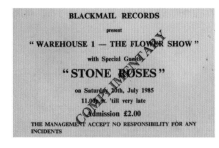

14. 'So Young' / 'Tell Me' single label detail, 1985.

'We'd always said we'd split everything five ways and then it came out that Ian and John wanted their names as songwriters' Pete Garner

15. Ticket for the Roses' first Manchester warehouse show, 1985.

'The Roses already had a small nucleus of followers – just mates, people like Cressa' John Breakell

16. The Patrol, on stage at Lymm Youth Club, 1980 (*from left*: Squire, Couzens, Brown).
'John wrote a lot of the lyrics in The Patrol. He was the only one of us who could play anything really; he'd had guitar lessons' Andy Couzens

17. In rehearsal at International II, 1987 (*from left*: Squire, Brown, Garner).
'Pete was definitely more sensitive than the others. They all had tougher skins. It's a classic album, the one they made with Hannett. Even now' Slim

18. In rehearsal, 1987 (Brown).

'I didn't see Ian again until almost twenty years later, and he is the lead singer of The Stone Roses. That motherfucker is more famous than me'
Geno Washington

19. On stage, 1987 (*from left*: Squire, Garner, Brown).

'Pete was like an indie encyclopaedia: he could tell you who played on what
record and it moved from that into independent films. He was a brilliant cataloguer
of all the important things' Howard Jones

20. On stage, 1986 (Brown).

'Have you seen how many haircuts Ian's had? Blond hair, red hair, different haircut every couple of weeks' Pete Garner

21. On stage, 1986 (Reni).

'The girls loved him'
Andy Couzens

22. On stage, 1987 (Reni).

'A lot of drummers are always pulling a face or straining. Reni was the
exact opposite. He made it look easy – he was always icy cool and graceful'
Jon Brookes, The Charlatans

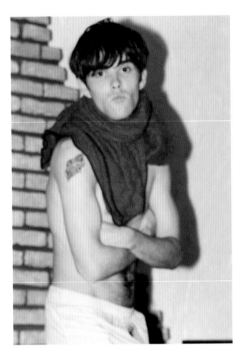

23. Brown, showing off his
Union Jack tattoo with 'England'
written across it, 1988.

'I remember someone interviewing Liam
Gallagher and saying, You think you're a
bad boy? You want to get along with Mensi
and the Upstarts and you'll find out what
a bad boy is' Mensi, Angelic Upstarts

24. Mani, 1987.

'Of the band, Mani was the one who
was 100 per cent outgoing, like Tigger,
always a smile on his face'
Eileen Mulligan

25. The Roses' second warehouse
party, Manchester, 1985 (*from left:*
Squire, Couzens, Brown).

'There was hardly anybody there,
only fifty people. Now everyone
says they went. It's like all these
people who say they saw the Sex
Pistols at the Free Trade Hall
and there were only twenty-six
people there' Sue Dean

26. Outside the International II, 1988 (*from left*: Mani, John Leckie, Brown).

'I was working with The La's and somebody said there's a band in Manchester looking for you and they are called The Angry Young Teddy Bears. Then I found out later it was The Stone Roses' John Leckie

27. Outside the International II, 1988 (*from left*: Mani, Gareth Evans and Tim Booth).

'Years later Gareth would claim all this was a cunning plan and each of these grotesque mistakes he made because of his total lack of knowledge of the music business and bonkers nature was part of the master plan' John Nuttall

28. Signing the contract with Evans in an Italian restaurant in Rusholme, 1987
(*from left:* Garner, Squire, Reni, Brown).

'As far as they were concerned it was a done deal. They were going to be successful – it
was only a matter of time and the public catching up with them' Anthony Boggiano

29. Band signatures/contacts, as requested by Steven Howard, 1988.

'I had them sign this piece of paper during the talks about them signing
to Jive/Zomba. I often think with a band you can imagine them as cartoon
characters, and each of the Roses you could see how they would
translate as cartoons' Steven Howard

was a pal of their roadie Slim, and knew the circle of girls that gravitated around Sue Dean. It sounded like fun and he was flattered, to some extent. Money wasn't discussed.

Hook arranged for New Order's engineer, Mike Johnson, to assist on the production of 'Elephant Stone' and booked studio time at Revolution in Cheadle, Stockport. He had never worked in this studio before, nor had he met the Roses until they showed up there to record. Reni was impressed to find Hook on the phone to Ian McCulloch, singer with Echo & the Bunnymen, making plans for a New Order and Bunnymen tour of America. 'When we went in to record it, if anyone was being the rock star it was probably me; bragging and showing off,' said Hook.

Hook suggested to the Roses that 'Elephant Stone' needed a break in the middle to open the song out and the band happily accepted his direction, even the inclusion of a sound created by banging a dustbin lid. Reni was one of the best rock drummers Hook had ever encountered, 'as good, if not better, than Stephen Morris was in Joy Division. Reni's drumming lent such a character and identity to the songs. Ian and John had got it with the melodies and lyrics but they were lucky to get Reni because he took them from being a traditional, normal rock band into the stratosphere with other great groups.'

Hook did have his reservations about Reni though, finding his strong personality overpowering, particularly in relation to recording the vocals. It had taken Hook a little time to get his head around Brown's sound, but he had come to the conclusion that what he lacked in virtuosity, he made up for with soul. 'He could reach you immediately as a person.' Reni handled the backing vocals with great skill but 'thought he was a better singer than Ian', said Hook. 'I think there was a struggle between him and Ian, more so than anyone. Reni was always in your ear, asking to sing, saying he could do it better.'

Hook had further problems with Reni when he refused to play sixteenths on the high-hat through the entirety of 'Elephant Stone' – 'I thought it would make it swing,' Hook said. So, after the basic song was recorded, Hook arranged for Shan Hira, the drummer of Stockholm Monsters, to play the part. He and Hira went to Strawberry Studios to add the overdub on Christmas Eve. 'Shan's playing away and I thought, Oh great, this is just what this song needed. And then over my shoulder this fucking head comes in: Hiya Hooky, Merry Christmas! I looked round and it was Reni. But he took it on the chin like a proper man and he said, Right, it does sound better, but let me in, I'll do it better. He went in and played on it and he did do it better.'

Factory had never paid Hook for his production work and he was on £100-a-week wage with New Order. After finishing the recording of 'Elephant Stone', plus two B-sides – 'The Hardest Thing in the World' and backward track 'Full Fathom Five' – he was surprised and delighted when Evans peeled off £1,000 from a wad of cash to pay him for his efforts. The band, he noted, also took advantage of Evans's largesse. 'If Ian's kettle blew up, he'd phone Gareth, who would buy him a new one and take it round,' he said. 'Mani would go, Oh, my hi-fi's broken, and Gareth would buy him a new one and take it round.'

Squire delivered the artwork for the single to Geoff Travis at Rough Trade. It was his first Jackson Pollock-style effort, with an instruction for Letraset typefaces for the lettering: Grotesque 9 and Grotesque outline. Squire first became aware of Pollock's abstract expressionist work while flicking through a Clash photo book. 'Pennie Smith had made a comment about Jackson Pollock with reference to a photo of Paul Simonon, and how they used to drip paint on their clothes and on their guitars early on,' he said.

When Travis received the finished mix of 'Elephant Stone', done at Hook's own Suite 16 studio, he suggested, and the band agreed, that it needed a bit more work. Hook had sat in the Rough Trade office with Travis listening to the mix and was forced to agree, although the poor quality was down to cheap cassette tapes the tracks had been copied onto.

To remix the single, Travis booked time at Power Plant studios in Willesden, north-west London. A Power Plant engineer heard

'Elephant Stone' and tipped off Jive (Zomba) Records, a major pop label who were based in the same studio complex, to the potential of the Roses. When they next played live, in January 1988 at Dingwalls in London, Jive's A&R staff were out in force. One of them, Roddy McKenna, arrived late but saw enough to make him want to pursue the band. He had a keen interest in dance music, while his superiors made sure he kept an eye on finding the 'next U2'.

McKenna arranged to meet Evans in Manchester privately, to discuss his interest. Evans turned on the charm and McKenna came away not only with the impression that it would be a 'real blast' working with him but also with the knowledge that nothing was yet signed with Rough Trade. McKenna also picked up on the fact that Evans was devoted to his son, and on subsequent visits to Manchester he always brought a gift for Mark – a single, CD or a T-shirt. It was this gesture, more than anything else, that would have an influence on Evans's sudden volte-face regarding Rough Trade.

The Roses, unaware of Evans's clandestine meeting with McKenna, were already talking up 'Elephant Stone' now that demo tapes of the single were circulating. They were featured in an article in Dave Haslam's *Debris* in December 1987 where 'Elephant Stone' was described as having 'golden melodies, a harder sound than "Sally Cinnamon", brilliant beat, and sparkling, crystal candy guitar'. The article was written by Andy McQueen, who worked at Eastern Bloc, a record shop that would soon overtake Piccadilly Records to become Manchester's key music outlet. In it, McQueen mentioned how the city's tastemakers were still split over the Roses, citing *City Life*'s omission of 'Sally Cinnamon' from the magazine's 1987 end-of-year Top 40.

'A lot of bands in the city dislike us because of the way we are,' said Brown. 'All we are is a big local band, we're not known nationally. So you get "the inflated egos of the Stone Roses" and we have got inflated egos – that's an important part of being a good group. I don't want to slag anyone off but you don't hear people going, God, I hate The Railway Children, because they're not the sort of band you hate, whereas I think we are, because we're of some value.'

The photograph in *Debris* was of Squire and Brown, separated by a Pollock-style paint-splattered guitar in front of a similarly decorated giant backdrop. It was the work of Ian Tilton, who had been introduced to the band by *Sounds* journalist John Robb. Robb, like McQueen, was another major local supporter of the Roses and, badgered by Evans, he wrote the first lengthy feature on the band for *Sounds*, which appeared in January 1988. In the interview the band said they were thinking of calling their debut album *Bring Me the Head of James Anderton on a Plate* (Anderton was Manchester chief of police), and Brown named the Happy Mondays as the 'best group in Manchester'.

After Dingwalls, the Roses played the International II on 26 February. It was another packed-out night and Roddy McKenna brought along his boss Steven Howard, the young managing director of Jive Records and the affiliated Zomba Music Publishing and Zomba Management. 'What staggered me was I saw the poster listing upcoming events at the International and the Roses' ticket price was as high as Simply Red's, who had broken through by then,' Howard said. 'As an A&R guy coming up from London, it was like, What is going on here?'

Howard was also blown away by the sight of the queue outside. 'It was all these kids in baggy jeans, flared jeans,' he said. 'I thought, If they've got this kind of cult fashion thing going on, there's a whole lifestyle. That, coupled with the fact the ticket price was high, the venue was larger than it should have been – my antennae were well and truly turned on. The show was, dare I say it, the second coming. The band was incredible. I spoke to Clive Calder [the owner of Jive Records] the next day and said, Look, I think we might have a U2 here.'

What Howard had seen, in terms of a lifestyle emerging and coalescing around the band, was a movement dubbed (tongue firmly in cheek) 'The Baldricks' and led by Cressa, Al Smith and Little Martin. The Baldricks had been mentioned in *i-D* magazine as early as 1987 and called part of 'a surreal youth cult roaming the Haçienda'. Cressa, Smith and Little Martin were photographed (by Ian Tilton) wearing flares and big outdoor jackets for a feature about the Baldricks in *i-D* in April 1988. Followers of the movement were defined by 'a love of

1960s psychedelia and acid that had instinctively drawn them to house music', the feature said. With a lineage drawn from Perry boys, casuals and scallies, the Baldricks were celebrated for initiating the return of flared jeans. The 24-year-old Happy Mondays lead singer Shaun Ryder was interviewed for the *i-D* piece: 'It's just a way of life,' he said.

Howard returned to Manchester to meet with the band, who were under the impression the deal with Rough Trade was going ahead. To confuse matters, no one had told Howard of Rough Trade's interest. 'It was an odd one,' said Howard. 'I was really embarrassed because here I was talking to these rock 'n' roll guys from Manchester, and Jive Records was best known for Samantha Fox.' Howard quickly established there was no other major label interest in the band, but was crushed when the band informed him of Rough Trade's offer. 'I just thought, There's no way we can compete with Geoff Travis,' he said. 'Here's a guy rooted in credibility versus these guys who've basically got Samantha Fox and Billy Ocean.'

To Howard's surprise, he found some of the Roses were open to working with Jive Records: 'They actually liked the fact that we were in the mainstream because they viewed Rough Trade, even though it was very credible, as very "indie". They wanted to be the biggest band in the world and they felt Rough Trade couldn't deliver that, whereas by being on Jive, because we're putting some of these pop records onto the top of the charts, they figured if they could do it with us, it could actually work for them.'

Jive Records, formed in 1981, was part of the Zomba Corporation, which had been established by Clive Calder and Ralph Simon in 1975. They'd had huge success with Zomba Music Publishing, representing a diverse roster of acts including the Joy Division catalogue; and Zomba Management, most closely associated with esteemed producer Mutt Lange. Jive Records had success in the early 1980s with pop acts such as Flock of Seagulls and Tight Fit and had ridden on the back of the popularity of hip-hop and rap. The label was, as Howard said, best known in the UK for launching the singing career of former Page 3 model Samantha Fox.

Squire was not convinced. There was a discussion between the band and Evans at Reni's flat in West Didsbury where the merits of Jive/Zomba and Rough Trade were debated. 'I wanted to sign to Rough Trade and everyone else wanted to sign to Zomba,' Squire said. 'Rough Trade seemed like a better label than the one Sam Fox was on to me. There wasn't much to talk about as far as I was concerned.'

Unfortunately for Squire, due to internal difficulties regarding their distribution arm Rough Trade had still not produced a contract. Jive/Zomba had moved with speed and their contract was already in Evans's hands. Evans had the backing of the rest of the band and, with a sizeable advance on offer, was eager to sign. He liked McKenna, felt a little intimidated by Geoff Travis at Rough Trade, and was satisfied in his negotiations, having bumped up the advance from £30,000 to £70,000. Evans would not go back to Rough Trade, as would be standard practice, to see if they could match the deal Jive/Zomba had offered.

'There was never a proper negotiation,' said Travis. 'He never said, They've offered me this, why don't you match it, or, Offer more and we'll sign to you – which would be a normal sort of conversation. I would have matched any offer. We wanted to do a serious deal for a number of albums. We knew this was a once-in-a-lifetime band.'

Evans paraded the Jive/Zomba paperwork around in triumph. He would pull it out of his briefcase, flash it at associates and then scamper off. The finer points of the contract were lost on him and he turned it over to his solicitor, Geoff Howard, for advice. Howard was a couple of years older than Evans and ran his practice from premises in Sale. He was not a music business lawyer and specialized in property. Evans and Cummins had bought and sold a lot of property with his help.

Zomba boss Clive Calder, on the other hand, was an incredibly shrewd operator, one who would go on to amass a £3 billion fortune, and the contract Evans and Howard were looking over was in fact just a 'draft', an amalgam of all the toughest clauses in the various contracts Calder had come across over his many years in the business, such as the one which stipulated the band didn't get paid on the first 30,000 records sold. Jive/Zomba fully expected the draft contract, which tried to tie the band up for an incredible eight albums, to be considerably amended – any competent music business lawyer would have ripped it to pieces. Evans, though, was eager to finally nail the big deal, and wanted to get it done fast. Nothing was changed and the contract went through as it was, which would have severe consequences. It was, famously, one of the worst recording contracts in history.

Evans took the Roses into Rough Trade for a marketing meeting about 'Elephant Stone' and later the same day had the band sign with Jive/Zomba. 'We all passed round this telephone directory of a thing and said, We haven't got a clue, giggled and signed it,' said Squire. Evans and the Roses had signed to Jive Records for recording, and Zomba Music Publishers Ltd for publishing, for territories encompassing 'the world and its solar system'. The advance of £70,000 was split between the two companies: 50 per cent against the publishing contract and 50 per cent against recording.

The news left both Geoff Travis and Lindsay Reade stunned, as Travis explains: 'It was one of the biggest disappointments of my entire life in music. I certainly felt very used. I don't think they ever paid us back for the recording costs for "Elephant Stone". They just took the single away.' Reade was 'absolutely disgusted' by the turn of events and told Evans she wanted him out of her life. 'We were musicians,' said Squire. 'We wanted to get on with it. We weren't interested in the business side and we weren't interested in business people. So Gareth would take care of that and report back to us. We knew what he was like, of course we did. But we had a good time with him.'

8.

Leckie

As news of the Roses' deal spread around Manchester, one of the rumours was that Evans had bought a fleet of ex-Post Office Range Rovers with the advance money. Evans himself started many of the rumours; all publicity was good publicity as far as he was concerned. There was some truth, however, to others, such as how he was still dealing in gold bullion and had a yacht in Puerto Andratx in Majorca.

The best story about Evans, and the one that seemed to exemplify his approach to life and business, was about a skiing holiday with Bernard Sumner of New Order and their respective girlfriends. Evans insisted on taking on the most challenging slope, despite never having skied before. Ignoring protestations, he shot off down the slope and was found at the bottom stuck in a tree hanging over a fast-running river. 'Barney was saying if he'd fallen off he'd have been dead,' said Peter Hook. 'Gareth was off his rocker. The group used to try and keep him in check.'

Having enjoyed working with Hook on 'Elephant Stone' the Roses wanted him to produce their debut album for Jive/Zomba, but commitments to the next New Order album, *Technique*, prevented him from accepting the offer. Instead, the band turned to John Leckie, who in a twist of bitter irony had initially been recommended to the Roses by Geoff Travis at Rough Trade before the band had abandoned him.

Leckie may not have been first choice, or even the band's choice, but he was the right choice. In the early 1970s, he had worked with artists such as Syd Barrett and John Lennon in a junior studio capacity, and by the end of that decade was producing acts such as XTC, Simple Minds, Magazine and Public Image Ltd. More recently, he'd produced three albums with The Fall and had just completed work on the notoriously difficult debut album for The La's.

McKenna invited him to meet the band in Manchester. 'I stayed at Gareth's farmhouse in Knutsford,' Leckie said. 'Gareth told me it was one of his many farmhouses and if I wanted one it was £300,000. As soon as we got there he jumped in the car and drove off again, and left me in this farmhouse.' The next day Leckie went to see the band rehearse on the stage at International II. 'They were very welcoming towards me,' he said. The Roses were less welcoming of Reni's new look. He'd returned from a short holiday with fake dreadlock hair extensions, and they teased him remorselessly until he removed them. Leckie watched the band rehearse from mid-morning until four in the afternoon, when that evening's featured band arrived to soundcheck, and he agreed to return north to watch the band play live the following week at International II.

Leckie had never worked with Jive Records before and was wary of the label's lack of credibility in the rock world, although there were now plans to set up a separate guitar label for the Roses. The incongruity of bringing the band to market on the Jive label had troubled the band's A&R man McKenna and his boss Steven Howard. McKenna said he didn't trust the marketing team at Jive 'to handle such a cool act'. Howard was having 'panic moments' about the situation. 'The *NME* was the most powerful media publication that you needed to get on side for your band, and Jive as far as they were concerned was an absolute joke,' said Howard. 'So, talking with Clive Calder, I said, We need to have an indie label that becomes a home for guitar bands, just in the eyes of the *NME*, where we can be perceived as indie and they don't smell the whole Jive thing behind it. Clive got that in a second and said, Let's do it.' Howard travelled to Manchester to discuss the idea with Evans and the band. 'That was a very hard sell,' he said. 'They had chosen Jive because it wasn't an indie label – but the bottom line is they went for it.'

Clive Calder approached Andrew Lauder to front and run the new Jive/Zomba 'indie' label, and inked a deal with him on 18 April 1988. Lauder was reluctant to take on the Roses, because he was more into the blues, but quickly began 'to smell and feel the groundswell of opinion from some of the tastemakers that this band was the real deal'. He was thirty-six and already had a distinguished career: in the 1970s, as head of A&R at United Artists, he had signed bands such as Can, Motörhead and Buzzcocks. He had co-founded his own label, Radar Records, home to Elvis Costello, and, during a brief stint at Island Records, signed U2.

On 30 May 1988, Leckie returned to Manchester to see the Roses play live at International II. 'It was jam-packed, you couldn't move in there,' he said. The Roses were supporting fellow Manchester band James and the night was an awareness raiser, organized by Dave Haslam, for the Anti-Clause 28 movement. 'It was pretty chaotic,' Haslam said. 'You'd have thought dealing with Gareth in a club he was connected with would have been easy but for some reason it made it even harder.' Brown described the gig as 'perfect'. James had been on Factory Records, and tipped as the next big thing, before defecting to a major label Sire in the US and Blanco Y Negro in the UK, and failing to fulfil their promise commercially. The band were at a low ebb but retained a strong local following.

Evans had been to work on the fly-posting, 'putting the Roses in huge letters and James really small', he said. He also delayed the Roses start-time until 10.30 p.m., so that by the time headline-act James played, half the audience were on the bus home. 'We completely stole the scene,' he said. The reviewers must have also been on the bus because there was no mention of James in either the *Melody Maker* or the *Record Mirror* reviews that followed.

Both reviews were positive, but the gig wasn't what Leckie expected. 'It was a lot more of a rock kind of thing. It was loud and Reni was centre stage. I thought, Oh, this band is all about the drummer. Reni would be taking off, singing and playing, and all the lights would be flashing on him. He was all energy and showing off.'

In June, the Roses played the International II again. In the review by *Sounds*, Brown was said to have thrown 'pints and sarcasm over the audience'. The same month, there was a small interview with the band in *NME* that promised 'Elephant Stone' would be out shortly. The band was quoted as saying, 'We want to be the first band to play on the moon. We want to be bigger than The Beatles.' In July the Roses appeared on the cover of local fanzine *M62*, their first front cover since *Buzzin'* over a year before. They boasted of their deal with Jive Records and talked up a next single, 'Made of Stone', a new song that they intended to couple with 'I Wanna Be Adored' as the B-side. For their debut album they were now thinking of the title *The Stone Roses Are Coming*. The band also provided the answer to a question that had troubled Geoff Travis: why sign for Jive over Rough Trade? 'We've got to get in the middle of big business to shake it up,' Brown said. 'We want to become huge popstars and shake things up our own way.'

The cover photographs for the *M62* piece had been taken by Ian Tilton, who'd first photographed the Roses for *Sounds*. Tilton chronicled this period in the band's development, climaxing in shots that graced the debut album cover. The shots used for *M62*, of the four Roses sitting on a futon in Tilton's studio gesticulating towards camera, saw the band's look inching closer to the finished article – with Brown's crew cut now growing out. The session had been Mani's first proper shoot with the band. 'Mani was like a fish out of water,' said Tilton. 'We had to give him a bit of guidance. He was just a lad.'

Leckie had remixed 'Elephant Stone' as his first commitment to the Roses project, basically just double-tracking what Peter Hook had done for the 7-inch version of the single. Of the band, only Brown made fresh contributions to the track, rerecording his vocals with Leckie at Zomba's Battery studios in Willesden. The studios were almost exclusively used for Zomba product and operated twenty-four hours a day. 'It was quite corporate, quite serious,' said Leckie. The Roses' A&R man Roddy McKenna was dubbed 'the headmaster'. 'He'd talk to Ian and wag his finger at him as he was talking,' said Leckie. 'But Ian really respected Roddy because of a lot of the black music he was doing for Zomba.'

Attention turned now towards recording the band's album and future singles for Jive/Zomba. In preparation Leckie had the band in Stockport's Coconut Grove studio working on pre-production. They had been busy. 'We wrote most of the first album in the few weeks after inking the deal, because we'd blagged the record company,' Brown said. 'We told them that we had about thirty or forty songs, but we only had about eight.' New songs the band were developing included 'Bye Bye Badman', 'Made of Stone', 'Shoot You Down' and 'I Am the Resurrection', all credited to Squire and Brown. '"I Am the Resurrection" started out as a piss-take of Paul McCartney's bass on "Taxman",' said Reni. 'Mani used to play that riff every day, in reverse. I'd come in and John would doodle some Fender over the top and we'd do it for a laugh in soundchecks. Finally we said, Let's do it properly, this joke song actually sounds really good.'

It was at Coconut Grove that Leckie discovered just how new the new Roses songs were. Lawrence Stewart was the studio's in-house engineer/producer, and he worked on pre-production sessions that lasted two days. 'Leckie went into the live room to listen to the band play and came back out with his face red,' said Stewart. 'He told me to turn off the recording equipment. He went back inside the live room and told everybody to shut up. He went through the musicians one by one – and told them what to do. He drilled them. When they first struck up, the timing was all over the place, to the point where it was incredible that somebody of Leckie's stature would work with them. It was much, much worse than anyone could ever fathom. Once Leckie had finished with them they were a different band.'

'That's kind of what I do really: tell them it's shit and to pull it together,' said Leckie. 'I was used to shambolic bands. Most of the time it's that they don't listen to each other, they can't hear the whole thing. They play as individuals rather than as a band and you just get them together. The Roses' strong point was that they all wanted to be the front man and somehow we made them into a group.'

For Leckie there was one event from these pre-production sessions that would be hard to forget. On the second day, Reni had phoned the studio at one in the afternoon to tell Leckie he had just got up, but would be over in twenty minutes in a taxi. Reni didn't have any money and wondered if Leckie could pay the £10 taxi fare. 'I said, Yeah yeah, just come.' While Reni was on his way to the studio, Evans turned up. 'Reni walked in and came straight up to me and said, Have you got that tenner, the taxi driver's waiting outside?' Evans grabbed hold of Reni by the throat and said, Don't ever ask John Leckie for money, if you want money come to me – and whacked him. Reni's nose was bleeding and then Reni started hammering out. They were on the floor kicking and punching each other. I'm standing there holding this tenner and Gareth disappeared, vooomph, he was gone.'

Both Reni and Evans were flamboyant and there had been a clash before this incident, but it developed into a palpable mutual dislike. 'I don't think Gareth had his favourites in the band,' said his girlfriend Sue Dean, 'but he didn't like Reni, and Reni thought Gareth was an idiot.'

After Leckie's pre-production drilling, the band were well prepared to start recording the album. 'Everything was worked out,' Brown said. The sessions started in July 1988 at Zomba's Battery studios and would conclude in February 1989. Working with the band in the studio alongside Leckie would be Jive/Zomba staff engineer and producer Paul Schroeder, who'd worked at Battery since 1985, recording with artists such as Detroit techno pioneer Kevin Saunderson and new jack swing master Teddy Riley. They had specifically requested a dance engineer.

The early sessions were done at Battery 2 studio, where Bob Marley and Queen had recorded. Initially the band was kept on a tight budget and booked into cheap night-time sessions, starting at seven in the evening and finishing at nine in the morning. This would become draining. 'We'd work on two or three songs a week,' said Schroeder. 'Then take some time off and do that again.' The first block of tracks recorded included 'I Wanna Be Adored', 'Made of Stone', 'Waterfall' and 'She Bangs the Drums'. Leckie was meticulous and inventive in the studio, initially focusing on the drum sound. Reni's unconventional approach of rarely playing the same thing twice could be as frustrating as it was rewarding.

He didn't notice that 'Made of Stone' had a similar vocal melody to the title track on The Dukes of Stratosphear album *25 O'Clock*, a psychedelic pop homage he'd produced with XTC in 1985. It was the album that, prior to meeting him, had persuaded the band Leckie was the man for them. Nor that the riff in 'Waterfall' strongly echoed the Simon & Garfunkel song 'April Come She Will'. It was clear to him that the band was channelling a 'freakbeat' sound, influenced by bands such as Nazz, The Bryds and Love, as were other indie bands of the 1980s such as Primal Scream. 'That dusty 1960s kind of thing, that's what I do, my mark, my era,' said Leckie.

Leckie began to grow in his understanding of what made the band unique, despite the label's pressure to produce singles that would be radio hits, with the vocals high in the mix. 'I started to think, Hang on a minute, this is a band, it's four guys, and you've got to give them equal importance,' he said. 'Although yes, you want the vocal so you can understand it and hear it, the other three elements are equally important. That's what guided me. They all want to be in the foreground.'

McKenna was under pressure from his bosses not only to produce hits but to keep a tight control on the budget. Leckie was being paid for his time but Schroeder worked for the company, and to save money McKenna suggested the band record B-sides for future singles with Schroeder alone. Already Leckie had been messing about playing tapes backwards with the band to create a new melody and proposing to record other stuff over the top, but it would be Schroeder who produced 'Don't Stop', the album's famous backwards track. It was the result of an incredibly productive weekend. As well as 'Don't Stop' the band cut 'Going Down' and 'Mersey Paradise'.

'With "Don't Stop" we flipped the tape over and I did a basic mix of what we could use and what we couldn't, and then we just added elements,' said Schroeder. In order to keep in with the backwards idea, all the mic'ing was done back to front. Cymbals were recorded from underneath, guitar amps were recorded from the back. 'Then we used a lot of the backing vocals and it actually sounded like "Doooon't stop", fantastic,' Schroeder said. 'So we put extra vocals in the right way and mixed them with the backwards vocals for this dreamy effect. Then we put the bass line through a gate that was triggered by Reni playing sticks on the floor, so every time he hit the stick on the floor the gate would open up and you'd hear the bass sound. With a bit of jiggery pokery we came up with the lovely bass-line bit for the ending, which was Ian Brown's favourite section of a record ever.'

The band, as a rule, didn't take drugs in the studio. They made an exception for this moment. 'When we finished that, we knew it was good and we rolled a great big spliff and put it on massive speakers,' said Schroeder. 'We all lay down on the floor in front of the desk and listened to it. It was absolutely gorgeous.' It was ultimately far too good for a B-side.

Five tracks down, Roddy McKenna left to set up a Jive / Zomba office in Chicago. The band applauded this brave musical move. His departure allowed Andrew Lauder to take a more hands-on approach. By now the new label Jive / Zomba had set up to accommodate the Roses had a title: Silvertone, named after a vintage guitar. Squire had chosen it.

The early sessions at Battery had been fruitful; a second batch of recording had seen starts on '(Song for My) Sugar Spun Sister', 'Bye Bye Badman', 'Shoot You Down', 'I Am the Resurrection' and 'This Is the One', and the band would make frequent returns to the Zomba-owned studio before the album was complete. The Roses took a break from recording in October 1988 to promote the release of 'Elephant Stone'. The band were happy with their work. Evans had them put them on a weekly wage of £70 each, enabling them to finally sign off the dole after three years. Squire was relieved, as the DSS were weeks away from finding him regular employment. They had money in their pockets for weed, were responding well to Leckie's laid-back approach, and, in Manchester, had it easy at their

HQ at International II. Brown and Squire were supremely relaxed and in solid relationships, and all four of the band felt, finally, their self-prophesying greatness was about to become a reality – and the last laugh on all those who had doubted them would be truly sweet.

Zomba's plan to launch the band on Silvertone, with the respected Lauder at the head of the label, worked well. The perception of it as a new indie label was enhanced by the fact that 'Elephant Stone' was promoted as being produced by Peter Hook. 'It worked a dream,' said Jive Records managing director Steven Howard. 'They were coming from out of the underground into the overground, the *NME* loved it, it was a label they hadn't even heard of, very indie, and with someone from Joy Division and New Order behind the group. It just caught fire.'

The press release for the single tried to make purchase out of the band's earlier 1985 warehouse gigs, linking the band with the explosion of illegal acid house warehouse raves now dominating headlines. No guitar bands as yet were being associated with these new raves, and for many, acid house signalled the end of guitar music. For Brown it was the opposite. 'Pop music was saved by the advent of acid house and rap because whites [white guitar bands] have done nothing for ten years.' In early 1988, the drug Ecstasy, the smiley face logo, and London clubs such as Shoom and Spectrum and The Trip had heralded the beginning of a new era. By what was being labelled 'the Summer of Love' acid house had exploded into the national consciousness. The *Sun* ran front pages chronicling the 'evils' of the scene as the first outdoor raves such as Sunrise became massive. 'We didn't play acid house music but we did enjoy it,' Brown said. While in London, he, Mani and Reni had been at the acid clubs, and back in Manchester they enjoyed a similar experience at the Haçienda and the Thunderdome. 'We saw some of the spirit of Paris 1968 reflected in the acid house movement,' Brown said. 'People were coming together and governments don't want that.'

The release of 'Elephant Stone' coincided with the first big illegal acid house rave in Manchester, at which Brown was present. Sweat

It Out on 5 October 1988 was organized by the young Donnelly brothers, Chris and Anthony. 'Ecstasy made that period what it was,' said Chris. 'At the Haçienda, Mike Pickering bringing music back from Chicago and New Order had a big influence, but it was Ecstasy that made acid house explode in the city.' The brothers recall the first shipment of 200 pills arriving in Manchester and being distributed at a club called Stuffed Olive's on South King Street. 'After that night no beer got drank for about a year,' said Anthony. For Sweat It Out, a railway arch was bolt-cropped, a stage was built, and five or six strobe lights installed that never stopped until ten in the morning. 'The police didn't have a clue what was going on,' said Anthony.

'Football hooliganism got finished overnight,' said Brown, who was an Ecstasy convert. 'Just the strength that we felt with each other, just en masse, you know what I mean, beautiful. It was a community thing. We'd had the Tory government, we'd had the miners' strike, and here's the people all laughing and dancing. You're trying to finish us but look at us.'

'Elephant Stone' reached number 27 in the indie charts. The band had sold the majority of the 2,000 records in Manchester. Due to the switch from Rough Trade to Jive/Zomba and then to Silvertone the single had been on hold for six months. The band were already keyed up to release 'Made of Stone', but a game plan had been formed and 'Elephant Stone' was seen as an incremental step forward. 'Album out early next year,' teased the press release. Andrew Lauder had arranged for Philip Hall at independent PR company Hall Or Nothing to handle the group's publicity. Hall had already won a *Music Week* PR award for his campaign for The Pogues and was working with bands such as The Waterboys, James and The Beautiful South. With Hall on board the profile of the Roses in the three main weekly music papers began to improve.

There was a small but largely disparaging *Melody Maker* interview published on 12 November. Brown was quoted as saying, 'You can make yourself everlasting by making records.' In the *NME*, Manchester writer Sarah Champion penned the band's first serious career overview, chronicling the 1985 graffiti outrage and warehouse gigs at length. 'Elephant Stone', she wrote, had enjoyed phenomenal regional sales. 'If I thought we'd remain selling 2,000 records I'd give up now – I think we're going to be huge,' Brown told Champion. Hall would continue to build the band in the press on the back of a steady series of glowing live reviews in the coming months. Lauder knew to really break the band nationally he would need exposure on radio and TV and wanted Gareth Davies of Beer Davies (who had represented The Smiths) to handle this key element of the band's career.

Lauder sent Davies to Manchester to watch the band rehearse at International II. There was also a boy of nine or ten watching the band that day, having strolled in uninvited on his way home from school. When the band stopped to chat with Davies, Reni handed the kid his drumsticks so he could have a go on his kit. 'I'd never come across a band that would just let a kid who had wandered in play their instruments,' said Davies, who would become the band's TV and radio plugger for their entire career. 'They were just about the least arrogant and most friendly band I've ever dealt with, completely different to the way most people perceived them.'

Davies immediately arranged for the group to film their first TV show, an interview and mimed performance of 'Elephant Stone' for indie show *Transmission* made by Music Box, a European cable and satellite channel owned by Virgin and also seen on several terrestrial TV channels, most significantly ITV's Yorkshire Television. The Roses were interviewed and filmed in their dark cellar rehearsal space at the International II, which Squire had bedecked in a Pollock-inspired backdrop. The band mimed to 'Elephant Stone' enthusiastically; Reni's drum kit was now Pollocked, as was Squire's guitar and Brown's shirt. The band's classic look was taking shape, although there was no Reni hat, Brown's hair was still short of its heyday and the jeans were narrow at the ankle. Squire and Brown, the only two featured in the interview, were awkward and defensive. Asked what 'Elephant Stone' was about, Squire deadpanned, 'Love and death. War and peace. Morecambe and Wise.'

'Rachael Davies was doing the interview,' said Davies. 'John and Ian were standing beside one another and they both had their hands behind their back, just swaying from side to side, like shy schoolchildren. They were very slow with their answers and it all seemed very difficult. Rachael came up to me afterwards and said, God, did I do something to upset them? They very quickly picked up on the fact that you can create your own sort of mystique about yourselves by not talking.'

There was also a handful of gigs to support 'Elephant Stone'. In November the band played in Brown's hometown of Warrington, in St Helens, at London Polytechnic and in Chester. Evans, unbeknownst to the band, was often out the day before handing out free tickets and manically putting up fly posters. In December the Roses played the London School of Economics, reviewed by *Melody Maker* and *Record Mirror*, the latter calling the Roses 'indie's great hopes of 89', then Belfast and Edinburgh. The dates marked a shift in the band dynamic. Cressa had left the Happy Mondays to take up a permanent position on Squire's side of the stage, grooving his funky dance behind the largely static guitarist. His task was nominally to change patches on Squire's guitar effects, but it was more about the look.

'There were only three or four songs I would have to change his effects on more than once,' Cressa said. 'John could have done it with pedals like everybody else.' With Cressa came fellow 'Baldrick' Al Smith as the Roses built a new touring crew, corralled chiefly by the indefatigable Steve Adge. He involved a strong presence from his part of Manchester, Hyde, including Phil Smith and Chris 'The Piss' Griffiths – nicknamed because at gigs he would urinate wherever he wanted (in people's pockets was his forte).

There was a new addition to the management set-up as Evans was introduced to the Los Angeles-based Greg Lewerke, a friend of Andrew Lauder. Lewerke had previously been head of International at United Artists, and Lauder hoped he would help Evans understand the American market, where Jive/Zomba product was distributed by major label RCA. Lewerke was impressed in

Edinburgh as the Roses drove the crowd crazy in 'a tiny room that was hotter than hot, dripping sweat off the wall'.

Lewerke agreed to represent Evans in America, for a percentage of his commission. In Edinburgh Evans was selling band T-shirts, and told Lewerke the band didn't know how many he sold and that he was keeping the money. 'I should have known from the beginning,' said Lewerke. 'But Gareth was as much part of the myth of the Roses as anything else.'

9.

Blackpool

The band kicked off 1989, the 'year of the Roses', with a defining performance on the Tony Wilson-hosted show *The Other Side of Midnight*. It was a booking that had nothing to do with their newly appointed plugger, Gareth Davies. This was strictly a Manchester thing.

'When we started, Factory was the Manchester mafia,' Brown said. 'The Smiths had broken through but even they needed the say so of Tony Wilson and the rest. You had to play the Haçienda as a sort of homecoming. But we really believed we could do it our way. In a way we were wrong, because it wasn't really until *The Other Side of Midnight* that we were accepted and things started to happen.'

How the famed boss of Factory Records ended up with the Roses on his Granada TV show (he admitted during his introduction that he'd 'seriously disliked' the band 'for four or five or six years') can be attributed to producer Steve Lock, who had only recently arrived in Manchester. Lock quickly discovered that two bands were being talked about: the Happy Mondays and The Stone Roses. 'They were in very different camps. Tony hated The Stone Roses, absolutely hated them.' Evans rang Lock and invited him to see the band rehearse; he was impressed but had no joy in persuading Wilson of the band's worth.

The Other Side of Midnight was often put together at the last minute, and it was only when an act dropped out of the show that Lock was able to force Wilson to reconsider. 'I had a big row with Tony,' he said. 'He said, I don't want a fucking goth band on. They'd obviously been around for a while in a number of different guises, so the band he hated may not have been the band they were, but knowing Tony he wouldn't have let that get in the way of a good hatred.'

The show went out weekly and, although it gave the impression of being a late-night affair, was recorded between 11 a.m. and 1 p.m. on Thursdays in the Granada 2 studio, where the Sex Pistols and The Beatles had played. The show was transmitted on Granada and ITV regional networks such as Yorkshire and Tyne Tees. In London it went out in the early hours of Sunday morning on LWT and had a cult following due to Wilson's involvement and the fact that the critics Paul Morley, Stuart Cosgrove and Jon Savage sat in the studio and reviewed the show live on air. 'Although it may have been seemingly obscure, it was a very influential show in terms of the type of people who watched it,' said Lock. 'It was being written about in the music press all the time.'

The Roses invited photographer Ian Tilton to come to the recording, and the photos he took in the studio would end up gracing the band's album sleeve. 'So it was kind of a seminal moment,' said Lock. 'None of us had any inclination of that. It was just a local band coming into the studio and we were just a low-budget regional TV show who couldn't get proper bands on the show.' The band ran through 'Waterfall' a couple of times. 'The first time Reni didn't wear a hat and the second time he wore a hat,' Tilton said. 'I didn't even think about the hat. He just wore it, it looked right on him and that was that. I did colour and black and white photographs but didn't know what it was going to be used for. They didn't pay me, nobody mentioned money. I just did it.'

On the live version of 'Waterfall' that was broadcast, Reni's hat was in place. The studio was entirely white. Cressa did his groovy dance behind Squire's amp, Mani's Rickenbacker was Pollocked and – spare a few inches on the hair and trouser legs – the band's look was in place. The effect was electrifying, almost hallucinogenic: Reni's vibrancy behind the kit, Cressa's Bez-like grooving, Mani's dainty flick haircut and pouting showmanship, the melodic chime of the song, and Brown and Squire's staggering insouciance.

The band's growing sense of destiny was carried over into the conclusion of the recording of their debut album. They travelled to Rockfield studios in Monmouth, Wales, to begin the process on

5 January. Andrew Lauder had responded to the band and Leckie's requests to shift studios. Whereas company man McKenna had tried to keep the band recording in Zomba's Battery studios with an eye on the budget, the more independent Lauder green-lit the move to this residential facility. Some tracks, including 'Waterfall', were re-recorded in their entirety at Rockfield. 'It was exciting, they were passionate, they meant it,' said Leckie of this final phase of recording the album. 'It was energetic. There was a lot of energy and Reni's energy was important to it all.' Unlike the Hannett album, on which Reni didn't sing at all, now you couldn't stop him. 'Once he got on to harmonies he would saturate it, so you had to hold him back.'

One of the keys to the sound Leckie achieved on the album was the blending of Brown and Reni's voices to create something that could never be exactly replicated live. Much trickery went into this process. 'The vocals are well mixed. But it wasn't intentional to obfuscate who was singing what: it was just getting the best mix that felt good.' 'This Is the One' caused the most problems. 'It worked real well live, a bombastic thing that got faster and faster, but in the studio we had to work hard on getting the dynamics right and making the changes work smoothly.' The band spent most time on 'I Am the Resurrection'. It was the song they now concluded their live sets with. 'We wanted something epic to end the album so we literally built that massive crescendo piece by piece.'

'It was me who coaxed them to do that ending on "Resurrection",' said Brown. 'Only prog rock groups and players up their own arses did 10-minute guitar solos. But I kept saying to them, Look, you're great. Let's do a 10-minute song where you're just playing and playing and playing. For two days I watched them work out the ending to that song. It still sounds amazing. Me and Reni wanted John to be a guitar hero. He wasn't the usual sort of rock guitarist at that time. He was a real quiet, mellow kid and we wanted him to be the hero for that reason – talk with your fingers kind of thing.'

The final overdub sessions took place at Konk Studios in London, starting on 23 January. McKenna had flown back from Chicago and spent a day listening to the work. The record was £5,000 over budget and his Zomba bosses were not happy. He found Squire in a cramped back room by himself, while the rest of the band listened to obscure hip-hop, house and reggae tracks. Squire was working out the guitar part to 'Bye Bye Badman', recording into his Portastudio while sat on top of a cardboard box. 'We were getting right down to the wire in terms of time, and when I went in to record I still didn't really know the part,' Squire said. 'Then [Squire] came in and did it pretty much in one take,' said Leckie. 'At the end we had some pressure to get the album finished. Maybe there were things we could've done better. But it's character that makes a record special, not fine detail and technical tightness.' The mixing was done live, with everyone hands-on, and although time was tight there was an upbeat, celebratory vibe. 'We recorded and mixed the album in fifty-five days – on and off,' said Leckie. 'It's never enough.'

Upon finishing the album, Leckie told them, 'You're going to do really well, you know.' 'And we just said, Yeah we know,' said Brown. 'And we did. We just felt it. He was a bit taken aback by our confidence. But we knew we were good.' 'It did seem perfect, that album,' agreed Leckie. 'We had a few traumas but there was this fantastic underlying sense of self-belief. I just think the band knew they were making a classic. I really don't know how they could gauge such a thing. They'd never really done it before and for a while I thought I must be getting carried away, losing my objectivity. But it dawned on me during those sessions that this was something truly special. Strange tricks kept coming out of the recording.'

Squire and Brown had shared the writing of the vocal melodies and the lyrics on the album. Brown wrote the words to 'I Wanna Be Adored', 'Made of Stone' and 'I Am the Resurrection'. Squire wrote most of the words to 'Waterfall', while almost all the rest of the songs were a collaborative effort. The pair both admitted they had deliberately tried to conceal some things in the lyrics, so they would have hidden meanings. 'Even on songs we've got that are about a girl, there's always something there that's a call to insurrection,' said Brown. 'People have to tune in, we don't make it obvious because that would be less exciting for us.' That applied to all but one song on the finished record, 'Elizabeth My Dear', whose lyric Brown wrote. It is a song about assassinating the Queen sung over the tune to 'Scarborough Fair', a traditional ballad that dated back to 1670 but had been popularized by Simon & Garfunkel in the 1960s. 'We wanted the tune to be familiar so that people could instantly identify with it and then hear the lyrics clearly,' said Brown. The song ends with a gunshot. Perhaps because the sentiment was so clear, and the other song lyrics so open to interpretation, it was this track that would quickly become a focus of the Roses' 'political agenda'.

In February 1989, with work on the album all but finished, the Roses began gigging like they'd never gigged before. They had a new booking agent, Nigel Kerr, and he would have them on the road until the end of June. In these five months they would play around fifty dates, roughly the same number the band had managed to play in the previous five years. It was widely held that this was one of the greatest pop tours of all time. 'A big thing was happening in England at that time with Ecstasy, and we arrived exactly then,' said Brown. 'It felt great, righteous. I felt we were pure, that we weren't conning anyone. We were real and beautiful.'

'The E-scene is just going to explode this summer, people in the media just don't realize how massive it's getting in the provinces,' said Mani. The Roses were in the right place at the right time. From 17 February to 3 March they were back in Warrington at Legends, played Sheffield University on Brown's twenty-sixth birthday, then Middlesex Polytechnic (where Bob Stanley gave them a euphoric *Melody Maker* live review, calling the band 'four teenage Jesus Christs'), Brighton Escape club (where the band did four songs and walked off), Club Rio in Bradford, Cardiff Coal Exchange and back again to Legends in Warrington. They had now played this club in Brown's hometown three times in quick succession.

Sandwiched in this clutch of dates was a show at the Haçienda, on Monday 27 February, which had been arranged by DJ Dave

Haslam. 'Gareth said to me, can you get us a gig at the Haçienda?' said Haslam. 'In Manchester, playing the Haçienda was seen as one of the key stepping-stones.' More or less at the same time Paul Cons, who was in charge of entertainment at the Haçienda, asked Haslam about booking the band for the club. Haslam told both Evans and Cons he could sort it for £200 apiece. 'It would have been easy for them to pick up the phone and speak to each other, but they went through me and I earned £400 just for the introduction,' he said. 'There were those barriers, The Haçienda and Factory stood for something, and the Roses stood for something else. Then I phoned my friend Brenda Kelly at *Snub TV* and said, There's this great band called The Stone Roses playing at the Haç; you must come up.'

Snub TV was broadcast on BBC2 at six o'clock on Monday nights, and the Roses' appearance on the show would be another milestone. 'The band have so far concentrated on their hometown with their brand of ecstatic pop – crowds queue in the rain, concerts sell out, fans know all the words to the songs. Now on the verge of achieving national recognition, this is The Stone Roses live at the Haçienda,' ran the presenter's introduction to the band, who were shown playing an electric, perfect, 'I Wanna Be Adored'. A second song was also broadcast, the less effective live song 'Sugar Spun Sister'. Squire even smiled, and Brown, in a plain white baggy T-shirt, gave the lyrics an enunciation that was bluntly, unapologetically, northern. The Haçienda show was given glowing live reviews in both the *NME* and *Sounds*.

The band took time off the road in March to promote the release of a new single, 'Made of Stone', and to oversee the finishing touches to their debut album. The strength of the B-sides of the Roses' singles would become a selling point, and 'Made of Stone' (again in a Pollock-inspired sleeve by Squire) was backed by 'Going Down' and 'Guernica', the latter a backward version of 'Made of Stone' featuring the lyric 'we're whores, that's us'. It was a track Brown said had been inspired by trips to Manchester airport to watch the planes take off. 'Your eardrums sound like they're shredding with the volume of the engines and the fire coming out of the back,' said Brown. 'Bits of "Guernica" sound like planes. I'd love to have done it as an A-side.'

The band's plugger, Gareth Davies, accompanied Squire and Brown to an interview on Radio 1's *Newsbeat*. 'They told me they thought I was unhappy with the last interview with *Music Box*, so on the train they thought they'd write down some things they could talk about,' said Davies. Towards the end of the interview, when Brown and Squire were doing their usual yes/no answers, they were asked if there was anything else they wanted to talk about. 'They both said, No, not really; they didn't look at the notes they'd made at all,' said Davies. 'People thought they were very unhelpful but more often than not it was simply that they had nothing to say to the question that had been put to them.'

'Made of Stone' was the *NME*'s Single of the Week and entered the indie charts at number 4, and although sales were not strong enough to register on the UK Top 40 it raised awareness of the band, particularly in London. It was also a clear vindication of Jive/ Zomba's decision to form Silvertone; few in the media connected the Roses to their parent company and the band's ascendancy was aided by the perception of them being an 'indie' act.

Following fast on the heels of the single, the Roses' eponymous debut album was released in April 1989. The band were exuberant and had been proudly playing advance copies to associates in Manchester. They were particularly excited by 'Don't Stop', so enthused that few dared to point out The Beatles had done backward tracks decades before. The album provided the band with their first proper Top 40 hit, as it entered the charts at number 32 in its first week. It climbed no higher, plummeting out of the Top 40 the following week. For a major label act this would have been a disaster, but for an indie band a chart placing, however brief, was seen as real progress. The band were unhappy, however: the album had failed to set the charts ablaze, and there was little to suggest they had hit the mother lode. Nevertheless, in the music press Bob Stanley continued his canonization of the band with breathless praise of the album in

Melody Maker. John Robb nailed it in his *Sounds* review: 'In guitar pop terms, this is a masterpiece.' *Record Mirror* pondered a backlash to the Roses hype but decided against, awarding it four out of five stars.

There was only one major music press interview to promote the album – by the *NME*, which by now was seen as the most influential of the three music weeklies. It had damned the album with faint praise, awarding it seven out of ten. Brown toyed with a lemon throughout the interview and said he was listening to reggae and funk, Barry White, Adrian Sherwood and Black Uhuru. Squire was also into Sherwood and expressed a preference for the 1971 *Shaft* double album. 'Everyone I know has always liked rock music, dance music, punk and Northern Soul,' Brown said. 'I don't think it's unusual for our fans to be into dance music. Those dividing lines aren't there any more.' He also came up with another killer quote: 'It takes effort to sound effortless.' In Philip Hall, the Roses had a publicist who could play the press as apparently effortlessly as the band could their instruments. He was eyeing a front cover for the band, and, by granting just this one interview to the *NME*, had *Melody Maker* chomping at the bit.

The lemon Brown used as a prop in the *NME* interview was a reference to the three slices of the fruit featured on the cover of the band's album, which lit up a fairly nondescript green-hued Pollock-inspired painting by Squire, entitled *Bye Bye Badman*, with daubs of blue, white and red overlay. 'The lemons aren't part of the picture, they're real lemons nailed on because it was photographed on the wall,' Squire said. 'It ties in with the lyrics of "Bye Bye Badman", to do with the Paris student uprisings of May 1968. Me and Ian saw a documentary on it and liked the clothes: there was a guy chucking stones with a really nice jacket and desert boots. The students used to suck the lemons to nullify the effects of tear gas. That's why the tricolour is there.' The green of his painting was inspired by the water at the Giant's Causeway in Ireland, which the band had visited before their gig at Ulster University – and where Led Zeppelin had shot the cover for their *Houses of the Holy* album. The other Squire painting to be found on the album's inner sleeve, a crude but pretty amalgamation of the Union Jack and the Stars and Stripes, entitled *Waterfall*, was inspired by a more prosaic image: a pair of Sue Dean's trousers.

The band went back to the treadmill of small venues. After three dates in April, playing at Liverpool Polytechnic, Portsmouth, and Brunel University, there was barely a day without a gig in May. Following a return to Liverpool Polytechnic, the Roses arrived in Widnes where a local magazine wanted to know what it felt like to be big in Manchester. 'We're not massive in Manchester,' said Squire. 'There are a million and a half people in Manchester and we only get 2,000.'

Next stop for the Roses was a triumphant show in front of 2,000 at International II on 6 May. They played in front of Squire's Union Jack and Stars and Stripes hybrid backdrop, and Brown introduced himself ringing a bell like a town crier. There was now no need for Evans to give away any free tickets, as a new breed of genuine teenage fan crowded into the venue to worship the group. Support was The Charlatans, pre-Tim Burgess. 'I'd never seen that kind of relationship between a band and an audience before – it was messianic,' said the band's drummer, Jon Brookes. 'We couldn't understand how people knew all the lyrics to their songs.'

The Charlatans went on to play with the band at Junction 10 in Walsall, Warrington Legends and Trent Poly. Outside Manchester it was still hit and miss for the band. 'At Trent Poly there was a guy skateboarding inside the hall when they were playing, that's how empty it was,' said Brookes. 'It didn't seem to bother them, you never heard them moan, they just got on with it.' The Charlatans were deeply impressed and copied a great deal from the Roses. 'They wore flares and outdoor jackets which they kept on inside, zipped up. We thought that was the ultimate statement of ice cool. They were a gang, the band and the crew. From when they turned up with their gear, when they soundchecked, played, and when they went, it was all one cool movement – there was never anybody out of place. It was beautiful.'

Brookes was particularly observant of Reni, in his bucket hat and with his edited-down three-piece kit, a mixture of Ludwig, vintage and a big expensive Sonor snare drum – all customized in the Pollock style to match Squire's guitar and Mani's bass. 'He never pounded the drums, he used to caress them and get them to sing, he was that kind of drummer. It was great to just watch him, very poetic, beautiful motion, very light touch, at the same time very musical. And he was singing as well, these beautiful melodies, it was unbelievable. On the first album a lot of the spirit emanates from the drums. The album captured a man at the height of his creative powers rhythmically.'

In Leeds, Brown told a fanzine writer he didn't want to be just New Order big, he was aiming to be as massive as Michael Jackson. After Trent, Dudley and Tonbridge, a show at London's ICA saw the Roses playing to their biggest London crowd to date (500) and was reviewed euphorically by *Melody Maker* and the *NME*. Birmingham, Aberystwyth, Camden, Oxford, Shrewsbury and Preston followed before the band were forced to cancel dates in Milton Keynes and St Helens to finish the recording of B-sides for their upcoming single, 'She Bangs the Drums'. At the end of May the *NME* carried a report that the Roses had turned down two support slots in favour of headlining this run of smaller shows. The band were said to have turned down a UK support slot with The Pixies and a lucrative guest spot with New Order in America. 'The band have never supported anyone in their life and see no reason why they should now,' a spokesman said. 'Other bands would have jumped at the opportunity but the Roses have their own thing to do and don't want to play second fiddle to anybody.' The real story, as with much of the Roses' media hype, involved Evans.

'Gareth phoned me up and said, Hooky, you're big in America, aren't you?' said New Order's Peter Hook. 'I said, Well, yeah, we're doing quite well. He said, Who does your tours? I said, We've got our own American manager called Tom Atencio. Gareth said, I like him, I like the sound of his name, give me his number.' Hook put Evans in touch with Atencio, who planned a series of college dates for the Roses in America. 'Tom phoned me up a few weeks before

the tour and he said, Hooky, how well do you know this Gareth?'
said Hook. 'He said, He's just phoned me and asked, can I guarantee when The Stone Roses arrive in America they are mobbed like
The Beatles? Tom told him, Of course I can't guarantee that, they're
only a college band, they're only coming over doing 1,000-capacity
venues. Gareth said, Well, if you can't guarantee that, then they're
not coming – and cancelled the tour. Tom said to me, Don't send
me these nutters any more.'

In early June the Roses appeared on their first weekly music
paper front cover: *Melody Maker*. Brown was the sole band member
clearly pictured, doing an approximation of a Cressa/Bez-style
move in a rave-styled photograph. 'I'll be severely disappointed if
we haven't had a number 1 by the end of 1989,' Brown was quoted
as saying in the article. In a lengthy and unusually productive interview with just Brown and Squire, the talk veered from sexual
politics – where they batted back accusations of misogyny in the
lyrics – to homelessness, the royal family ('a bunch of castle rus-
tlers'), religion ('Jesus was the world's first communist'), the British
Empire ('sick'), working-class freedom or lack of, and their worship
of women. 'Man is weak, Woman is power,' said Brown.

It was in this interview for the first time that flared trousers
became a major topic of discussion. Brown, encouraged by Cressa,
was now sporting a pair. Squire spoke up in favour of parallels. 'I
think I've got divine knowledge and complete ignorance of everything except about clothes.' For Brown it was 24-inchers, 'for that
slight swish'. 'They're probably just as important as England falling,
actually, flares,' said Brown, who would soon narrow his vision to
21-inchers. Flares, and the downfall of the monarchy, would become
recurrent themes in the Roses' media briefs.

The strongest, most controversial, line in the *Melody Maker*
interview was Brown's. 'I'd like to shoot Prince Charles,' he said.
However he did it, writer Simon Reynolds had managed the first
and only serious discussion with the band in the pop press in their
entire career. Reynolds, agreeing with the general feeling of the
time, praised the band's live shows more than their debut album,

but made a note of saying how unusual it was to meet a band who had ideas about subjects away from music.

June was equally busy on the road, as the tour continued with fourteen shows, from Walsall to Glasgow. For a band that had never properly toured, this long stretch of UK dates was crucial in building a small army of fans who all felt part of something special and empowering. These fans were treated with the respect that The Clash had treated the teenage Squire. Tim Vigon, who was seventeen, was inspired to make a fanzine devoted to the Roses called *Made of Paper*. In Shrewsbury, the Roses' tour manager Steve Adge took Vigon's disposable camera off him and he feared it would be confiscated. Instead Adge took pictures of the band close up on stage and handed it back to the awestruck Vigon.

A teenage gang of girls dubbed the 'Bobs', because of their haircuts, were familiar faces. The 'Bobs' were Eileen Mulligan, her best pal Shirley McGurrin and sisters Colette and Theresa Shryane, and all were delighted when Brown wore a Co-op T-shirt on stage that one of them had gifted him. Colette would go on to marry Roses roadie Al Smith. Even in their early days the Roses never had a groupie thing going on – and this attitude continued to mark them out. Squire and Brown were still both involved in long-term relationships, and while the band exuded sex appeal it was tempered by a romance reflected in their lyrics. It was why the Roses always had a more mixed audience than the Mondays. Adge made sure nobody messed with the Bobs, and the atmosphere backstage was 'very innocent, very civilized and un-rock 'n' roll', said Mulligan.

The benefits of the band's first sustained spell of touring were evident when, in July, 'She Bangs the Drums' became the Roses' first mainstream Top 40 hit single, peaking at number 36. The A-side was the same version as on the album, but strong B-sides – 'Standing Here', 'Mersey Paradise' (which recalled The Byrds' song 'I'll Feel a Whole Lot Better') and backward track 'Simone' – made it a must-have. Limited-edition versions of the single also included prints and postcards of Squire's artwork.

Gareth Davies had the band back in London to promote the single with another radio interview – this time for BBC London with DJ Johnny Walker. Davies suggested that Reni, who was 'much more forthcoming and articulate in these situations', accompany Squire and Brown to the interview. In answer to Walker's first question, Brown nodded furiously but didn't say anything – not much use on radio. Walker asked the band about The Byrds, and there was more dead air time. What about Hendrix? Reni said his mum and dad had Hendrix's *Greatest Hits*. Brown was asked about the Roses' lyrics. 'He genuinely looked totally confused,' said Davies. 'He said, They mean whatever you want them to mean; which is so right, because that makes the songs more personal to everyone who hears them. If you know what it's about, everyone thinks of the song the same way. But if you don't tell people, they can make it their own. That to me was a genuine reaction.'

The Roses were slowly making an impact on mainstream audiences, and this was helped when they featured in the British tabloids. Another anti-monarchy quote from Brown, when he offered the opinion that there wouldn't be revolution in England unless someone put a bag over the Queen Mother's head (he'd offered to do it himself), had sparked a degree of controversy. The *Sun* newspaper hassled Brown's parents and their neighbours in Timperley, hoping for some gossip. The singer was unrepentant. 'I think Buckingham Palace should be turned into flats for old people who live in cardboard boxes.'

The release of 'She Bangs the Drums' landed the band their second music-press front cover, in *Sounds*. Brown proclaimed he believed in one love as a manifesto, and Squire registered his delight in having made the tabloids: 'If you want to be as big as we want to be then you've got to get in that forum.' There was talk of releasing a new single in September, called 'Any Time You Want Me', but, other than that, Brown and Squire gave little away. Not saying much in interviews was now becoming the talking point.

'After the first few interviews we were getting pressurized to open up and be more chatty,' said Squire. 'Sell yourself, treat it as a PR exercise. And we've resisted that.'

'People around us, press officers, said, You can't do that, you won't be getting any more interviews, people won't want to talk to you because you're not saying anything,' said Brown. 'About three weeks later it's, Oooh it's working, what a great angle. It's not an angle. It's us.'

The cover photograph for *Sounds* was taken by Ian Tilton, and saw the image of the band take another giant step forward, Brown's infamous 'money' T-shirt and 'monkey face' making debuts. 'He'd never done that face before,' laughs Tilton. 'He pulled the face and I said, That's weird, do it again. He's a good-looking bloke but he didn't give a shit about looking cool or looking handsome.'

There were now offers coming in from around the world for the band to perform. A string of European dates was being lined up, and in America there was talk of a free gig in New York's Central Park and one at the end of a pier in Santa Monica, Los Angeles. There was also strong interest for the band to tour Japan. The Roses, however, had other ideas and were planning a major date in Blackpool. Evans claimed it was his idea: the romance and unpretentious nature of the British seaside resort would fit with the band's 'street-level image'. 'The Roses still had an awful lot of doubters. Blackpool was something different. It was almost like pulling the band back from the hype and letting them play to their own – to the people who knew them and had helped them build. It was a thank you and good bye.'

'We wanted to give people a day out to finish their summer,' said Brown. 'When you live in Manchester and you've got no money there's nowhere to go. Blackpool is the local seaside resort. I've been beaten up a few times in Blackpool. We wanted to go one step beyond just a concert.' It was originally intended as part of a tour of seaside resorts (Southend, Scarborough, Morecambe). The venue was the Empress Ballroom – it had hosted The Rolling Stones but been off the circuit for many years. It was an awkward gig to produce, largely because the venue had a springy floor and an enthusiastic audience could easily shake down the PA system. Bruce Mitchell, who ran Manchester Light & Stage, managed the production. Mitchell had also trained up many of the Roses' crew, as the band preferred to use mates rather than seasoned professionals.

Dealing with Evans was 'like plaiting sand', Mitchell recalled. 'He changed his mind four times in a sentence.' Instead, Mitchell relied on the Roses' co-manager, Matthew Cummins – 'a quiet guy and absolutely of his word'. Crucial to the band's live impact was the lighting: a Quasar system that reacted to bass frequencies and zapped out lines from the back of the band into the audience.

It was Saturday, 12 August 1989 and the 4,000-capacity Empress Ballroom had sold out three weeks prior. The idea of playing other seaside dates had been abandoned. This was the must-see show. Steve Adge had booked a big American bus to transport the band from Manchester to Blackpool, and it was packed with crew and friends. After falling out with the driver, Adge drove the bus into Blackpool straight down the tram tracks, having lost his directions. Photographer Ian Tilton was on board. 'They wanted to have a good time, so you go over with your mates, everyone together and make a real thing of it,' he said.

The fans went to Blackpool with the same intention, and there was a festival spirit in the air – a celebration of the north. 'Having done a tour of Great Britain I've changed my mind a bit on Manchester because it's a place where things are happening, there is a vibe in the air here,' Brown said. Astonishingly, almost all of the 4,000 punters were now aping the look of the band, in flares, baggy shirts and what had become known as 'Reni hats'. The band were taken aback. 'We didn't know or expect that kids would dress like us,' Brown said. 'We were just trying to dress so we looked different from everyone else. Reni loved it; half the crowd had the hat on.'

There were no support acts. Instead, the crowd would be warmed up by Manchester DJs Dave Booth and Dave Haslam, whose Temperance night at the Haçienda was now big. 'The band had decided that they didn't want a support act because nobody was worthy enough to share a stage with them,' said Haslam. 'Also they hoped they would catch some of the kind of acid house atmosphere that you could experience at clubs in Manchester at that time.' The city had by now produced two of the era's best home-grown acid house tracks, 'Voodoo Ray' by A Guy Called Gerald and 'Pacific State' by 808 State. Acclaimed music video director Geoff Wonfor had four cameras and a crew of thirty at the gig, to film a video for the band's next single – although there was confusion over what that would be. The song Wonfor expected to film was not on the band's set list.

'The place was packed, the place was hot, the audience absolutely lapped up the music,' said Haslam. 'As a DJ you're working hard to hit that moment just before the band comes on when everybody is ecstatic and expectant. I played "Sympathy for the Devil" and that did the trick.' Brown strolled on to the stage in 1972 green corduroy Wrangler 21-inch flares, nonchalantly playing a light-up yo-yo, and declared, 'Manchester . . . International . . . Continental.'

'I don't usually think about anything while I'm on stage but about halfway through the set, I suddenly realized I'd been in this place before,' he told the *NME*. 'All through the soundcheck I hadn't recognized it but I had blagged my way in here years ago to see Tony Benn at the Labour Party conference.' Brown went on to say that he thought Benn deserved more respect than any pop group, and that he had been brought up to believe the aristocracy should be shot.

Haslam watched from the back of the stage, just next to where Cressa was grooving behind Squire. 'The volume and the intensity that was coming off the audience was phenomenal,' he said. 'It was hitting the stage; waves of love. For some people it could have been their first experience of that dance club vibe.' It was far removed from the traditional rock gig, with the whole downstairs dancing, not just bobbing up and down. 'Proper dancing,' said Brown.

Evans missed the show after his car broke down on the way over from Manchester. 'We got there for the last song, as they were doing "Resurrection",' said his girlfriend Sue Dean. The band's manager had missed something massive and unrepeatable. Reviews of the show glowed golden. *Sounds* and *Record Mirror* praised the band from the heavens, while the *NME* called it 'gig of the year'.

10.

'Fools Gold'

Jive/Zomba were growing impatient for new material. They had already taken 30,000 pre-orders on the next Roses single, whatever it was going to be. 'Some bands would have felt under pressure to deliver the goods in that kind of situation,' said John Leckie. The Stone Roses thrived on it. Leckie booked recording time at Sawmills studio in Cornwall. Paul Schroeder, the Battery studio dance-music expert, was also there.

Sawmills was one of the UK's first residential facilities and also among the most remote, located within a creek on the banks of the River Fowey. The only means of access was by boat or, when the tide was out, by walking along a railway line. 'If they tell you to be there at four o'clock to get the gear in and you turn up at five and the tide's gone, you have to wait twelve hours before your next chance,' said Leckie. 'Everything fits on the little boat and off you go.' Evans was caught short by these arrangements, and one evening he missed the boat back from the studio, then spent the night outdoors. Mani found him asleep on the grass the next morning.

Evans was the closest of anyone to the four Roses, but still found the bond between them impenetrable. The Roses shared a seemingly unbreakable sense of purpose and desire. What they did not have was much new material, nor any real sense of where they were heading musically. Five months of hard touring had knocked Squire and Brown out of their old songwriting routines. In the two weeks the band spent at Sawmills they recorded just two songs, 'Fools Gold' and 'What the World Is Waiting For'. Initially it was 'What the World Is Waiting For' that was thought to be the more promising. It was a familiar, golden guitar song that dripped melody and referenced lyrically the 1961 Leslie Bricusse and Anthony Newley musical *Stop the World – I Want to Get Off*.

'Fools Gold' was a more experimental track, initiated by Squire. He had written it after picking up a *Breaks and Beats* album from Eastern Bloc records in Manchester during a signing session for 'She Bangs the Drums'. It was one in a series of twenty-five *Breaks and Beats* albums that were popular with hip-hop producers as they featured drums for sampling. Squire had chosen it because he liked the photograph on the sleeve, of African American athletes Tommie Smith and John Carlos giving the Black Power salute on the medal podium at the 1968 Olympic Games in Mexico City. In what was a new way of working for Squire, he'd written the song over a looped break. 'I wasn't familiar with the song it came from. It was the repetition that made it work, that made it what it was.'

Mani added his own unique contribution. His all-night partying often met with disapproval from Squire at rehearsals, but Mani said clubbing was for research, and he was looking for 'things to pinch'. The bass line from the Young MC's club hit 'Know How' was a case in point, and it was used as further inspiration on 'Fools Gold'. Brown said the words were inspired by John Huston's 1948 film *The Treasure of the Sierra Madre*, starring Humphrey Bogart. The promo line above the film's title was 'They sold their souls for . . .', and the plotline was summarized by Brown as: 'Three geezers who are skint put their money together to get equipment to go looking for gold. They betray each other. They all end up dead.'

The loop Squire wrote the 'Fools Gold' riff over was taken from 'Hot Pants' by Bobby Byrd with John 'Jabo' Starks on drums, produced by James Brown. If the band and Leckie were unsure about the nature of 'Fools Gold', Schroeder had no such doubts. He declared it a 'fucking smash' on first hearing. 'Even just in the demo form, it was brilliant. It had the "Funky Drummer" loop, it had the bass loop, it had the lyrics so it was all pretty much there. I was into this idea of having the drum sample loop round kind of every thirteen bars, a very odd number of bars, so the beat would never be the same. Reni loved it. It meant he could dance around it with his kit.' The band responded to the vibe of the unique recording location, and the beauty and spirit of Sawmills seeped into the session as they experimented.

Schroeder also spent time on the guitar to 'Fools Gold', and the more work went into the track the better it sounded, until the band began to prefer it to the sublime control of 'What the World Is Waiting For'. 'It was more what we were about,' said Brown. 'Fools Gold' was a brave and radical departure for the band, more rhythmic and dance-orientated.

The vocals on 'Fools Gold', Brown's strongest to date, were recorded back in London in a tiled room in a studio in Muswell Hill. The groove of the track suited Brown, who displayed an astounding ability to lay back and ride a rhythm in the best reggae tradition. 'The natural echo you hear on Ian's vocal, that's not extra stuff being added, that's just him,' Schroeder said. 'I had the lights turned off, so he didn't know where the mic was, and he was dancing around really out of it. It worked a treat. It was just a condenser mic but I put it on "all round" so that it would pick up everything. I just told Ian to pretend he was sitting on top of a speaker looking down on people dancing. I said for him to imagine that he was in control of the dance floor while he was singing. I think he had that in mind while he was doing it. He had a big smile on his face when he came back in.'

Schroeder did a rough mix of 'Fools Gold' that he played to Jive / Zomba boss Clive Calder. 'He said, That's a hit record but it needs a remix,' said Schroeder. The recording of the single had already eaten up over a month. 'We'd do the mix with everyone together, the whole band and me and Paul in a room, and then, invariably, Paul would go off and mix it by himself,' said Leckie. 'He'd say, I've got next week booked to mix it again. It was like, Hang on, it's only one song.'

In late September, while work continued on the single, the band were filmed for the popular BBC2 pop show *Rapido*. The feature, scheduled to air on 7 October, captured the band in and around Battery studios looking cocksure and unkempt. The main focus was their debut album, which six months after its release was still picking up praise. Interspersed with footage from Blackpool, the band delivered an unparalleled example of their classic interview technique. 'It's hard to act interested when you're not,' Brown told the interviewer, bluntly. He went on to denounce the UK indie scene as certainly as Mani dismissed the psychedelic label the band had been tagged with.

In the background, as the band were being interviewed, Leckie and Schroeder were seen at the Battery recording desk working on 'Fools Gold'. Mani's distinctive bass line could clearly be heard. When *Rapido* was broadcast, Gareth Davies got a call from a BBC TV contact asking about the 'amazing' bass riff. The truth, Davies admitted, was he didn't know. The band remained cautious about 'Fools Gold'. It was very different thing from anything they'd done before, lacking not just the ripe melody and soaring chorus the band were known for but any traditional strong structure.

The Roses took off for Europe at the end of September, playing in Valencia, Milan, Deinze, Hamburg, Cologne, Amsterdam and Paris. Although lucrative for Evans, who would end the short European tour showing off a suitcase crammed with £100,000 in cash in various currencies, the Roses played to crowds more intrigued by them than participating in the party. The band's flares seemed even more incongruous on the continent. In Milan, Brown responded to the muted welcome by smashing the stage lighting. Paris, where they had played before, and Amsterdam, where a coach load of Mancunians made the trip on the Cess Express, organized by Mancunian character Cess Buller, were more like home.

Legendary *NME* photographer Pennie Smith had been invited to the shows in Europe. Famed for her work with The Clash, she'd already photographed the Roses at Reading Gaol for a Japanese magazine. Squire had been a fan of her work since he was a teenager, and Smith would continue to document the Roses for the rest of their career, as she had done with The Clash. The first thing Evans had said to her was, 'I know what I want out of the band – I want a helicopter. What do you want?' Brown had more artfully introduced himself by telling Smith 'you look like one of your photos'.

The most seen photograph of the band from this period, however, was not a Smith shot but one taken by Kevin Cummins, for the band's first *NME* cover. The *NME* trailed the band from Amsterdam to Paris for the cover feature, and Cummins photographed them in front of the Eiffel Tower. Evans had wanted him to photograph the band hanging off it. The *NME* cover story would not be published for over a month, in November. In it, the magazine would finally hail the Roses' debut album one of the decade's finest debut LPs, and Evans would have a starring role – described as 'streetwise, funny, like some awful Mancunian mutant cross of Arthur Daley and Tony Wilson'. It was a popular rumour that he was knocking out bootleg Roses merchandise outside the venues, often undercutting the official merchandise that he also controlled. Of the suitcase full of money, Evans was quoted in *NME* as saying, 'I've got hefty outgoings. These boys go through a lot of drugs.' The band said very little – as was becoming their standard practice.

In the weeks between the interview and the NME story appearing, Cummins decided he had not captured 'the essence of the band' in Paris and planned a further shoot back in England. 'What I'd always wanted to do was to do them as a John Squire painting,' he said. One of Cummins's Paris shots of the Roses would eventually appear on an *NME* front cover, but not until 1994.

Cummins had to wait to take the shot for the November 1989 cover, however, as the band were flying from Paris to Japan. *Rockin' On*, Japan's biggest and most influential music magazine, lavished fourteen full pages on the band to coincide with their arrival. The album was said to have sold 20,000 copies in its first week of release and the Roses had their first taste of being treated as stars – travelling in style on the bullet train and being chased by fans trying to pull their hair out. The four dates, in Kawasaki, Osaka and twice in Tokyo, were all hysteria-drenched affairs.

In England a succession of events would now propel the Roses to the forefront of a similar explosion. While the band had been away in Europe and Japan, Leckie had done a final mix on 'Fools Gold'. It had tested even his famous patience. 'Eventually I said, Look, just give me the tape and a day at RAK and I'll do it,' he recalled. 'I went in about noon, on my own, and came out about nine the next morning.' Even a disgruntled Schroeder, who had been refused co-production credit on the track, agreed that Leckie had done a brilliant job. 'I'm not sure it would have been as good if anyone else did it.'

Jive/Zomba planned on releasing the single as a double A-side, with equal emphasis on 'Fools Gold' and 'What the World Is Waiting For', but Gareth Davies, whose job it would be to deliver the single to radio, had his doubts. 'You can never really have a double A on vinyl,' he said. 'One has to be the B-side.' The band had wanted to go with 'Fools Gold' as the A-side, but the Zomba promotions people had said Radio 1 would never play the track. Davies felt they would and persuaded Andrew Lauder at Silvertone, who told him to re-sticker the promo records with 'Fools Gold' as the A-side while he would reprint the records in production. This was late on a Friday afternoon, and neither the band nor many of their key associates were aware of the decision.

Up to this point Davies had experienced little joy in getting the Roses' singles played on Radio 1, consistently being told he was six months ahead of the curve. But he was positive 'Fools Gold' would work. Richard Skinner, who had a Saturday afternoon show at Radio 1, was the first to pick up on the track, or rather his producer, Mark Radcliffe, was. 'I rang Reni up and said, Richard Skinner is going to play "Fools Gold" this afternoon,' Davies said. 'Reni said, No, Gareth, you've got the wrong track, they'll never play that, it's "What the World Is Waiting For". I said, No, they're going to play "Fools Gold". On the Monday I rang [Radio 1 DJ] Simon Bates, while he was on air, and he said, Yeah, bring it over. I took it around to him and rang [the band's publicist] Philip Hall to say Simon Bates is going to play "Fools Gold", and he too said, No, Gareth, you've got the wrong song. Radio 1 will never play that, it's "What the World Is Waiting For".'

From here 'Fools Gold' began to take on a life of its own, with promo copies also proving popular in clubs. There was no going back, and 'Fools Gold' became the undoubted lead track on the single that was scheduled for release on 13 November to coincide with the band's highly anticipated big London event at Alexandra Palace on 18 November.

At the *NME*, the cover story, started in Europe and planned to coincide with both the gig and the single, would now get its famous cover shot. Schedules were incredibly tight and the band only had a Sunday spare. Photographer Cummins rented a studio in Manchester and covered the whole place in polythene. The band arrived carrying five-gallon tins of paint. 'I thought John would then get a brush out and start painting each of them,' said Cummins. Instead Squire opened a tin of white paint and hurled it across the room at the rest of the band. Then he tipped it over himself. 'I thought, This isn't going to plan,' said Cummins. 'But I'm going to have to run with it.' Squire stepped out of the frame and threw a tin of sky blue all over the band before tipping the rest over his head and laying back in the shot. 'Then we put some yellow and red and black on, and I shot it in every stage. They were lying in it for two hours. It was a riot of colour. You look at that and you feel you could be on E.'

After the shoot the band were eager to shower, but everywhere in the building was locked. 'They went mental and left handprints down the stairwell.' Cummins kept Reni's hat as a souvenir, and that paint-splattered hat would subsequently adorn the sleeve of the tenth-anniversary release of the Roses' eponymous album. 'I knew when I was doing it that the picture would define The Stone Roses.'

With 'Fools Gold' picking up pre-release radio play, the band flew to Lanzarote to shoot a video for the track. The director was Geoff Wonfor, who had filmed them at Blackpool, and while in Lanzarote would also shoot a video for 'I Wanna Be Adored', which Jive/Zomba planned to release as an American single. 'Blackpool was chaotic but not as chaotic as Lanzarote,' said Wonfor, celebrated for his work with Paul McCartney and The Beatles. All his crew's equipment was impounded at customs, and the time it took to secure its release meant Wonfor had one day to shoot two videos. The band told him they wanted the video to look like it was shot on the moon. 'Then they said they wanted to do it at night. Which begs the fucking question, why are we in fucking Lanzarote when I could have been in Twickenham studios with a bit of volcanic rock? Then they had the great idea of lighting the mountain behind, which is ten miles away. I had a generator of about four foot square. By God, every fucker was on the moon and past it. We were all on Mars . . . We eventually found this wonderful place to shoot it and we'd just got into it when a cop came up on a motorbike and asked us to leave.' Wonfor stood his ground, but the cop started to finger his gun. 'I said, Don't even bother, because the only thing you can do at this moment in time is fucking kill me and right now that seems like a good option.'

Back in London, Wonfor edited the footage and showed it to the band. He was already known for his filming style, and the band walking towards the camera in slow motion was a familiar trick of his. 'They looked at it, looked at me as if I was a Martian, and said, No, man, it's not what we wanted.' Wonfor asked what did they want? 'They said, We don't know.' Wonfor stormed out of the editing suite and left the band there to make their own changes. 'The band didn't change a thing on it, not one shot.'

Alexandra Palace would be the Roses' first UK live show since Blackpool. The band had considered holding this major London showcase at a film studio in Shepherd's Bush used as a venue for an illegal rave by Energy, but that idea had stalled as crackdowns on raves by the police intensified. 'Ally Pally,' said Brown, was the 'best legal alternative'. The venue, famous in the 1960s for hosting acts such as Pink Floyd, had been off the circuit for decades. The Roses would be the first band to play there after its recent reopening. The woman in charge of the venue had heard of The Stone Roses and was petrified by the prospect. 'But I was there with the cash and they were at least going to get the press,' said the promoter Phil Jones, who was close to Evans.

Although Blackpool had been a major success, and there was a growing buzz around the band, it was difficult to gauge if this would translate to numbers in London. Jones intended to poster prime sites there, but on the morning tickets went on sale, all 7,500 sold out immediately. The posters never went up. 'We were like, Shit, this thing has transferred to London,' said Jones. The Berlin Wall had fallen on 9 November and Brown was full of insurrection talk, suggesting that a revolution was possible in England. Maybe, even, the Roses could provide the spark. 'Anything is possible when people come together,' he said. 'I'm talking about people who are constantly being had over, sold short, misled, had the wool pulled over their eyes. Eventually they will say they are not having it any more.' He talked of a raised consciousness. Something, he suggested, was 'in the air'.

At Alexandra Palace it was the hot air leaking from the band's pricked ego, as they were forced back down to earth. The gig was held on the same Saturday night that the Happy Mondays played the Free Trade Hall in Manchester, and Bruce Mitchell of the Manchester Light & Stage company Lighting (who had handled production in Blackpool) opted to work on the Mondays' show. 'Gareth had wound me up so much, I didn't want to be down there with him,' said Mitchell. 'So I did the Mondays.' He also knew Alexandra Palace was a terrible venue. 'You can only fix the sound by spending more than the gross of the door,' he said.

On the day of the gig Cummins's classic shot appeared on the front cover of the NME but little else went to plan. Mitchell subcontracted the Roses job to a company who had hired expensive hydraulic lights, but they didn't know how to make them work. Nothing could be done until the lights were up, and they were still being erected at quarter to five. When finally the band could soundcheck, promoter Jones discovered the PA team hadn't brought a radio to communicate between the front of house and the stage. In the cavernous great hall, the sound levels for the band were achieved by shouting instructions back and forth.

'It was a very stressful day, mainly because we couldn't get these lights up.' When the doors finally opened Jones realized that the 7,500 tickets he'd been allowed to sell barely filled half of the venue. 'The punters only went back as far as the mixing desk. The venue could have held three times the number.'

As at Blackpool, the Roses didn't have a support band, relying on Dave Haslam and famed Balearic/acid house DJ Paul Oakenfold to warm up the crowd. This decision to open with DJs was seen as further evidence of the Roses' open-mindedness to the cultural shift heralded by acid house. 'All roads were open, all things were considered,' said Haslam, whose set was disrupted by the chaos surrounding the production. 'Equipment was still coming on and off stage. I played "Good Life" by Inner City and it jumped about three or four times. Every time it jumped I winced and threw a dark look at Steve Adge.'

After missing Blackpool, Evans made a show of himself at Alexandra Palace. 'Gareth had the worst knitted jumper on that I'd ever seen on anyone in a position of influence in the music industry,' said Haslam. 'It was a Christmas jumper with a Santa on it.' Evans had demanded £70,000 to allow Steve Lock, the Granada producer who'd got the band their break on *The Other Side of Midnight*, to film the gig. The price was still being negotiated, but they came to an agreement that Lock would film two or three tracks. Lock's overriding memory of the event was of seeing Evans after the show. 'He had bin-liners full of cash that he was putting into the boot of his car from the merchandise he'd sold.'

When the band took to the stage to the familiar strains of a loop from 'Small Time Hustler' by The Dismasters, itself based on a sample from the 1970s track 'Sport' by Lightnin' Rod of late 1960s rap pioneers The Last Poets, the vast venue was half empty and the gig stalled and stuttered, failing to generate the spirit of the packed Blackpool show. This was a dark, damp night, not a summer's day out, and the sound was as bad as Evans's jumper. The band played on manfully as the guitar went missing, the bass often became inaudible, the drums grated and Reni and Brown's vocals shot up and down. As the crowd grew bemused, Brown admonished them.

'You're not moving much. We need to be entertained too.' He responded to a heckler, 'It ain't where you're from, it's where you're at.'

Mani, bluntly, said the gig was 'crap' and 'a disaster'. It received mixed reviews. For many in the London media this was their first taste of the Roses, and it was puzzling. 'No matter about the vague sensation of déjà vu, the 1990s it seems start right about here,' ventured the Q magazine review.

'Ally Pally wasn't what it should have been,' Brown admitted. After the show he and Squire left in a car and didn't say a word for two hours. But they knew they still had an ace up their sleeve. They had 'Fools Gold'. In a sleeve that featured Squire's best artwork of the period, *Double Dorsal Doppelganger One*, the single charted the day after Alexandra Palace, on 19 November, at an impressive number 13 in the UK Top 40, giving the band their biggest hit to date. Squire had aimed to put the 'human touch' back into acid house, which to him sounded as if it had been written by a computer virus. Brown declared that if they'd had the confidence, more of the debut album would have sounded like 'Fools Gold'. 'We never intended to sound like a 1960s group.'

Three days after the single charted, the Roses filmed an infamous live appearance on BBC2's *The Late Show*. The arts programme went out at 11.15 p.m., in the 'graveyard slot' after *Newsnight*. Two minutes before the band went on to play live, Brown said he looked at the others and knew they didn't want to do it. 'We said a little prayer that something would come and get us out of it and it did.'

The band, at first glance, looked magnificent: Mani, with his hair scraped back into a ponytail and holding his Pollocked Rickenbacker bass; Brown still wearing the famous 'money' T-shirt; Reni in a leather bucket hat and leather jacket, over a yellow T-shirt, behind his thrown-together drum kit; and Squire, disinterested, concentrating on his guitar parts. They got through the first verse of 'Made of Stone' and were building into the chorus when the guitar and bass suddenly cut out. A beat later, and the camera fell on Reni, smirking.

He attempted to straighten his face but couldn't, and started to laugh.

'Hey, what's happened? Hey, *que pasa?*' Brown said. The show's presenter, Tracey MacLeod, appeared on screen to apologize for what looked like a power shortage. Behind her Reni snapped his fingers, whipping his hand towards Squire, who threw back the same 'wicked' hand gesture. Brown started shouting behind MacLeod, ending with, 'They ask you to come and then they mess you about.' As MacLeod began to introduce the next segment of the show, Brown, still visible behind her, appeared to be looking at someone off screen. 'We're wasting our time, lads,' he said. MacLeod turned to him and said that they would sort it out in a minute, then continued her preamble to the next piece. Brown strutted towards the camera. 'The BBC are a bunch of amateurs,' he declared. MacLeod flinched, but soldiered on with her attempt to keep the show moving. Brown interrupted again. 'Amateurs! Amateurs!'

Evans claimed it was all a set-up, intended to launch the band into the public's consciousness in a similar way to the Sex Pistols. It would certainly prove priceless in terms of publicity, but Gareth Davies, who had booked them on to the show, said that during the afternoon rehearsals there had been problems with the automatic cut-out switch, triggered by the band's volume. 'It was cutting in too quickly, which didn't give the engineers time to adjust things. So when it came to film the show live, the volume triggered the cut-out switch.' Brown had reacted impressively. 'If you look at the video,' Davies said, 'when the sound cuts out, Ian ducks down. He was looking to see if he was on the TV monitor. That's why he then started walking up and down shouting, Amateurs, amateurs, BBC are a bunch of amateurs. If you notice he didn't swear.'

The following day, on 23 November, the Roses were due to appear on *Top of the Pops*. Also booked to make their debut appearance on the show were the Happy Mondays. The Roses were staying the night in London at the YMCA on Tottenham Court Road, and after arriving back from *The Late Show* recording they told Davies they didn't want to do *Top of the Pops*. The band realized that the impact of their aborted appearance on *The Late Show* would be positive. Davies tried to persuade them that doing *Top of the Pops* would throw them into the mainstream, and that the band's fans would love seeing them on the show. The Roses' main doubt was over the show's strict rules that no band could have any amps on stage, and they were afraid of looking naff. 'They were insistent on having amplifiers, just to make it look vaguely real,' Davies said. It was smoothed over when a couple of the Roses' crew charmed the TV crew into letting them set up.

Evans arrived first at BBC TV Centre and told Davies the Roses were following right behind. Then he made one of his famous quick exits. 'He said, Tell them I've gone for an urgent meeting – and ran away down the corridor,' said Davies. 'The band arrived in two cars. John got out of one and came up to me to say that the cars were waiting for a while, because if they didn't like how it looked, they were going. But they went into the studio, saw the amps and they were fine. The only instruction I had from Gareth was not to let the band out of my sight because he was convinced the Happy Mondays would spike their drinks with acid.'

For Mani the show 'felt like a vindication for the city of Manchester'. The Roses and Mondays converged backstage and turned the whole of the studio 'into a massive rave', terrorizing the other bands on the show such as the Fine Young Cannibals and Five Star. 'We caused chaos.' Powder, pills and booze were freely consumed.

For this, the band's only appearance on *Top of the Pops*, Squire spruced himself up in a baggy long-sleeved top, decorated in crucifixes, and big jeans. Unlike *The Late Show*, when he played live using a brown Gibson with a capo, for *Top of the Pops* he held a paint-splattered guitar. Mani was dressed in huge jeans and mimed his distinctive bass part with a cocksure strut. Reni was in a white bucket hat and a maroon sweatshirt.

It was Brown, however, who looked like he had benefited most from some backstage primping. He wore the same top as he had at Ally Pally, a red zip-up jacket-style top braided in black and gold, big loose-fitting parallel jeans, and his hair and face shone holy. He played games with the microphone as he danced his monkey dance, holding it above his head and mouthing the words to camera in a posture that was as defiant as it was blessed. His hair, his top, his face were all pop perfect. The song washed over the audience, as the effortless spectacle, swagger and voluminous jeans drowned all senses. The following week 'Fools Gold' rose to number 8.

II

Madchester

Top of the Pops was the spark that ignited a frenzy for all things Manchester. The Mondays had brought 'Madchester' into the public domain with their new EP *Madchester Rave On* (produced by Martin Hannett), and the term became a catch-all to describe what would become a golden age of Mancunian cultural dominance.

Keith Jobling, the Mondays' video-maker, coined the word while writing a music-driven film script called *Mad Fuckers*. Factory Records boss Tony Wilson ran with it from there, forcing the word on a reluctant Mondays. 'It did sum up an atmosphere,' said Jobling. 'Manchester stunk of marijuana everywhere you went. It was a very lawless period, hedonistic, and it did go a bit mad.'

Brown would become the face of Madchester, and his street stance was widely imitated. Unlike his Mondays' counterpart Shaun Ryder, Brown had the poster-boy looks and distinctive cartoonish style that, in the business of commercial pop, was paramount. He was on his way to becoming an icon. 'I'm not particularly keen but I'm aware it could happen, probably will happen,' he said. 'I'm aware there's people who will use my face to fill their wallets, who can suck me in, then, when they want to, shit me out again.'

Gareth Davies now fended off demands for the Roses to appear on TV programmes as diverse as *Panorama* and *Blue Peter*. The band said no to all, and *Top of the Pops* was to be their final performance together on British TV. Interviews to the press would also now be sparse, though deft handling by Davies and publicist Philip Hall kept this non-compliance well hidden. The band did come close to appearing on Channel 4's *The Last Resort*, hosted by Jonathan Ross – even after Ross slighted them on TV. 'We had planned to rehearse in the normal way and go through the whole thing,' said Davies. 'Then when it came to cuing them in live on TV, the band would just rest their instruments against the amplifiers and walk off, and there'd just be white noise. But they decided not to do [the show] in the end.'

There had been talk of a gig at Manchester's 9,000-capacity GMEX Centre before Christmas 1989, but the band would not play live again for nearly six months following Alexandra Palace. They didn't need to. In the UK, their album – which had dropped out of the Top 40 a week after its release – began selling again, and the popularity of the band's T-shirts became a licence to print money. T-shirts, above all else, became a key market, as Madchester became as much about the look as the music. Jobling created two of the best: 'Madchester' and 'Just Say No To London'. Leo Stanley, at the Identity shop based in Afflecks Palace, produced the 'AND ON THE SIXTH DAY GOD CREATED MANchester' T-shirt and other variations thereof. For many, the cloth became mightier than the chord. The Roses admitted to being obsessed with clothes but stuck to expensive, and rare, French, Spanish and Italian T-shirts and tops. The top half of the band may have been continental but the bottom half was Madchester – flares and baggy jeans were firmly set as the scene's key signifiers.

Local brand Joe Bloggs hit the jackpot with their popular jeans, heavily logoed sweatshirts, hooded tops and T-shirts. It was estimated the company was worth £60 million. More to the Roses' taste was Gio-Goi, a fashion label started by the Donnelly brothers, Chris and Anthony, who had done 'official bootleg' T-shirts at the Mondays' recent Free Trade Hall show that took place on the same night as Alexandra Palace. They were now pumping out their own T-shirt, in collaboration with the Happy Mondays' sleeve designers, Central Station, and would soon develop a full range of clothes. 'Finally it had landed and there was a fortune out there to be made,' said Anthony.

Another clear winner in the Madchester gold rush would be the Inspiral Carpets, a band who embraced the Bloggs brand and were managed by Anthony Boggiano, who had worked for the Roses' manager Evans at the International in the mid-1980s. 'The pecking order was the Roses, then the Mondays and then the Inspirals,' said Boggiano. 'They weren't as sexy as the Roses and they weren't as rock 'n' roll as the Mondays.' The Inspirals too were cashing in on the T-shirt bonanza, with their infamous 'Cool As Fuck' T-shirts, and, as Manchester became a Mecca for A&R men, they signed a lucrative deal with Mute Records.

The Roses' own label Jive/Zomba was no less eager to capitalize on the Madchester craze, and saw a possibility of breaking the band worldwide; America being the real cash cow. 'It sort of exploded,' said Jive's managing director Steven Howard. 'And we focused everyone on the Roses in America.' In New York, Jive/Zomba had an office with a core staff of around fifteen run by Barry Weiss, today the chairman and CEO of Island Def Jam and Universal Motown Republic Group. He had astutely appointed the young Michael Tedesco to oversee the Roses' product, specifically for his understanding of the 'alternative' rock scene. Tedesco had already been working hard on the band. He had used imports of the UK 12-inch of 'Elephant Stone' to 'seed the soil' with America's alternative-rock radio stations such as WLIR in New York, KROQ in Los Angeles and LIVE105 in San Francisco. Jive/Zomba had subsequently pushed import copies of 'Made of Stone', and then given a first Roses American release to the single 'She Bangs the Drums', which sold poorly. Essentially the American operation had been tracking the pattern of UK releases. This had changed when Tedesco held back on releasing the Roses' album in America and lifted 'I Wanna Be Adored' to release as a stand-alone single.

'"I Wanna Be Adored" was a significant next thrust at modern rock radio,' said Tedesco. 'But it wasn't boom, the way it was happening in the UK. It was just making progress.' The Roses' album was released three months after the UK release, but sold poorly and was largely ignored. Then came 'Fools Gold'. As in the UK, the single was a huge catalyst. 'It really was the record that ignited The Stone Roses' career, the most effective and influential record the group had,' said Tedesco. In America 'Fools Gold' was both released as a 12-inch single and used as a marketing tool to sell the album.

Tedesco put the track on the end of the album and re-released it in late 1989. 'We knew there was so much more life in the album, and we also knew "Fools Gold" was just a watershed moment.'

Tedesco needed the band in person and made repeated attempts to persuade the Roses to visit America for promotional duties or live dates. 'I would speak to Andrew Lauder daily. I would also speak to Gareth, but the bigger they started to become in England the more difficult it became to get straight answers. Then we heard that they were not coming to America until they could do Shea Stadium.'

This was the New York venue where The Beatles had famously played in 1965 to 55,600 people, an attendance record subsequently broken by Led Zeppelin in 1973, and where The Rolling Stones had recently played a six-night run. The idea was absurd, and palpably beyond where the band were at in America. 'This is when dealing with Gareth, who was actually a very likable character, became frustrating,' said Tedesco. 'He was probably in a little over his head and didn't always know what the best next move would have been.'

RCA, who licensed and distributed Jive/Zomba product in America, had not put their full might behind the Roses. Clive Calder had interceded, but the major label's priority remained more mainstream material such as the soundtrack to *Dirty Dancing*. Alternative rock was not yet considered big business. In RCA's Los Angeles offices, however, there was a small core who were wildly enthusiastic. Evans's American representative, Greg Lewerke, was also based in Los Angeles and was a regular at RCA, trying to boost the band's profile and importance to the label: 'It took a while but they finally caught on. I dealt with a lot of RCA people all the way up to the top.'

One of the band's supporters at RCA was radio plugger Bruce Flohr. 'These guys didn't give a fuck,' he said. 'We were doing everything we could just to track them down on the phone, to find out what we should be doing. It was just a mad scramble to keep up with the explosion. It was out of control. Nobody at RCA, not in PR or anything, could get any access to the band.' Robbie Snow was the Roses' product manager at RCA. 'The question of the day, every day, was, When are they coming?' he said. Snow felt Evans was not relaying to the band the message of how important it was for them to have a promotional presence in America. Accompanied by Lewerke, Snow flew to the UK on a mission to talk to the Roses directly. He couldn't get through to Brown and Squire, but spoke with Mani and Reni. 'I thought they got it, they knew what I was talking about,' he said. 'I came back thinking, They know there's demand. We did communicate it to them. But it was not easy.'

The idea that the band could play Shea Stadium, and everybody in America would come to that one show, betrayed either breathtaking arrogance or a genuine naivety at the heart of the Roses. Either way, the band's resistance to flying to America to promote their records initially fuelled anticipation in the country. 'I used to think, in the early stages of it, they were being really smart,' said Snow. 'I kept thinking, They're going to come, but six months after everybody thinks they should have come. But in those six months they're going to build up so much more demand that it's going to be the hottest ticket going. I did believe there was a method to the madness at first.'

In the UK, demand for the group was unquenchable. The Roses featured in *Smash Hits* for the first time, with Brown commenting on the rumour that the band had turned down a lucrative tour support with The Rolling Stones. 'They should be bloody supporting us,' he said. The same month, December 1989, the Roses stared out from the front covers of *Melody Maker*, *The Face* and the *NME*. Oddly, both the *Melody Maker* and the *Face* articles were negative, although at least *The Face* had Glen Luchford's sumptuous photographs, with Brown on the cover and a band portrait inside.

The *Melody Maker* cover story was by Jon Wilde, who had first seen the band in 1985 and still wasn't impressed. His article was an all-out attack, claiming the band typified 'the late 1980s rock malaise'. Wilde labelled Brown and Squire, who did the interview, as 'pitifully inarticulate'. The *Face* cover story echoed the sentiment.

Written by Nick Kent, after meeting both the Mondays and the Roses at *Top of the Pops*, he expressed unease with the Roses' statements of intent, such as their belief in 'positive thinking'. 'We want to keep moving,' Brown said. 'The world's too small. It's doesn't end at Manchester.'

'The next album will be more positive, tidier, looser, better,' Squire said. 'The idea with the first album was to make each song extremely different from the last, but we didn't get it. So that's the aim with the second. We don't want to sound like a band.' Brown elaborated on why the Roses had turned down the Stones – one of Kent's favourite bands. 'We said no to the Stones because everybody else would have said yes. We're against hypocrisy, lies, bigotry, showbusiness, insincerity, phonies and fakers. People like Jagger and Bowie, they're so insincere now they're just patronizing.' Evans later said that he'd made up the story about the Roses turning down the Stones as a press stunt: 'We sat in the International trying to think which band we could refuse to support,' he said. Nonetheless, the Stones and Bowie were the latest acts Brown had impressively trashed. He had already called U2 'drivel', Lou Reed 'a miserable bastard', said Bruce Springsteen 'always sounds like he's having a shit', and labelled another of Kent's favourite acts, Guns N' Roses, 'redneck rubbish'.

In the *Face* article, Kent wrote about an interlude backstage at *Top of the Pops*, with Tony Wilson holding court and chastising the Roses for being unprofessional at Alexandra Palace due to excessive drug use. Evans 'softly but firmly put his hand over Wilson's mouth and whispered something in his ear that caused Wilson to stiffen momentarily'. Wilson turned to Kent to tell him, 'You should know The Stone Roses don't take drugs.'

Evans had previously attempted to play up the link between drugs and The Stone Roses. The band maintained it was overplayed. 'We were never strung out,' said Squire. 'A lot of the drug stuff came from Gareth,' said Brown. 'We never even smoked in front of him, but he was just trying to be a rock manager, trying to make us notorious.' 'Ecstasy wasn't the band's fuel,' said Squire. 'That was the desire to succeed and create.'

The cover story in the *NME*, head cheerleaders of the Madchester scene, was more positive. The band were interviewed and photographed amid snowy scenes in Switzerland. They had gone there, reputedly, so that Evans could stash the money he'd made from the International in a Swiss bank account. The five-year-running Dougie James court case over ownership of the International was close to being decided. The *NME* cover line was 'Top of the World', followed by 'The Stone Roses: Band of the Year', and the article was a puff piece, best summed up by a quote from Reni: 'No-one can ever get the right impression from a picture and a 1,000 words. You can't compress the whole of four people into that. When you do, you end up with misinterpretations like "Scallydelic" and nothing could be further than the truth.'

'We're the most important group in the world, because we've got the best songs and we haven't even begun to show our potential yet,' declared Brown. In the same edition of the *NME*, 'She Bangs the Drums' was named Single of the Year, with 'Fools Gold' at number 2 and 'Made of Stone' at number 5 in the magazine's Top 50 singles. The Roses' album, which had now sold close to 75,000 in the UK, came second in the NME's Top 20 albums of the year, behind De La Soul's *3 Feet High And Rising*.

The critical acclaim and growing commercial success, however, had not translated into financial reward. Just before Christmas 1989, Steve Lock went to visit Evans at a serviced office complex in Knutsford. It wasn't a proper office; Lock wasn't even sure it was Evans's office. Lock was putting together a documentary about the Madchester scene for Granada TV, and was trying to negotiate use of the Alexandra Palace filming for the programme. Evans was holding out for £70,000, and an agreement eluded Lock. After the meeting, Evans asked him for a lift back to town. He wanted to stop off in Didsbury to drop something off for Reni. 'This was the week The Stone Roses had been on the cover of the *NME*, that classic Top of the World shot,' said Lock. Evans invited Lock into Reni's flat to say hello.

'We go in and Gareth goes to Reni, This has been a really, really good year this year, really good, so I'm just dropping off your Christmas bonus,' said Lock. 'He gets out his wallet and he counts out, I think it was £150, might have been £200, and his next line was, Now if this all carries on after Christmas you're going to have to think very seriously about getting your own . . . I was expecting the next word to be accountant, or lawyer. And Gareth said, Your own bank account. I was just gobsmacked. You read old rock 'n' roll stories about Colonel Tom Parker, or whoever, ripping off young bands. I was close to [Tony] Wilson where it's all 50/50, no contract, and everyone still gets ripped off anyway – but at least there's some kind of semblance of fairness. With Gareth and Reni it was just the classic musician getting ripped off.'

The Roses and Evans had been aware for some time that they had entered into a bad contract with Jive/Zomba. It was now particularly apparent that their percentage on record royalties was not good. When the cash should have started to come through, it just wasn't stacking up. This was only on record sales. Brown and Squire were beginning to get their publishing money as songwriters. This extra revenue stream for Brown and Squire was pronounced, as record sales weren't generating what Mani and Reni had expected, and potentially divisive. Evans had already discussed the record contract with Andrew Lauder and Roddy McKenna, and they both agreed it needed fixing. Following the success of 'Fools Gold', Evans met with Mark Furman, Jive/Zomba's young business affairs executive, and John Fruin, former boss of Polydor and Warner Bros in the UK and one-time chairman of the BPI (British Phonographic Industry), who was now a consultant to Clive Calder, to discuss the issue further.

The lack of financial pay-off for the band as record sales rocketed resulted in the Roses becoming increasingly hostile towards Jive/Zomba. The situation was not helped when Jive/Zomba removed Gareth Davies from the Roses' set-up, in favour of using in-house pluggers. They only reneged when Radio 1's support for the band dried up, reinstating Davies. The Roses relied heavily on Evans as their conduit to the label, and Jive/Zomba said Evans never fully disclosed to the band their readiness to renegotiate.

Jive/Zomba sanctioned, as a show of good faith, a £40,000 Christmas bonus for the band in 1989. Evans said the company intended it as a 'stop-gap' and it was possibly an attempt to appease him over his demands for contract renegotiations. 'We should have been negotiating on a massive scale, not quibbling over a £40,000 Christmas bonus,' he said. 'They thought I was some Cheshire bumpkin. That's when I started to plan ahead. I knew I had to be two steps ahead of Zomba and one step ahead of the band.' Evans had spent heavily on the band, and perhaps felt he was owed the lion's share of that money, or needed it for future band dealings, as he counted out the band's Christmas bonus of a few hundred pounds from his fat wad.

For the Roses, 1990 was the year to deliver on the hype. 'Fools Gold' had established them as the hottest act in the UK, they were media darlings and Brown was an iconic face. Madchester fever had gripped the music world. Their debut album was back in the Top 40 in January, climbing to its era high of number 19 in February. America was theirs for the taking, and Reni recalled with pride how Pink Floyd's Roger Waters had applauded the band. 'The Roses remind me of us twenty-five years ago,' Waters had said. 'They've got loads of bollocks and arrogance and won't take any shit.'

But the year started badly and would get progressively worse as business not music began to dominate their lives. The mishandling of the band's affairs by Evans seemed to be at the crux. Their earlier career had been marked by what Pete Garner referred to as one step forward, two steps back, and history appeared to be repeating itself. In December 1989 Paul Birch, boss of the band's former record label FM Revolver, had re-released 'Sally Cinnamon', backed by a new video. The band had only recorded the one single for the label in 1987 before walking out on them. Birch, who had been unsure of the band's worth then, was now certain. His original deal with the band had been for two singles and an album; he had considered taking them to court to claim damages, but had been quoted legal fees of £150,000.

'Sally Cinnamon' had been selling well throughout 1989, to fans interested in the Roses' back catalogue. It was only when Birch switched the independent distribution of the single to major label BMG, and shot a video, that the interest of Jive/Zomba and the band was aroused. 'We didn't consider it to be a reissue, we just changed the distribution and as soon as we did it went onto the charts at number 46,' said Birch. Dave Roberts, the A&R man who had signed the band to FM Revolver, took a cameraman to Manchester to film the video, including shots of Madchester temples such as Afflecks Palace and kids in flares. It ended up being shown on popular Saturday morning programme *The Chart Show*. The band took offence to the video, with Brown calling it 'insulting'. Zomba took FM Revolver to court to stop it being shown, but after three days in the Old Bailey it was ruled they could still use the video.

Around Christmas 1989, Evans visited FM Revolver to discuss the matter with Birch. According to Birch, Evans said, 'Paul, I don't know what's happening at Jive/Zomba, we're in a terrible mess, the band have got no money, we're not getting paid – yeah, there's a lot of publicity and on the surface it looks like the band is successful, but we can't get any money out of them and we're desperate; is there anything you can do to help us?' Birch said, 'In the circumstance that we had found ourselves in, what am I likely to say? But I still gave him a cheque for £5,000.' Birch was unnerved by Evans, whom many members of FM Revolver's staff found intimidating. 'It was just nonsense, ranting and madness. But you'd always be frightened that the chap was going to pull a gun on you. You always felt he was about to harm you in some way.' The Roses were never made aware of this £5,000 payment, just like they had been kept in the dark about the Jive/Zomba Christmas money.

The situation with Jive/Zomba was clearly complex, but the situation with FM Revolver seemed black and white, and on 30 January

1990 the Roses decided to take matters into their own hands. Driving between Manchester and Rockfield studios, in Wales, to begin recording new material, they decided to pay Birch a visit at his Wolverhampton record label HQ, where he also lived.

'When the band turned up, Olivia, my girlfriend, went to the door,' said Birch. 'It's 7.30 in the evening, the accountant's working in the back room. My office was upstairs, and she came in and said, The Stone Roses are at the door.' At first Birch didn't believe her, and it was only when she returned five minutes later that he went downstairs. 'All hell broke loose,' he said. 'It's quite a narrow passage into the house. There they were and they covered us in this bloody paint and it went everywhere. They threw it all over the cars and smashed the windows of the cars. I had a Dobermann and he slept all the way through it. The band weren't in their right minds when they attacked us. They were high. And also there was the road crew. What really scared us was we found tins of Nitromors, paint stripper, outside.'

The paint stripper was for the cars, not him. But the band were angry and aggressive. Squire said the stunt was his idea, and the damage could have been a lot worse. 'They answered the front door of the office and Reni got in first, then the rest of us, and we just started chucking paint around, but they locked the door into the rest of the building and called the police,' he said. 'He thinks we're just puppets, performing monkeys that he can earn a buck off,' Brown said a few months after the incident. 'He told us to make an appointment and that's when I kicked off. He's earning a lot of money off us and he tells us to make an appointment.'

Roberts had left the office and was at the company's base in London with a press officer at hand. 'I got a call from Paul; he was really upset,' said Roberts. 'His voice was shaking. We rang up the *Sun* and they wanted to run it as an exclusive. It snowballed from there. They sent someone up to Paul to do photos and an interview, and then it appeared the next day as a major news story.' Roberts tried to speak to Evans, but it was all 'a bit threatening': '"You don't know who you're dealing with", that kind of stuff,' Roberts said. 'Then I got phone calls on my mobile with no one speaking on the other end for about a month.'

Birch accepted he was fair game, but felt that his accountant and girlfriend were victims. 'For the longest time they both went through very difficult trauma. The paint got into Olivia's hair, she had to have it all cut out, and had to use pumice stone to get the paint out of her scalp.' In his view the Roses were also victims. 'As far as they were concerned they only know what they're told,' Birch said. 'They were robbed of the opportunity to make their own decisions and judgements. Young men from Manchester who have talent, hope, aspirations, dreams, and they're looking for someone who is capable, who can steer them through the entertainment industry, which is not exactly known for its good nature. And they had Gareth.'

After attacking FM Revolver HQ, the Roses drove to Rockfield studios, where producer John Leckie was waiting for them. They turned up covered in paint, with the police on their tail. 'We were meant to be starting the album at Rockfield,' Leckie said. 'Steve Adge came in and said, The cops are coming — any minute now, they're going to find out where we are.' That evening the band recorded the guitar, bass and drums of a fresh Brown/Squire composition, 'Something's Burning', covered in paint. It was the first new song they had come up with since 'Fools Gold', and would surface as a B-side to their next single, 'One Love'. 'What you hear on "Something's Burning" was recorded that night,' said Leckie.

The next morning the police turned up at Rockfield and arrested Squire, Brown and Reni. 'The police woke me up and found a pile of paint-covered clothes next to my bed,' said Squire. The same day Mani and Steve Adge walked into Monmouth police station to give themselves up. Adge was released without charge. The Roses spent a night in the cells and then on 1 February all four were taken to Wolverhampton Magistrates' Court to face charges of criminal damage estimated at £10,000.

The *NME* were in court to report on the day – although there wasn't really much to report. The case was adjourned to 6 March and the Roses released on bail. 'It's the worst hotel I've ever stayed in,' said Brown of his stay in the cells, mimicking Mick Jagger's famous quote after his night in Brixton Prison following the Redlands bust in 1967. 'I didn't know abstract expressionism was an offence,' said Squire. The story made the front page of the *Manchester Evening News*, under the headline 'Pop Stars in £10,000 Raid Quiz'. As the band were having their fingerprints taken, they joked with police about which papers they were going to be in next morning. 'It'll be in the *NME*,' Mani said. That issue just happened to come with a free poster of the Kevin Cummins photograph of the band covered in paint. 'Just the sweetest irony, unreal,' said Mani. 'We signed the poster for the coppers and wrote "Exhibit A" on it.' The band could afford to joke. They expected nothing more than a slap on the wrist and an avalanche of publicity.

12.

'One Love'

After being released on bail the Roses returned to Rockfield to continue recording new material. 'Something's Burning' was a further
exploration of the groove and rhythm they'd begun to ride with
'Fools Gold'. The track was as grown-up as the Roses had ever
sounded, mining a funk that suggested they might take off in
George Clinton's 1970s Mothership. But this promise of channelling
the essence of Funkadelic/Parliament quickly evaporated as the
band drew blanks in the studio. With 'Fools Gold' they'd ridden out
into the middle of the ocean with such pioneering spirit that now
they found themselves a long way from dry land.

Changing their classic sound was seen as essential for a band keen
not to ride on the back of their own reputation, but 'Something's
Burning' was the full stop on that journey. Squire and Brown had no
new material. The only other track they recorded at Rockfield was
'One Love'. It was essentially 'Any Time You Want Me', the song
they'd talked about releasing before 'Fools Gold', with a new chorus
tacked on. The song had a melodic chime, which suggested it would
be another Roses classic, but they wanted it to be more than that.
They wrestled with the song. 'The idea was we were starting the
new album and they just had those two songs and that was it,' said
Leckie. 'One Love', based around programmed loops of bass and
drums, was the song Jive/Zomba pencilled in as a new single, but
the recording of it would prove frustrating and fractured – and
would eat up the remainder of February, March and April. Evans
was now in the habit of telling the band it didn't matter when the
next record came out, the longer the better. 'He kept telling us to
slow down,' said Squire.

Although Leckie didn't want him there, the band insisted Paul
Schroeder act as engineer on these fractious sessions. ' "One Love"

was difficult to record,' Schroeder said. The mixing process would go on endlessly. 'They were a difficult band to have in the mixing room. They'd all be trying to get something out of it; Reni telling you to turn the drums up, John telling you to turn the guitars up, all these little ideas.' Schroeder produced a series of mixes of the track. 'I did a punk mix, very monofied; it was pumping and very tough,' he said. But it wasn't used. Adrian Sherwood, from the influential On-U Sound Records, revered for his experimental punk, avant-garde, dub and reggae releases, was also sanctioned to remix 'One Love'. Unlike the Mondays, who had embraced remix culture, this was the only remix of a Roses track done with the band's say so while they remained with Jive/Zomba. Squire said the Sherwood remix made the band sound like Janet Jackson and stamped on the tape.

After recording 'One Love', Leckie had left England for Seattle to produce an album by American alternative rock/power pop band The Posies. During the time he was away, the Roses remained in stasis. This apparent slow death of the band's creativity had not gone unnoticed at Jive/Zomba. The label further alienated the band with their haste to capitalize on the success of 'Fools Gold'. In February 1990 they'd re-released 'Elephant Stone' as a single and it peaked in the UK at number 8, despite zero promotional support. The same month 'Made of Stone' was re-released in the UK, reaching number 20, followed by a re-release of 'She Bangs the Drums'. Jive/Zomba was also busy working Roses product around the world, such as Germany, where a singles EP was released. The band had not been consulted on, nor supported, any of these releases.

They had, though, finally agreed to a short tour of America. A series of dates was being organized for Los Angeles, New York, San Francisco, Chicago and Detroit – a city the band had insisted on playing due to its dance-music legacy. In late February the Roses acquiesced to two days of international interviews at London's Tara Hotel to talk up these plans. The British press was not invited. 'The Manchester scene is a convenient myth to sell product, whether it be records or newspapers,' Squire told *Rolling Stone*, America's most influential music publication. 'We feel we're the only British group worth exporting since the Sex Pistols, definitely,' Brown said. 'We don't want to be an English phenomenon,' said Squire. 'There's a lot of other British groups doing well in America,' said Brown, 'but we think we're better, so we want Americans to see us and hear us. It's just as important to be big in New York as Manchester.'

It was during this short period of promotion at the Tara Hotel that Evans, and the Roses' American manager, Greg Lewerke, met and hired lawyer John Kennedy, a decision that would deeply affect the future course of the band. A fierce litigator specializing in music business law, Kennedy would be the ideal man to assist in the renegotiations regarding the Jive/Zomba contract. It would seem a shrewd move by Evans, but the decision had been forced on him when his preferred lawyer, the property specialist Geoff Howard, was brought before a Law Society tribunal in December 1989 and accused of practising while uncertified, accounting deficiency, and bringing the profession into disrepute. On 27 February 1990 the tribunal had found the allegations to be substantiated.

Lewerke asked the new lawyer, Kennedy, about the possibility of the band escaping Jive/Zomba and signing to a different label. Kennedy, who knew and respected Clive Calder, said that although the Jive/Zomba boss would be tough on renegotiations, 'it's always better if you can work out a deal and stay on the label'. Evans handed over the contracts, and Kennedy was amazed. 'The contracts were so bad, they were the like of which you didn't see any more. One of the most damaging things was the combination of the recording and publishing agreements. They were two very tough agreements, both of which in their own right might have been vulnerable – but the fact that they were together, and linked in a number of ways, made it dynamite in terms of vulnerability.'

A week after hiring Kennedy, the Roses were back at Wolverhampton Magistrates' Court for the FM Revolver paint incident, arriving from the ongoing mixing sessions for 'One Love', which were now taking place at RAK studios. Surprisingly the band's legal representative was Geoff Howard, and things didn't go well. A small crowd of fans had gathered outside the court, and again the *NME* was present – this time putting the band, on the court steps, on its front cover. It was proposed the case should be referred to the Crown court because of the seriousness of the offences: estimated damages had risen to £23,000. Howard raised no objection but said the band would fight the charges.

Crown court was, as Reni said, 'big lad's court', where penalties were much more severe than in the magistrates' court. Only serious offences were taken to the Crown court and, if found guilty, the band would be facing a prison sentence. The Roses nonetheless spent forty-five minutes posing with fans and signing autographs afterwards, as Evans flogged 'Ian Brown is innocent' T-shirts. 'We're going to get our bottoms smacked good and proper,' said Squire. 'That's when it hit us that we'd done a pretty bad thing. Mani was making jokes about us getting raped in prison.'

The new Roses single, 'One Love', was expected in May to coincide with the recently announced Spike Island date. But the single continued to prove problematic; rehearsals and songwriting attempts between court appearances also faltered. The band reappeared on 12 April at Wolverhampton Magistrates' Court with over a hundred fans and chaotic scenes awaiting them. FM Revolver's Paul Birch was 'jostled, nudged, punched and elbowed' in the gallery overlooking the courtroom. The case was adjourned until 26 April, and it was then that the trial was finally committed to Wolverhampton Crown Court. The case was expected to come before the court in September and the threat of prison was stark. Geoff Howard was replaced with Paul Reid QC, a specialist in crime.

Andrew Lauder at Silvertone was now under increased pressure from his Zomba bosses to get the band restarted on the new album. He had requested a list of studios and recording dates from Leckie while he was away in Seattle. In late April he faxed back twelve possible locations around the world and a schedule that began in June and concluded in September. Among the studios Leckie suggested in New York, Malibu, Paris and Dublin, he listed the Rolling Stones Mobile and 'a little eight-track in New Orleans at Mardi Gras'. On his return from America, Leckie was amazed to find the band still mixing 'One Love'.

'I came back after six weeks and they were still doing it,' he said. Leckie took charge of the new single and completed a final mix of 'One Love'. There were now difficulties with the cover art. Suggestions of a swastika could be detected in Squire's design, reported the *NME*. It was more than a suggestion, and the single cover and thousands of promotional T-shirts had to be destroyed. The man responsible for making the Roses' T-shirts was Johnny Bolland, who had known Squire and Brown since his scooterboy days leading the Stockport Crusaders. 'We all said straight away it looks like a swastika,' he said. 'You could make it out. We'd done a few thousand T-shirts and somebody went to a venue in town and got refused entrance.' The wilfully provocative Squire said he was trying to 're-appropriate' the swastika. It was a serious error of judgement, and it was left to Brown to apologize.

The band also had problems making a video for the single. They had hoped the Happy Mondays' video team, the Bailey Brothers, would work with them. Unlike the Roses, the Mondays had already followed their chart breakthrough with a massive new single, 'Step On'. It had put them in the UK Top 5 for the first time, and the Bailey Brothers had shot the much-played video in Barcelona. It featured Shaun Ryder wrapped around a huge neon E sign. The Bailey Brothers were keen to work with the Roses, and an idea had been loosely formed to shoot the video for 'One Love' on the top of a building with a helicopter.

Tony Wilson put a stop to any such plans. 'Wilson said, There's fucking no way you're doing it,' said Keith Jobling, one half of the Bailey Brothers. 'He said, It's not right for the story about the war of the bands, the Mondays and the Roses.' The Roses took the news stoically. 'They said, Oh don't tell us: because of Gareth?' said Jobling. 'We said, Yeah, Wilson hates Gareth, get rid of Gareth and we'll do a video.'

The May release of 'One Love' was postponed. The Roses had sold out Spike Island by April, but the cost of organizing the event would eat up any profit. In that sense it was cold comfort, as not just the Happy Mondays but a slew of other bands capitalized on the Madchester boom. The Inspiral Carpets' debut single on Mute, 'This Is How It Feels', had gone Top 20 in the UK, and their debut album *Life* was at number 2, selling a quarter of a million copies. Primal Scream had also hit the payload with their radical new single, 'Loaded'. The Charlatans single 'The Only One I Know' was at number 9. Steve Lock's Granada TV documentary *Celebration: Madchester – Sound of The North* was also a hit in May. 'Manchester is now the music capital of Britain, some say Europe, some say the world,' ran the opening credits to the documentary. But the jewel in the crown, the Roses, didn't feature in it. 'The Stone Roses were a glaring omission really,' said Lock, who never reached agreement with Evans to include the Alexandra Palace footage in his documentary.

While the Mondays et al worked towards their album releases in autumn 1990, the Roses were going nowhere. They hadn't responded to Leckie's faxed suggestions for the new album: the band had neither the material nor the inclination, because of the ongoing contractual renegotiations with Jive/Zomba. All they had was Spike Island – and some famous Manc lip. The Roses' attitude towards the scene they headed had begun to harden. Brown had previously declared it healthy. 'It needs more than just one group to change things – it needs loads of them,' he had said. Now he decreed, 'We've never gone out of our way to align ourselves with the so-called Manchester scene. We've never understood the supposed connection between us and all these other bands. It's a media thing. People are people, your attitude is your attitude. It ain't where you're from, it's where you're at.'

'I felt like we were flogging something for somebody, but I didn't know what it was or who they were,' said Squire. 'A lifestyle, I suppose. An attitude.' Brown poured water on the idea of it being 'Christmas every day' in the city, and, in May, he also dampened the expectations of Jive/Zomba that the band's plans for America would run smoothly, telling *Q* magazine, 'America isn't that big a deal to us.'

As a continuation of the band's policy to play outside of the traditional circuit, Spike Island was a huge success. It suggested the band had the potential to take the world. Spike Island also provided ample evidence that, although there was much to admire about Evans, their manager was also wildly out of control. At a time when the Roses most needed solid, down-to-earth advice, as fame affected their own egos, Evans's ego shot through the roof. With the Italia 90 World Cup approaching, he was dismayed that New Order were dominating the coverage – having recorded the England team's World Cup song, 'World in Motion'. Evans plagued the band's plugger, Gareth Davies, with early morning calls demanding that the Roses get equal prominence.

'I was usually in the office by 6 a.m.,' said Davies. 'And he realized this, and he would start ringing me at half past six.' It prompted Davies to approach BBC sport show *Grandstand*, and an instrumental loop of a Roses track from their 1989 album was used during the BBC's coverage of the World Cup. Despite this result, Davies found many other suggestions from Evans ridiculous. He, too, worried that Evans was neglecting to relay important messages to the band. 'I concluded that if you wanted to get things to happen, basically you had to avoid Gareth.'

Following Spike Island, the Roses played the Provinssirock Festival in Seinäjoki, Finland. Brown took offence at a Confederate flag waved by a crowd member, demanding that the person waving it be removed. This was followed by shows at the Mayfield Leisure Centre in Belfast and Glasgow Green in Scotland. In their desire to avoid traditional venues, and to help create a rave atmosphere at their shows, the band played in circus big tops. In front of 8,000 fans in Glasgow, on 9 June 1990, with sweat dripping like rain from the tent roof, the band played what would not just be their final show with Reni but also one of their best. 'The best ever,' said Brown. 'We all looked at each other on stage, and then just went up to another level,' Mani agreed.

It went downhill quickly from there.

'I came home from Glasgow Green and didn't see any of them for eighteen months,' said Cressa. 'But you know, shit happens.' The release of 'One Love' continued to be held back, purportedly due to the switch of cover art. Others suggested the band were prolonging the suspense, in an attempt to guarantee the single entered the charts at number 1. There was now a video for the single, filmed in a huge studio at Vector Television in Heaton Mersey, Stockport. It was a disheartening effort, the band miming the song as if live in front of a fire backdrop super-imposed with crude technical skill.

The Roses' plans for America grew more confusing, as the dates they had lined up were unceremoniously cancelled. This was despite the tickets for the Los Angeles gig, at Hollywood High, having sold out in seven minutes. 'America doesn't deserve us yet,' Brown said. 'We're just naturally stubborn,' said Squire. 'If we get pressured into going to America, which we have been, we'll turn it down.' The band's American manager, Greg Lewerke, said the small amount of money on offer for the shows made the dates financially unappealing to the band, and 'Ian's quote was just a cop-out'.

'The dates being cancelled was a travesty,' said Michael Tedesco. The Roses' album sales were in the region of a quarter of a million in America, and all at Jive/Zomba, including Barry Weiss and Clive Calder, thought they were poised for a breakthrough.

Contract renegotiations between the band and Jive/Zomba were ongoing. The label was willing to make an improved offer, but for boss Clive Calder there was a limit to what improvement there was going to be. For Evans, Spike Island had been the 'defining gig of a generation', after which every 'top record man in the industry' was on the phone to him, suggesting the band was now worth vast sums of money. He had expected that Jive/Zomba 'would rush back to London and immediately start setting up a big new package'. When they didn't, and renegotiations continued to be tough, his mind was made up. Evans was now gambling on being able to get out of the contract, and intent on making a new, massive money deal for the Roses with a different label. It was a huge risk.

Evans sent Squire and Brown to the Mull of Kintyre to write new material. He thought it sounded good in meetings. 'I liked the idea of sending them to this remote place. I just thought it had rock star class.' He even suggested that Brown should fake his own death while there, washed away at sea. Once the news made the front pages, Evans envisaged Brown returning from the dead to further headlines.

Along with his business partner Matthew Cummins, Evans flew to Los Angeles where Greg Lewerke had set up a series of meetings with the intention of securing a new deal for the Roses. 'The band, everybody, was pulling in different directions,' said Lewerke. 'Everybody had a different agenda.' Warner Brothers had paid for the flights, but Lewerke also took Evans and Cummins for meetings with PolyGram and Geffen Records – whose HQ happened to be just over the street from his own office, on Sunset Boulevard. 'It was all just talk, and the talk was if we could get free of Jive/Zomba, are you interested?' said Lewerke. It was an indication of how serious Geffen Records were in their pursuit of the band that boss David Geffen, one of the richest and most successful entertainment moguls of the twentieth century, label president Eddie Rosenblatt and senior A&R figure Gary Gersh met with the Roses' managers at an upmarket Italian restaurant in Los Angeles, Matteo's.

'It was a big lunch,' said Lewerke. 'It was a big deal. And Gareth was great. They loved him. I remember Eddie saying to me, How did you get teamed up with these guys?' Brown had been right in his initial appraisal of Evans over three years ago. He wasn't afraid of anybody, and he commandeered the lunch – regaling Geffen, Rosenblatt and Gersh with tall tales of Madchester. Geffen was the man who, while Evans was running hairdressing shops, built an empire with Asylum Records (with acts such as Joni Mitchell, Jackson Browne and The Eagles), and, after selling the label for $7 million, had re-emerged in the 1980s with his Geffen label, signing acts such as Aerosmith and Guns N' Roses. The ink was still drying on a deal that had seen Geffen sell Geffen Records to MCA for $540 million, while allowing him to keep control of the company.

Geffen was aware of the Roses and the Madchester scene and had been recommended the band by Rough Trade boss Geoff Travis. But it was A&R man Gary Gersh who appeared keenest, having been left drooling by 'I Wanna Be Adored', the single Jive/Zomba had chosen for the band in America. He called it 'one of the best songs I've ever heard in my life'. From that moment on, Gersh wanted The Stone Roses. 'We were told, rightly or wrongly, that the situation as it related to their long-term contractual obligations was up in the air and clearly sceptical at best,' said Gersh. 'And David and Eddie were nothing but unbelievably supportive and we were on a mission to bring the band to Geffen.'

Evans would claim that he left the lunch with a cheque for $350,000 as a down payment. Rosenblatt, Gersh and Lewerke do not recall that. But it was true Geffen signalled their intent to pay $4 million up front for the band. The rumours did not take long to filter back to Jive/Zomba. 'Gareth would be saying one thing to one party and one thing to another,' said Jive/Zomba's Steven Howard. 'I've no idea what he conveyed to the group, but he didn't encourage our relationship with them. He was divisive in terms of that relationship, because it strengthened his position.'

Money was the issue. Now that $4 million dollars was on the table, Evans was hell-bent on grabbing it. Any improvements Jive/Zomba were prepared to make on the original contract would never match that figure. Howard was busy overseeing other aspects of Zomba's growth, and the key men dealing with the Roses contract on the business side (including now a new boss of Jive Records in the UK, Steve Jenkins, a former Stock, Aitken and Waterman associate) had no real feel for the band. 'It was all about money,' said the Roses' A&R man Roddy McKenna. 'They wanted Zomba to come close to the kind of money they were being offered from Geffen.'

'The negotiations with Zomba were not fruitful,' said the Roses' lawyer John Kennedy. 'The Roses may have been the hottest band in the country but Zomba's Clive Calder is a tough cookie and quite a lot of money had been spent on the band already. Maybe they thought the band were running into a bit of a brick wall, because some recordings had taken place which hadn't been successful. So you've got this fantastic first album and you've got quite a lot of money having been spent, and the label were wondering where this band were going to go for the future. A bit of doubt had crept in.'

Finally, on 2 July 1990, a new Stone Roses record was released, eight months after 'Fools Gold'. The A-side, 'One Love', had the same title as the Bob Marley & the Wailers 1977 hit, and included the same lyric – 'one love, one heart'. The *NME* made it Single of the Week, but there was no appetite from the band to promote the record. Largely, this was a reflection of the chaos caused by doubts over their future with Jive/Zomba, but the band were also dissatisfied with the song itself. Squire called it a disappointment.

'We tried in vain to cover all bases – we wanted to appeal to everyone in clubs and indie kids and whoever, but it was a poor chorus,' said Brown. An opportunity to promote 'One Love' on the prime-time *Wogan* talk show on BBC1 came up. Brown and Squire were initially jubilant at the news. 'I was convinced, because there were always rumours about [the show's host] Terry Wogan having a wig, that the Roses were going to try and pull his wig off,' said Gareth Davies. 'Around the world they'd be known as the band that pulled that bloke's wig off.' The band pulled out of the show, however, when they discovered that the episode would be pre-recorded. This refusal to appear on *Wogan* was widely reported. 'Terry's worried about being the next Bill Grundy,' reckoned *Sounds*, referring to the Sex Pistols' foul-mouthed appearance on an early evening Thames TV show, *Today*, which launched the band. 'Roses Boycott Wogan' was the *Daily Star* headline, the band called a 'rebel four piece' whose 'new single is expected to rocket to next week's number one'. 'Terry obviously doesn't have enough bottle,' Brown was quoted in the *Daily Mirror*.

The Roses did appear on the cover of *Smash Hits*. 'We're the best band on the planet' – a Mani quote – was the headline, and on 14 July Brown, alone, was on the cover of *Number One*. In the *Smash Hits* interview Squire expressed concern about the impending criminal-damage court case, and Brown declared flares over: 'Too many sheep.' The band had already expressed their pleasure at featuring in the tabloids, and perhaps appearing in the teen magazines was another step in attaining the hugeness they aspired to: 'bigger than The Beatles, The Rolling Stones and Madonna put together'.

It was also time for reflection. 'Some people say we're a lads' band,' said Brown. 'Some people say we're a 16-year-old girls' band; they say a lot, don't they? But they say fuck all.' Fame was not an easy fit for the now 27-year-old Brown. He had always said the star was the audience, and that he was not to be worshipped. 'I Wanna Be Adored' was a song about sin, not a declaration of his own desire. He had talked about destroying the way that fans looked up to pop and rock stars like Bono, wanting to kick over those false icons. Squire spent a day crawling around his house on his belly after the *Smash Hits* cover attracted four teenage girls to camp outside the terraced house he shared with his girlfriend, Helen.

There were no further interviews as the band went into lock-down. Despite the lack of promotion, 'One Love' entered the UK charts at number 4, their highest position to date. There was no celebratory *Top of the Pops* performance to propel the single towards number 1. On the back of the success of 'One Love', however, 'Fools Gold' climbed back into the charts, reaching number 22. The Roses were persuaded to perform 'One Love' for the syndicated *Hit Studio International*, broadcast on the satellite station Super Channel, and shown in Japan and Europe but not the UK. It was unclear if the band were supposed to play live, as many bands did on this show, or mime. Brown walked off stage during the filming.

'One Love' was strangely anticlimactic. The song lacked any real club thump, and its sentiment was out of step in the context of the gang violence now taking hold of Manchester. Madchester was still a global attraction, but in the city the glory days of 1988 and 1989 were over, replaced by an era that would be dubbed 'Gunchester'. There was to be no 'Third Summer of Love' in Manchester, no 'one love', no love at all. Already the police had closed the Thunderdome club, following a drive-by shooting, and the Gallery venue, a favourite haunt for the notorious 'Cheetham Hill gang'. The Haçienda had become the focal point of a series of drug wars, door wars, gang wars, and in a few short months would be forced to temporarily close. The International clubs that Evans and Cummins owned, although more associated with the student crowd, were not immune to the darkness spreading across the city. Brown had been present at a reggae night at the International when shots had been fired.

With a new student hot spot, the Academy, recently opened on Manchester University campus, it was a good time to get out of the business. Evans and Cummins did. Dougie James had the pair up in court and, finally, won his long-running case against them. James was ruled to be a legitimate partner in the International and took outright ownership of the club. Another interested party bought Evans and Cummins out of International II. Although they had to pay a reputed £133,000 in court costs, it was offset somewhat by the sale of their shares in both clubs. Evans's personal wealth at the time of the court case was £1.7 million, and James estimated Evans and Cummins had taken as much as £3 million out of the International in the five years he'd been locked in a legal battle with them. In the International's accounts he came across £28,000 in video royalties meant for the Roses. 'They didn't know about it. I sent it to them. I felt very sorry for the kids because with a man like Gareth you can never have success.'

13.

Geffen

In August 1990 the first reports surfaced in the UK media concerning the Roses' precarious relationship with Jive/Zomba, claiming the band had 'left their contract' and been poached by an as yet unnamed company. In September Jive/Zomba responded by seeking to put an injunction on the band, preventing them from recording for another label. 'They were worried we were going to walk away and we did not really resist that injunction,' said the band's lawyer, John Kennedy. 'We agreed we wouldn't release anything but we wanted to be able to record, that was the important thing.'

The trial would not come before the High Court until March 1991. The Roses would be, effectively, in limbo for six months. The band's entire career would hinge on the result of the court case, and even by Kennedy's estimation it was a gamble. 'The thing you should know about litigation is you're fairly certain what your strategy is, you know what you're doing, but you're never certain about the outcome.'

Kennedy's case that the Roses' recording and publishing contracts were unreasonable and unenforceable was built on a body of law called restraint of trade. There were several clauses within the Roses' recording contract that were highly dubious. Key was the fact there was no positive obligation on Zomba's part to release the band's records, meaning the company could effectively sterilize the output of the group – a restraint of trade. Zomba had signed the Roses for one year, to be followed by six possible option periods that could be exercised at the whim of the company, meaning they could tie the group up for as long as thirty-five years, or even, possibly, due to certain loopholes, for ever.

The band were now taking this very seriously. Although Geffen had made a verbal offer, they had not signed anything – after all this the band could end up still tied to Jive/Zomba. 'We weren't confident of winning,' said Squire. 'But we were determined to do or die. If we'd never been released from that contract we wouldn't have worked for them again, so we were discussing plans to only release bootlegs, or to just tour.'

'It's not much fun falling out with your record company if somebody then tells you you've still got to work with them,' said Kennedy. 'That was one of the biggest issues. The Roses were cool, confident, and expressed detachment, but were actually fairly fazed by having to be involved in this. In a sense, of course, they're also competitors, so they wanted to win as well. I suppose it was quite appealing that it was a Sex Pistols-type move against the establishment.'

'It was bitterly sad,' said Steven Howard at Jive/Zomba. 'A classic case of lunatics running the asylum. They were courted by Geffen Records, who had never even seen them and who offered them an untold fortune, which was music to Gareth's ears. Geffen was prepared to pay this huge advance way out of any proportion to what they should be getting. And there were people on our side in the UK dealing with it by saying, Oh we'll leave it to the lawyers, the lawyers will sort it all out. And that's not how you go about these things. It was such a mistake.'

The criminal-damage charges that had been hanging over the Roses' heads since April were finally heard at Wolverhampton Crown Court on 5 October. Fans outside the court wore 'The Manchester four are innocent' T-shirts. Paul Reid QC, defending the band, called the Roses' actions 'stupid', but added, 'They believed the release [of the 'Sally Cinnamon' video] to be damaging to their professional reputations, so decided to take the law into their own hands. These four young men are not merely fussy but obsessive about the quality of everything associated with their name. They want to be the best at what they do and they are never satisfied with second best. It is a genuine desire on their part that their fans should not be ripped off.'

Judge Mott QC delivered his verdict: 'I can understand the indignation you felt, but the way in which you went about it was immature to the point of childishness,' he said. 'I think a prison sentence, suspended or otherwise, might lead to notoriety for you and ultimately be to your benefit and I certainly don't want to contribute to that.' The Roses escaped being sent to jail and were merely fined £3,000 each. Squire summed up the band's relief: 'I'm just glad to stay out of the nick,' he said.

In a year they should have dominated, the Roses were now beginning to be left behind. In October, Primal Scream's third album, *Screamadelica*, would see them cement their place as the era's most elegant acid house rock outfit. The Charlatans' debut, *Some Friendly*, made number 1 in the UK. Even James had revived, taking their *Gold Mother* album to number 2. The Mondays' third album, *Pills 'n' Thrills and Bellyaches*, hit number 4 in November. During this period the music press could only speculate on the Roses, as the band held a media blackout. *Melody Maker* suggested the Roses were being 'crucified by their own messiah complex' and had a 'peculiar death wish'. Brown was rumoured to have always wanted to be in a band that became really massive and then never did anything again.

Having only recorded two songs all year, it was a testament to the Roses' incendiary rise to prominence that there continued to be a belief that the band would deliver – nowhere more so than in America, where other English outfits including Jesus Jones, EMF and The Charlatans were scoring with variations of the Roses' sound. In December 1990, in the *LA Times*, in an article titled '20 bands that matter', chief pop-music critic Robert Hilburn named his top four as: U2, Guns N' Roses, Public Enemy and The Stone Roses. Of the Roses, he wrote:

Some rock groups take time before they display commanding vision, but many demonstrate enough of a glimmer of greatness in their first albums to stamp them as significant forces: for example the Sex Pistols, Talking Heads, R.E.M. and U2. The Roses, who have yet to tour the US, may never make another album as good as their 1989 debut, but that collection spoke with a youthful innocence and independence that suggests the Roses are capable of leading more than merely the Manchester, England, scene.

The Roses reconvened at the expensive Bluestone rehearsal facility – an isolated, converted farm in Pembrokeshire – on 13 January 1991 to brew up some more of their steamy funk and folk-rock magic. 'The first two weeks was just like an expensive record player,' said Mani. 'We just sat smoking weed and listening to tunes at a grand a day, then we went sledging on antique silver trays. Did a bit of mountain biking. Suddenly we've done five weeks in the studio.' Mani's father had died from a heart attack two months earlier and he was in a distressed state. Reni was the only one who noticed. Yet Squire and Brown, for all their self-absorption, were not concentrating on songwriting. New songs were not flowing in the way they once had. Their partnership had run dry. The band came back from Pembrokeshire empty-handed and with heavy hearts to face the Jive/Zomba court case, which began on 4 March and would run until the 26th.

Proceedings at the High Court of Justice were highly complex and detailed. *Melody Maker* reported Brown as saying that if the case went against them the band would give up music and go on the dole. While the case was in its early stages, Kennedy nailed down the deal with Geffen. His initial concern was to secure funding for the court case and his litigation team. These negotiations took place at the Halcyon Hotel in London with Geffen representatives Gary Gersh and Eddie Rosenblatt. The pair faced one late and surprise contender for the band's hand in the form of flamboyant cape-wearing Maurice Oberstein, the managing director of PolyGram. 'I don't know how he found us,' said Kennedy. 'He came to the hotel and said, Look, this is what we will do, we will match whatever deal Geffen offer and in addition, to make it interesting for your clients, we will sign the contract on Concorde.' Oberstein had signed The Clash to CBS in a similar cavalier fashion.

Kennedy told the band about the offer from PolyGram and continued negotiating the deal with Geffen, who agreed to fund the court case. Rosenblatt admitted Geffen were taking a huge risk. There was no guarantee the court case would be won, so they might only end up with a substantial bill for legal costs. He also admitted that the label had not heard any new Roses material. 'The court case could go either way and we were taking a risk,' said Gersh. 'It was very intense and complicated. John Kennedy negotiated masterfully, as he does.' The Roses felt that Gersh was someone they could work with, specifically because he had previously signed Sonic Youth to Geffen. It was the first time Gersh had sat with the band together. 'Some of them were very outgoing and loud and boisterous, and then some of them were very quiet and introverted. It was much harder to get through to Ian and John than to get through to Reni and Mani. They warmed up throughout the day and it got easier. We were literally negotiating from room to room. And Obi [Maurice Oberstein] was there too. I remember coming out of a room with Eddie and walking smack bang into Obi – and there was nothing to do but just laugh.'

'It was hard, but we got to the end of the negotiation on the Sunday night,' said Kennedy. 'I said to the band, Look, this is really a good deal with Geffen, we need to start making some decisions. I remember being quite irritated – when I went to see them for their decision, they were watching [the film] *Twelve Angry Men*. It was halfway through and they said they wanted to see the film all the way to the end before we had the discussion. It's now ten o'clock on a Sunday night, I'd been away from my family all weekend, and I wouldn't mind going home. I was their friend, I was working on their behalf, but at the same time they wanted a Sex Pistols-type edge.'

The film finished. Kennedy advised the band he had done what they'd asked and negotiated the deal with Geffen. If they won the court case the deal was said to be worth $20 million spread over the course of five albums, with an initial payment of $4 million. 'Then somebody said, What about that PolyGram offer? What about going on Concorde?' said Kennedy. 'I said, Well, it's fantastic to go on Concorde but you don't want to choose your record company because you're going to get a trip on Concorde. They said, No, no – you don't get it. We get on Concorde and when we're halfway across the Atlantic we say we've changed our mind. I drew the line there.'

Instead the Roses came up with the idea they wanted to sign to Geffen on a London double-decker bus. Rosenblatt was at the end of his tether. He'd worked with some of the biggest recording artists in the world, spent a weekend doing all he could, and now wanted to go home. 'It was just too much for him,' said Kennedy. 'I said, The band are quite capable of saying no. So the contract was signed on the bus.'

Kennedy now had to inform the High Court of the development with Geffen – and was warned by his own QC he could have overstepped the mark. If the judge agreed that it was a breach of the injunction, Kennedy would be in contempt of court and facing jail. Thankfully, Zomba's lawyers looked over the documents and agreed Kennedy had stayed on the right side of the law.

The band tended to keep away from court, except Brown, who was there most days but getting restless. 'At least I'm beginning to understand their double-speak,' he said. It was more entertaining when there were witnesses in court, and all the Roses travelled down from Manchester to hear the testimony of Geoff Howard, their lawyer at the time of signing to Jive/Zomba. Dougie James was also there that day. Zomba had approached him for dirt. James knew that Howard had been up before the Law Society, and he asked Zomba's lawyer to ask Howard if he was a man of integrity. 'He had to say no,' said James.

Howard was not the only man to have his integrity questioned on the stand. The Roses' QC Barbara Dohman described Evans as 'inexperienced in the music business' and it was revealed he had paid the band an initial wage of £70 per week, rising to £200, before tax. Peter Prescott QC, representing Zomba, attacked the length of Evans's ten-year management contract, and claimed the Roses' manager never supplied the band with detailed accounts of the finances of his company, Starscreen Management. That Gareth

Evans was not his real name was also made public. It was also stated that Jive/Zomba via Silvertone had approached Evans over the summer with possible amendments to the original contracts and that he'd never discussed these amendments with the band.

Jive/Zomba requested the unfair elements in the contracts be severed, leaving those parts of the contract which were fair intact. Zomba boss Clive Calder had doubts going into the case, but as the proceedings went on, some of the testimonies seemed to be in his favour. 'We started to feel more confident that we had a chance of winning,' said Michael Tedesco, who was in daily contact with Calder. Roddy McKenna, the A&R man who had originally signed the band to Jive/Zomba, said Evans tried to dissuade him from testifying in court. McKenna also asked the Roses if they had received their £40,000 Christmas bonus from Jive/Zomba. The band told him Evans had given them £500 each.

Evans seemed to register that the details revealed in court would permanently damage his relationship with the band, and was now preparing to be sacked. 'The breakdown in the band's relationship with Gareth started then,' said Kennedy. 'There had been more tension than I knew between them and it came to a head during the case.' For Kennedy, the court case was an all-or-nothing gamble. 'If I lost I was going to be considered very damaged goods. A good friend of mine was regularly getting messages from executives at Zomba, making clear they thought I'd mucked up really, really badly.'

The judge retired to consider his verdict. 'You don't know when that decision is going to come,' said Kennedy. 'Is it going to come in a week? A month? Six months? You have no control. So you're just getting on with life.' Three weeks later Kennedy spent the weekend in Ireland at his father's funeral. 'I'd come back on the Sunday evening to a message saying, Judgement tomorrow,' he said. 'I froze.' The judgement was delivered on 20 May. 'During the first twenty minutes reading his verdict, the judge gives all the signals we've lost. It's really cliffhanger stuff. Then he suddenly turns the corner. Things just started getting better and better and better.'

The Roses were released from their recording and publishing contracts with Jive/Zomba. Judge Humphries found both contracts legally unenforceable, calling them 'oppressive', 'unfair' and 'entirely one-sided'. 'Suffice to say in almost every clause it is the name of Zomba which is being provided for,' he said. Jive/Zomba immediately appealed the decision, but it would not amount to anything more than a gesture.

Squire hailed this court victory as perhaps the Roses' most significant contribution to music. The fact the band had taken on the music industry, and won, established new moral parameters in the way companies would make deals with bands. 'It's probably a greater contribution to popular music than anything we've ever recorded,' he said. Brown saw it as justice done: 'The week after, the director of every single record company was saying what a disgrace the result was. We were attacking their whole industry.'

For Evans, the court triumph was a pyrrhic victory. No representatives of Geffen had attended the proceedings, so all they heard was good news. A new Roses single was planned for release on Geffen as soon as possible, a new album scheduled for mid-autumn 1991, and the press was told to expect a big show in England during the summer. 'A massive surprise on the scale of Spike Island,' said Evans, who now also hoped to finally launch the band in America. 'We were planning on doing big shows,' said the band's American manager, Greg Lewerke. 'We were going to do one at Madison Square Gardens in New York, one at the LA Forum and one in San Francisco. Start off big, Gareth would say – they've got to be big, what's the biggest thing they can do? Some things came out in court that portrayed Gareth in a bad light, but he always seemed the same. He was maybe a little more nervous and shifty than usual, but he was always shifty and nervous.'

Evans admitted to now feeling unstable, having to deal with 'the might of the American music industry in one ear' and 'having to listen to the band planning my demise in the other'. 'The case had highlighted how badly we'd been managed because we'd been allowed to sign the original contract,' said Squire. Evans claimed the band broke into his farmhouse and threatened him, demanding monies they felt he owed them. Reni had wanted rid of him for years, and now Squire wanted Evans sacked, but the band were no longer a close-knit unit and making decisions about anything would take time. After all, the band had always known what Evans was like. But the idea of he and Cummins collecting their 33.3 per cent share of the massive Geffen deal was unpalatable. Brown, despite everything, retained a soft spot for Evans. There was talk, initially, of Matthew Cummins being axed and Evans being put on a more modest 20 per cent.

Evans had, by plan or blunder, contributed to the band being in the position where they had signed the most lucrative deal in recording history. The monies being quibbled over paled in comparison to what the band would now share. Evans had toiled on behalf of the Roses for four years, and felt he had done the best he could for them. Behind the hyperbole, he also saw them as friends – all in it together – and was shocked and hurt by these developments. He was excited about the band finally breaking America, and wanted to share in that ultimate triumph.

Instead, Evans was now busy collecting legal papers and testimonies to protect himself and his business partner Cummins and their remarkable 33.3 per cent share of the Roses' gross profits. They employed their own lawyer. A popular rumour was that the band wanted to sack Evans because he had stolen £1 million from them, with the intention of buying a Lear Jet, and it was only the band intercepting him at Manchester Airport that had prevented him from doing so. A good story, but untrue. Geffen, meanwhile, were keen to cement their plans for the group but the contact number they had for the band was Evans's farmhouse, where his disabled son, Mark, would often answer the phone. Eddie Rosenblatt was not comfortable speaking to a child with Down's Syndrome about his multimillion-dollar investment.

The Roses retained the services of John Kennedy, and he acted as the key adviser to the band. 'It was a proper debate as to what the next steps were,' he said. 'It was complicated. Different people had different views of Gareth.' For Greg Lewerke the situation was a nightmare. He had played a vital role in bringing the Roses and Geffen together, but his deal was with Evans. If the band were now going to cut Evans and Cummins out of the Geffen deal, his share would also go up in smoke. Although Lewerke never saw any money, above his expenses, Evans had used Lewerke's involvement as the reason why he had needed to take so much money from the band. 'Gareth was up to no good at the end,' Lewerke said. 'He didn't know what was right or wrong and I think he just took too much – and they caught him.' However, as he went on to say, 'The Roses shot themselves in the foot by being a little too clever . . . The money from Geffen destroyed them. It was very depressing.' He said the band should have retained Evans, and simply put him on a 'tighter leash'. 'There's all this money here, guys, we've all worked so hard to get to this point. Can't we just follow it through? What are you getting rid of the guy for? Just so you can make more money?'

The American dates Lewerke had worked to set up were cancelled. The Madison Square Garden date had sold out, but the Roses stubbornly refused to play the prestigious date on the principle that Evans had arranged it without asking them first. 'The Roses were tilting on the brink of being the biggest British band since The Beatles in America,' Evans said. 'They got rid of me six months too soon. They could have played those American gigs and then they could have sacked me. They got it horribly wrong.'

'It's easy to say we all became lethargic and pulled those big American dates,' said Squire. 'But we were a band who had got to where we were with a particular body of work, a particular style. Now we had to move onwards. The danger was that we would continue to play the same set and become very tired, dull. It might have raked in the money for Gareth, but it wouldn't have been natural. We all knew it.'

The cancellation of the American dates set alarm bells ringing for Geffen A&R man Gary Gersh. He had already allowed for the possibility of 'some insanity' going on with Evans and the band, but thus far Evans had delivered on every promise he made. 'Gareth was saying that those gigs seemed like they were going to happen and we believed him,' said Gersh. 'We felt like Gareth was the kind of character that the band needed: visionary and wily.' Now it was apparent that there were 'a lot of complications', and Gersh was growing anxious to get the Roses in the studio. The rumour was they had two albums' worth of material ready to record.

'I kept saying to Gareth, You have to believe, and they have to believe, that they're the greatest band in the world and they have to make the next record, that's all there is,' said Gersh. 'There's just the next record. It should be the second record in a long line of records, not the most important thing that's ever happened in their lives.' Geffen's plan to release a quick single, and an album in the autumn, was the first of many to be abandoned. Gersh could get no clear answers from Evans. 'Everyone around the world was just waiting for the Roses' record. We had gone through this whole process – signed the band, made this big commitment – and nothing was happening.'

After seven years without any, the Roses now had money. The $4 million [approximately £2.3 million] advance from Geffen was being carefully managed by John Kennedy and a new band account-ant, Patrick Savage, who worked for the OJ Kilkenny company (the industry's leading financial advice firm, who most famously looked after U2). The individual band members were said to have received £125,000 each. Reni treated himself to a flash new Saab car; Brown walked around Manchester handing out £20 notes to the homeless. Plans for a summer show in the UK were postponed. Instead, the band took off for a holiday together in the South of France, hiring a helicopter and staying in £500-a-night hotels in Nice, Cannes, St Tropez and Monte Carlo. Squire took Super-8 footage of the trip that would later appear in the 'Love Spreads' video. Back in Man-chester, real-life events delayed any definite decisions over their future. Squire and Reni became fathers, and all four Roses invested in property. The band splintered, following their own separate ideals, with Mani and Reni staying in Manchester, Squire moving to the Lake District and Brown buying a farm in rural North Wales overlooking Cardigan Bay and backed by views of Snowdonia. The days of living in each other's pockets, of strolling to rehearsal at International II, of dreaming of nothing but the band, were over.

Mani couldn't see the sense in moving to the countryside. 'If you are away from the action it's like over, really.' Squire and Brown did make attempts to reinvigorate their songwriting, and they were still close, but things were changing. Nothing came of their efforts, and Squire found he was making more progress with songs on his own. 'Ian was quite happy with that,' said Squire. 'He'd tell me he was sitting at home sending me positive vibes to help with the song-writing.'

The only people able to make any clear purchase out of the Roses in this period were, ironically, Jive/Zomba, who began to recoup some of the reputed £1 million – according to *Q* magazine – they'd lost on the court case. The Roses' contract with the label was only void for the future. All the material the band had already recorded for them remained with Zomba. In September 1991, 'Elephant Stone' was re-released as a single, reaching number 20 in the UK charts, and 'Waterfall' reached number 27. This was followed, in October, by the re-release of the Roses' album, in a limited vinyl gatefold edition of 50,000, and on cassette and CD with extra tracks, 'Elephant Stone' and 'Fools Gold'. A video of the band's Blackpool Empress Ballroom show, never intended as a concert film, was released in December.

Although the demand for Roses product remained high, the media's interest in Madchester had cooled. The Happy Mondays provided the movement's final hurrah, with their own Spike Island moment, headlining a massive gig at Leeds United football ground in the summer of 1991. It was the band's last significant perform-ance before disbanding. In Manchester, gang violence, gun crime, and even ram raids on clubs, became national news. The Haçienda had reopened with gun detectors on the door. Factory Records was on the verge of collapse. A new musical phenomenon called 'grunge' and a new city, Seattle, stole the limelight. Nirvana were signed to Geffen by the Roses' A&R man Gary Gersh in December 1990, and the band's album *Nevermind*, released in September 1991, exploded worldwide, on its way to selling 30 million copies.

In January 1992, under the headline 'Roses' Muse Dying on the Vine', the *NME* reported there would be no new album until the end of the year. A source claimed the court case had blunted their creative edge and that new songs, written by Squire, had been rejected by the rest of the band. 'Summit meetings' between Evans and Geffen were planned to iron out strategies. Gersh was now fully aware of the difficulties that lay ahead. 'I could tell it wasn't going well,' he said. In February 1992 Evans was officially dismissed as the Roses' manager. He would claim unfair dismissal, but it would not be until 1995 that this case would come before the High Court. 'I want £1 million,' he said. 'The Stone Roses have a five-album deal with Geffen. If they are successful, it could net them anything up to £50 million. I simply want monies that are owed for the part I played in thrashing out the deal. Right from the start I was out hustling and bustling every day for them.' With no records or gigs to promote, the Roses remained silent.

14

Second Coming

It was almost a year since they had signed with Geffen, and over two years since they had recorded 'One Love', when the Roses finally started to record a new album. They were free of Evans and Jive/Zomba but, in the process of achieving this, had lost the momentum that had propelled their rise to the top.

The Rolling Stones Mobile had been one of the twelve studio ideas John Leckie had mooted when he had planned on recording this album in the summer of 1990. Now he tried to talk them out of the idea, suggesting more traditional studios in New York or Paris. The Rolling Stones Mobile was essentially a studio built in the back of a van. It had an impressive pedigree: the Stones had used it to record *Sticky Fingers* and *Exile on Main St.*, and Led Zeppelin for *Led Zeppelin III*, *Led Zeppelin IV*, *Houses of the Holy* and *Physical Graffiti*. Bob Marley and Deep Purple had also cut albums with the mobile unit.

Bowing to the band's request, Leckie hired the Stones Mobile and parked it outside the secluded Old Brewery in Ewloe, Wales, where Leckie, the engineer, the band, and tour manager Steve Adge, would all live during this first four weeks of recording, beginning on 25 March 1992 and continuing until 22 April. The Old Brewery was on a hill next to Wepre Park, where the ruins of the historic Ewloe Castle stood. The Old Brewery was now run as a bed and breakfast by Sandy Finlay, and the Roses would record in the cellars underneath the main house where there was a natural echo. The main benefit was seclusion: Evans had threatened to burn down any studio he found the Roses using.

Finlay was delighted to have a solid booking for a month and tried his best to accommodate the band. 'He said he used to be a chef but the food was terrible and it was always late,' said Leckie. 'Anything you didn't eat the night before came back at you the next day with a layer of mash and melted cheese on it,' said Mani, who admitted that following the death of his father he was in no fit shape to record. 'My head was totally done in; a million miles away from where it should've been.'

Unlike the first album they'd recorded with Leckie, when they had all the songs virtually nailed down, for this new album the band only had three songs so far, all solo efforts by Squire, and they intended to use the time at Ewloe to conjure more. Brown was keen for the band to continue in a more groove-orientated direction. Squire had spent the better part of a year hooked on Public Enemy's classic 1990 album *Fear of a Black Planet*. He had leaned on Simon Crompton, who made acid house records under the name Vanilla Sound Corps, to help him get to grips with sampling and sequencing. But now the idea of deconstructing and reassembling music in the vein of Public Enemy had lost its appeal. 'Too much like a science lesson,' he said.

The songs he brought to Ewloe ⌐ 'Ten Storey Love Song', 'Breaking into Heaven' and 'Driving South' – bore that out. Squire had gone back to guitar music 'in any form that it came', he said. 'No matter what the trousers and haircuts were like.' Brown was now almost exclusively listening to rap music, while Reni kept a foot in both camps. 'Reni wasn't an elitist in any way with regards to what he would listen to,' Squire said. Lyrically these Squire solo compositions appeared to be playful and optimistic. 'Breaking into Heaven' seemed to take a sly dig at their new label-mates Guns N' Roses, a band Brown had aggressively dismissed. 'Driving South' reanimated the age-old theme of selling your soul to the devil in exchange for musical prowess, as first explored on 'I Wanna Be Adored'. It featured the lyrics 'Well you're not too young or pretty and you sure as hell can't sing, any time you want to sell your soul, I've got a toll-free number you can ring.'

The band's routine was to work through the night, retire to bed around eight or nine in the morning and start recording again around three or four in the afternoon. Leckie acknowledged that the Squire songs – apart from 'Ten Storey Love Song', which he called a 'traditional Roses song' – were radically different from the band's previous material, but the recording of them went well. 'My version of "Breaking into Heaven" was probably "Fools Gold" and "One Love" revisited,' he said. 'It was done to the same drum loop, anyway.' Brown thought the song sounded good but recalled it being written over an Eric B. & Rakim beat. One thing all could agree on was that Reni was ready to roll. 'When we started recording we had Reni playing the drums for 40 minutes and it was out of this world,' Brown said. 'I remember John Leckie turning around with a big beam on his face and saying, Can't this be the album?'

'Reni was always thinking of new ways of adding to the songs,' said Leckie. 'And it took very little time to do his drums. He'd bought lots of Tibetan cymbals and he used a lot of them on the "Breaking into Heaven" intro.' Leckie had hired engineer Brian Pugsley, fresh from working with experimental dance outfit The Shamen, to give the group scope to explore sampling, drum machines and loops. As well as Public Enemy, the band were in thrall to Barry Adamson's 1988 album *Moss Side Story*, particularly the track 'Man with the Golden Arm'. It had a dense, rich sound, which the band sought to mine. 'The atmosphere was quite experimental,' said Pugsley. 'We had fun with loops and various weird samples. Most of the loops came from Reni's playing, with maybe a few off vinyl. The band hadn't played live for a while and there were all kinds of very distracting stuff going on in their private lives. I think they wanted the space to experiment and see what came up.'

Out of this process came the album's most radical track, 'Begging You', the only song on the album to be credited to Brown/Squire, and one that sounded like the perfect solution for a band searching for a musical direction. It was original and powerful, more danceable than Squire's solo compositions. As Pugsley remembers it, 'We did not see very much of John Squire in the mobile. He was mostly writing in his room while the band worked on the tracks we had to go on.'

The Roses worked hard and the mood at Ewloe was upbeat. The band relaxed playing games of Jenga, and Finlay gave them archery lessons. They also explored their remote surroundings and found a small outhouse on the property which was lived in by Geoff Dwight, half-brother of Elton John, and a prodigious cannabis smoker. 'Ian and the band used to talk to him,' said Leckie. 'He hand-made acoustic guitars and mandolins.' The Roses used some of Dwight's instruments while indulging in late-night recording fun, jamming with a piano, violin and mandolin on a tune that would surface as a secret track on *Second Coming*.

Beside Public Enemy and Barry Adamson, the band's listening also included Led Zeppelin, who had recorded the bulk of their 1970s material with the Stones Mobile unit. There were screenings of Led Zeppelin's *The Song Remains the Same*, and talk of Reni's love for the album *Led Zeppelin IV*, and of the Roses creating monster riffs to match Led Zeppelin – as Squire was attempting on 'Driving South'. There was even talk of Peter Grant, Led Zeppelin's infamous manager, being approached to replace Evans. Grant was said to have replied, 'How wide do you want the flares to be?'

Brown was deeply suspect of this fixation: 'I'm watching them watching Led Zeppelin and thinking, You're all over these guys. They've not got that funk. They've not got what we've got. I thought, Don't they realize where we are in history, who loves us? We were better and bigger than Led Zeppelin. We weren't trying to be them old blues guys. I felt I was the only member of the band who knew how great we were, how much we meant to people. It was stupid sitting around worshipping lesser bands, really stupid.'

To complete the album a second session with the Stones Mobile unit was booked at Ewloe to begin in July. The band had planned to record 'Where Angels Play' on the album but had been forced to abandon the idea as Zomba continued to plunder the Roses' back catalogue, including a rough demo of the track on a compilation album of A- and B-sides, *Turns into Stone*. Already in March 1992 Zomba had released 'I Am the Resurrection' as a single that peaked at number 33 in the UK charts and re-released 'Fools Gold', which reached number 73. *Turns into Stone* was out in July and peaked at number 32. Zomba also released a singles box set, and even issued

'So Young', the band's 1985 debut single, on CD. This release prompted Brown and Steve Adge to visit Strawberry Studios and buy back the album they had recorded there the same year with Martin Hannett, intending to prevent its release.

When they reconvened at Ewloe in July, no new songs had been written in the two-month break. Leckie felt the band was missing the guiding hand of a manager: 'Everything had fragmented. It was chaotic disorder.' Squire often played guitar by himself to a click track or a drum machine. 'Then it was endless overdubs,' said Leckie. 'John would go back to his room. Reni might go home to his kid. Mani would get stoned and go to the pub. Ian would hang about. John would say, Is this going to be the demo? And I'd say, No, it's not – it's the real thing.' With money no object, and no new songs to work on, the Roses picked apart the already recorded material.

Leckie called Gersh at Geffen. 'I told him, We've been here for three weeks and haven't done anything. He'd say, Don't worry, John, just carry on, let them be, how's everything, how's your wife? And change the subject.' The session ended on a down when Evans showed up at the Old Brewery. 'We were in the kitchen having some cornflakes, eight o'clock in the morning, and this car draws up through the farmyard and parks up over the back,' said Leckie. 'Everyone ducked and peeked though the curtains.' Evans, and another man, sat outside in the car for a while and then drove off. 'The next thing Steve Adge turned up with this security guy, a big tough army type, and he lived with us there for the next four or five days – and then we left. That was the end of Ewloe.'

The band were not looking for any input from Geffen, but Gersh was unconvinced by the Roses' efforts. 'They were the very rough beginning of something that sounded like a band in the process of making a record,' he said. 'I believe a fear had crept in. I've never really asked John [Squire] that question, but I believe that's what happened and in some way, somehow, somebody became paralysed. That is the worst place to try and make a great record from.'

Gersh, like Leckie, felt the band needed management and advised them to meet with Peter Mensch and Cliff Burnstein, who managed Metallica, Def Leppard and Shania Twain. 'They kept saying they wanted a manager but there was no real attempt to get one,' Gersh said. Brown would later admit the band's lack of a manager meant 'we had no one to get us in line . . . It was just four chiefs and no Indians.'

Squire admitted the band made a 'big mistake' by sticking to the idea that the album had to be done before they did anything else. 'We should have written a bit, recorded a bit, toured a bit, and I think the record would've come out a lot sooner. We were guilty of saying, Let's sort everything out and then carry on. We lost momentum.' Post-Ewloe, Squire became more insular, said Brown. 'He cut himself off. I carried on writing my own things but he refused to work on anyone else's stuff.' Squire was having personal problems, as he dealt with being a new father and his long-term relationship with his partner Helen broke down.

He fed some of the pain and realism of his life into new songs, and the Roses began looking for a place to rehearse and record them. Just before Christmas 1992 they chose Square One studios in Bury, a small market town only eight miles north of Manchester. It was an unglamorous location but an impressive and expensive studio. Previous clients had included Take That, Ronnie Wood and Keith Richards, and Public Enemy's Chuck D. The studio was experiencing financial problems and there was talk of the Roses buying it off owner Trevor Taylor, with a view to running it as their own personal rehearsal and recording space. The band called Leckie in the New Year to tell him they'd booked the studio for a year. He had worked at Square One with The Fall, visited in February and agreed to return to the studio in June to continue recording the second album.

It would mean a break of almost a year between the end of the Ewloe sessions and his recommencement of the album. According to Leckie, there was an array of factors behind this faltering progress: 'The new songs weren't ready. People were ill. Reni would go on holiday. Ian's girlfriend was having a baby. John wanted more time to write songs.' Before Leckie returned in the summer, the band began rehearsing at Square One. Studio owner Trevor Taylor said the band seemed unsure of themselves and expressed strong anti-Geffen sentiment. It was now coming up to two years since Geffen had signed the band, and President Eddie Rosenblatt was growing increasingly impatient. 'I imagine I was less polite to Gary Gersh, saying, What the hell is going on here?' Gersh, the Roses' champion, flush from the success of Nirvana, was now on his way out of Geffen – having accepted an offer to become the president of Capitol. Rosenblatt handed Gersh's A&R role with the Roses to another major Geffen A&R figure, Tom Zutaut. If Gersh was on the Sonic Youth–Nirvana axis, Zutaut was firmly in the Guns N' Roses camp.

Geffen scheduled the Roses album for release in autumn 1993. Rosenblatt's only point of contact with the band was John Kennedy, who was equally keen for the band to record. He had already told the band that they needed to make two albums for Geffen before the deal started to make real financial sense. The Roses had incurred costs on the Jive/Zomba court case. 'I made that clear at the time to the band,' he said. 'This is all about getting to album two, and then you've got one of the best deals in record company history. They were so laid-back about that. They'd had some sessions in the studio that were expensive and not productive, and I was telling them to get on with it.'

In Square One, the band worked up the backing tracks of four new Squire songs: 'Love Spreads', 'Severed Head' (which would become 'How Do You Sleep'), 'Tears' and 'Tightrope'. While they did this, Brown spent time hanging out with studio owner Taylor. 'What I liked about him was he had this Salford boy image, bit of a bad boy, but he wasn't,' said Taylor. 'He was sound as a pound.' One night the two were heading back from the pub and came across a guy lying in the gutter. Taylor told Brown it was the local drunk. 'This guy wore the most ridiculous toupee you'd ever seen and, as he'd fallen over into the gutter, his toupee had slipped off and he'd

30. Dennis Morris's studio, 1989 (*from left*: Mani, Brown, Squire, Reni).

'They looked like they had been around for twenty years. A good word for it was effortless. You know why? There probably was no effort. If they were planning that look, I'd be amazed – because that's how they woke up' Anthony Donnelly, Gio-Goi

31. Dennis Morris's studio, 1989 (*from left:* Reni, Squire, Mani, Brown).

A scheduled September 1989 single, 'Any Time You Want Me', was abandoned, despite Geoff Wonfor being hired to film a video for the track at Blackpool Empress Ballroom.

MODERN ENTERPRISES
ARTIST AND EVENTS MANAGEMENT
90 PINE ST. SUITE 701
SEATTLE, WA 98101
TEL. 206-467-8656
FAX 206-467-6937

TO: ANDREW LAUDER
℅ SILVERTONE RECORDS

FROM: JOHN LECKIE USA

RE: STONE ROSES RECORDING
L.P. SUMMER 1990

AS REQUESTED I PUT FORWARD THE
FOLLOWING SUGGESTIONS IN NO ORDER OF PREFERENCE AND PENDING DISCUSSION
WITH THE BAND:

1) STUDIO MIRAVAL — SOUTH OF FRANCE — (JACQUES LOUISIER'S PLACE) NO NUMBER

2) THE MANOR — OXFORD — 08675 - 77551

3) PARIS — STUDIO PLUS TRENTE — 1 - 4202 - 2102
   OR STUDIO DAVOUT — NO NUMBER
   OR STUDIO DAVOLI — NO NUMBER

   STAY AT REGYN'S HOTEL, MONTMARTRE (PHONE MY HOME (435-2932) FOR NO.

4) TOPANGA SKYLINE — MALIBU, CA. USA. 213 - 455 - 2044 (JOHN EDEN)
   INDIGO RANCH — MALIBU 213 - 456 - 9277 (MICHEAL HOFFMAN)

5) ABBEY ROAD — STUDIO THREE + NEW APARTMENTS — 286 116 (

6) ICP — BRUSSELLS — ACCOMADATION INCLUDED 01032-2-6492206 (JOHN HASTRY)

7) BATTERY N.Y.C. — USA.

8) DUBLIN — WINDMILL LANE — DUBLIN 772008

9) ROLLING STONES MOBILE + RECORDING PREMISES / ACCOMADATION 0753 656337
   0753 653482
   (MICK MCKENNA)

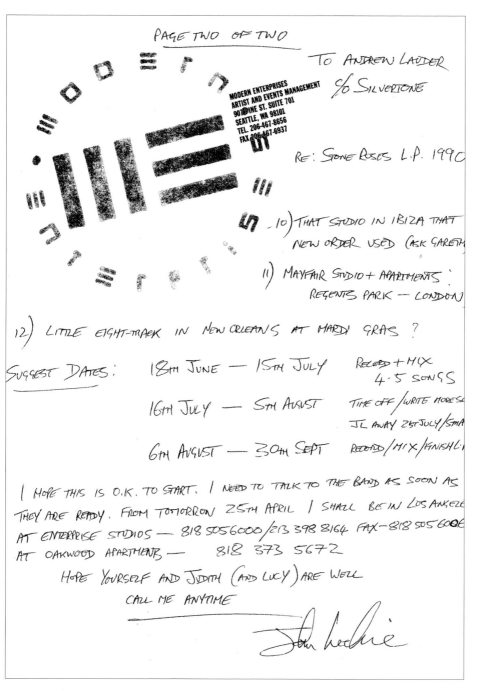

TO ANDREW LAUDER
℅ SILVERTONE

MODERN ENTERPRISES
ARTIST AND EVENTS MANAGEMENT
907 PINE ST. SUITE 701
SEATTLE, WA 98101
TEL. 206-467-8656
FAX 206-467-6937

RE: STONE ROSES L.P. 1990

10) THAT STUDIO IN IBIZA THAT
NEW ORDER USED (ASK GARETH

11) MAYFAIR STUDIO + APARTMENTS:
REGENTS PARK — LONDON

12) LITTLE EIGHT-TRACK IN NEW ORLEANS AT MARDI GRAS?

SUGGEST DATES:

18TH JUNE — 15TH JULY   RECORD + MIX
                          4·5 SONGS

16TH JULY — 5TH AUGUST   TIME OFF / WRITE MORE S
                          JL AWAY 25TH JULY / SMA

6TH AUGUST — 30TH SEPT   RECORD / MIX / FINISH L

I HOPE THIS IS O.K. TO START. I NEED TO TALK TO THE BAND AS SOON AS
THEY ARE READY. FROM TOMORROW 25TH APRIL I SHALL BE IN LOS ANGELE
AT ENTERPRISE STUDIOS — 818 506 6000 / 213 398 8164 FAX - 818 505 600E
AT OAKWOOD APARTMENT — 818 373 5672
HOPE YOURSELF AND JUDITH (AND LUCY) ARE WELL
CALL ME ANYTIME

John Leckie

32. and 33. Fax sent from Los Angeles by John Leckie, outlining studio suggestions
for recording the Roses' second album in the summer of 1990.

'I sat and scribbled it out because I urgently wanted to do it. One of the
suggestions was The Rolling Stones' Mobile and recording premises with
accommodation, and that's what we ended up with. But we didn't start
the album for another two years' John Leckie

34. Fans at Spike Island, 1990.

'There were just gangs of indie kids en masse buying up a totally different wardrobe, a different record collection and a totally different lifestyle' Dave Haslam

35. The band's dressing room, Spike Island, 1990.

'It was chaos but really beautiful chaos, rock 'n' roll chaos, totally out there' Geoff Wonfor

36. Crowd shot from the stage at Spike Island, with the River Mersey in the background, 1990.

'The Roses took the energy of who and what they were and managed to get that on to record – so you had a sense when you listened to their tunes that you felt you knew them' Lawrence Stewart

37. On stage, Spike Island, 1990 (Squire, Brown).

'Once Geffen were involved Johnny kicked up an extra gear. He knew that the Roses on Geffen could be as big as The Eagles – they could be the Fleetwood Mac of the next generation' Howard Jones

38. On stage, Spike Island, 1990 (Brown).

'The Stone Roses' attitude was "don't fuck with us", and everybody said, Okay, that's cool. Can't wait to see what they're going to do next' Bruce Flohr

39. On stage, Spike Island, 1990 (Brown).

'The most important thing culturally about the Roses was this charismatic front man who had a way of walking on stage, that whole Mancunian street stance. Every fucker started walking like that' Bruce Mitchell

40. On stage, Glasgow Green, 1990 (Squire).

'John was an incredibly visual, literate guy. The Roses had an intellectual bent and they played with that. Are we really very clever? Work it out for yourself' Keith Jobling

41. On stage, Glasgow Green, 1990 (Reni).

Reni was said to have recorded *Second Coming* on the same kit as he did the band's 1989 eponymous album – without even changing the skins.

42. On stage, Spike Island, 1990 (Brown).

'We focused everyone on the Roses in America: all the trendy, cool people in RCA would get the *NME* every week, and would see this band The Stones Roses, and think this is the new The Clash' Steven Howard

43. Glasgow Green, 1990.

'We talked a lot about how different the band was to other bands – they were playing in tents and fields. From the minute I heard "I Wanna Be Adored" I was not going to take no for an answer' Gary Gersh

44. On stage, Glasgow Green, 1990 (*from left:* Cressa, Brown, Reni).

'He knows how to ride a rhythm, that's the beauty of Ian' Dennis Morris

45. Stairwell, Dennis Morris's studio, 1994 (*from left*: Reni, Mani, Squire, Brown).

'It was almost like a comedy show. They were almost like a cartoon band then.
No one knew what they were like because no one saw them, so we all used to
imagine what they were getting up to' Jon Brookes, The Charlatans

The Stone Roses

Sessions

25th March - 22nd April 1992   Ewloe
6th July - 13th August 1992   Ewloe
1st June - 30th June 1993   Bury Marple
27th July 1993   Rockfield

Songs

1. *"Breaking Into Heaven"*
2. *"Drivin' South"*
3. *"Beggin' You"*
4. *"Ten Storey Love Song"*
5. *"Love Spreads"*
6. *"Tightrope"*
7. *"Severed Head"*
8. *"Tears"*

1. *"Breaking Into Heaven"*: 10.00

The Song starts with a 4:30 collage of sound FX, wild electric guitar and assorted percussion broken up by bursts of heavy drum loop. The song was unfinished when I left although the bass, vocal, main guitar, piano and all the effects, the introduction and arrangement were excellent and quote useable.
Ewloe 1st Sessions

Track Sheet

1. Bird FX	13. Congas
2. Bird FX (2)	14. Drum Loop
3. Crickets FX	15. Drum Loop (2) Heavy
4. Jungles FX	16. Bass
5. Zulu Warriors	17. Drums
6. Drone (1)	18. Drums double track
7. Drone (2)	19. Guitar (1)
8. Gtr Echoplex (1)	20. Guitar (2)
9. Gtr Echoplex (2)	21. Vocal
10. Gtr Echoplex (3) high	22. Vocal double track
11. Percussion (1)	23. Piano
12. Percussion (2)	

Slave reel made at Parr Street Studios - 21st June 1993

2. *"Drivin' South"*: 4:45

The song was recorded at Ewloe 1st sessions and later attempted at **Marple** as a live track in a different key. The guitar track from Marple was useable and the whole of the Ewloe was good but needed new drums and more guitar.

cont/...2

Track Sheet

1. Drum Loop	8. Gtr Zoom (1)
2. Synth (1)	9. Gtr (2)
3. Synth (2)	10. Gtr (3)
4. Bass	11. Vocal
5. Drums	12. Vocal d/t
6. Tamborine	13. Vocal (John)
7. Shakers	

Slave reel done at Parr Street - June 1993

3. *"Beggin' You"*: 4:30

This was an experimental track made by arranging and looping a number of samples from records suggested by the band. Some loops were also made from live drums and heavy treated guitar. This was done at Ewloe with Brian Pugsley and some vocals were later attempted at Marple.

Track Sheet

1. Loop (1)	5. Drums
2. Loop (2)	6. Guitar
3. Loop (3)	7. Vocal
4. Loop (4)	

The track needed finishing although the basic idea and arrangement was there. All programmed.

4. *"Ten Storey Love Song"*: 4:15

The basic track is useable but more work was needed to bring it up to scratch. This song was recorded at Ewloe (2)

Track Sheet

1. E. Bow Guitars	6. Drums
2. Guitar (1)	7. Drum Loop
3. Guitar (2)	8. Lead Guitar
4. Guitar (3)	9. Vocals
5. Bass	10. Vocals d/t

Slave was done at Ewloe

5. *"Love Spreads"*

6. *"Tightrope"*

7. *"Severed Head"*

8. *"Tears"*

These songs were attempted at Marple and Rockfield with a basic line up of guitar, bass and drums and guide vocals. Some percussion was overdubbed on tracks 5, 6 and 7 and various versions were recorded of each song. I don't think anything was useable although arrangements on most songs were OK.

46. and 47. Upon resigning from *Second Coming* in 1993, John Leckie was asked to list exactly what he'd done on the record to date.

'It all just fizzled out. I really didn't want to pursue it. I was happy and relieved to leave' John Leckie

48. Dennis Morris's studio, 1994 (Brown).

'I think they were afraid of America in terms of not getting the recognition they had in England. I don't think their egos could handle it'
Greg Lewerke

49. Dennis Morris's studio, 1994 (Mani).

'Our personal taste is a hundred per cent of the law. You can't try to fit into a certain trend, like a lot of bands in England do. That's bollocks, man. Then you're just a fashion accessory, aren't you? We do it for ourselves'
Mani, *Entertainment Weekly*, March 1995

50. Dennis Morris's studio, 1994 (Squire).

'John was one of those people who might not say a lot but when they do say something it's either incredibly funny or really vicious – but vicious with a smile. He's just letting you know you're being a wanker' Paul Schroeder

51. Dennis Morris's studio, 1994 (Reni).

'Reni is such a tremendous drummer, tremendous natural musician, I don't think there was much chance of loops sounding better than he did' Brian Pugsley

52. Dennis Morris's studio, 1994 (*from left:* Reni, Brown, Squire, Mani).
'I think the four members of the band, at the time, meant it was greater than the sum of its parts' John Squire, *NME*, April 1996

puked up inside the toupee,' said Taylor. 'Ian goes, Right, where does he live? I said, He lives just over there. So Ian said, Look in his pocket and see if his keys are in there. When we went to sit him up it was obvious he'd filled his pants as well. It was disgusting. I'm the type that would have walked on the other side of the street, but Ian insisted we carry this guy and put him in his house so he was safe.'

Squire had written the music and the lyrics for all the new tracks. 'He took my fun off me there,' said Brown. 'My fun was doing the lyrics and the melody.' But Brown figured that Squire had got 'a bee in his bonnet' and just needed to get it out. The Roses would make more albums for Geffen, Brown thought, so he would just let Squire get on with it and back him up on this one. And the lyrics were good. 'Love Spreads' controversially envisaged Christ as a black woman (Squire having been inspired by Rosalind Miles's book *The Women's History of the World* (1988), an elegy for the lost utopia that existed before patriarchy). 'Severed Head' was harder to decipher. It was easy to claim it was about former manager Evans, but Squire said it was aimed at 'the people who make decisions that are guaranteed to cost lives, like sending troops into battle'. 'Tears' and 'Tightrope', however, were deeply personal, dark and painful songs, and, said Squire, 'maybe that was something that Ian had a problem with'. Yet even when Squire's control of the songs extended to his writing the bass lines for Mani, as he had done for Pete Garner, there was no apparent grudge towards Squire from the band. 'John was being the prolific one, coming out with some great songs, so we let him get on with it,' said Mani.

The news that the Roses were recording in Square One quickly leaked, resulting in the band appearing on the front cover of the *NME* on 29 May 1993, under the headline 'Gotcha! The Stone Roses hunted down'. The piece relied on a snatched photograph of Brown that appeared on the cover. The band refused to talk: Brown told the *NME* it was 'too soon' and to come back in a few months when the album was finished.

On 1 June, Leckie arrived at Square One, expecting that the band had got the fresh material required and they would nail the album before he left at the end of June. He and the band would live together while recording, in a rented house in Marple, Cheshire, at least an hour's drive from the studio. The house 'was a loafer's paradise', said Mani. It had electronic gates, a snooker room, indoor pool, a sauna and jacuzzi. The band caused £7,000 worth of damage, it would later be claimed.

Square One was expensive and booked twenty-four hours a day. The band would rise around three in the afternoon, drive through the rush hour to Bury, organize food, and were ready to record around nine or ten o'clock at night. 'Then about three in the morning everyone would be a bit bored and want to go back to the house to go in the swimming pool, and stay up until eight o'clock,' Leckie said. 'Sometimes they'd turn up at the studio, have something to eat, chill out, strum a bit on the guitar and go home,' said Taylor. The air-conditioning in Square One was faulty or non-existent, and the studio was unbearably stuffy. 'Leckie wasn't happy with anything. I'd had him in before and he seemed quite a laid-back character, happy, but with the Roses there was a lot of trauma going on. John [Squire] wanted more say over what was going to tape. Leckie was a respected producer but it wasn't working – it was just a bad gel.'

After only a few days at Square One Leckie suggested they spend the rest of the month recording in the house in Marple. He had hired equipment from London, including the tape recorder and mixing desk, and it was transferred to the house. Reni was set up in the back room and they cut lacklustre versions of 'Love Spreads', 'Severed Head', 'Tears' and 'Tightrope' in Marple. They also re-recorded 'Driving South' in a different key. Squire's original version required Brown to sing high, like Led Zeppelin's Robert Plant, and Brown had refused. 'There was not much screaming or fisticuffs,' said Leckie. 'Sometimes, in terms of the music, or not getting a part right, but it was very rare. They always seemed to be mates. But they were in a rudderless ship, and just seemed to be drifting. The raw material they presented to me had no clear direction.'

By 30 June, with nothing really achieved, Leckie left Marple for New York. 'I'd exhausted all my suggestions,' he said. 'Although they'd spent all this time rehearsing the songs, I said they needed to do some demos as the band, without me, without my influence. I just said, Give me some demos of the songs.' They were due to reconvene at Rockfield Studios in Wales on 27 July, to complete the album. This time the Roses followed Leckie's advice, and booked into Manor Park Studios, in Tintwistle in the High Peak, to record demos. The band remained in the shared house in Marple, determined to nail down the eight songs they already had and to add more.

Manor Park Studios was based in a former working men's club, now operating as both a private club and studio. The live recording area was the club's main room, with a small foot-high stage and stinking of cigarettes and beer. The studio was £15 an hour and mostly used by indie bands hoping to get a demo done quickly and cheaply. It was not the sort of place you expected The Stone Roses to turn up.

The Roses worked with in-house producer, Mark Tolle. He was assisted by Al 'Bongo' Shaw, who wasn't a qualified engineer but knew where to get weed. The Roses had booked the studio initially for just a few days, but appreciated the relaxed atmosphere and spent three weeks recording there. The band worked long days, and Tolle was struck by both how the material echoed Led Zeppelin and their impressive work ethic. 'They'd try a middle bit for a song ten different ways for four or five hours, until they got what they wanted,' he said. 'John was in control but Ian wasn't sat on the sidelines or anything. There wasn't a whole lot of banter going on. It was pretty serious.' Squire bossed the sessions, and was protective of the master tapes, taking them away with him every night after they finished. He also asked Tolle to dissuade outsiders from coming in while the band were there. The band played as if live in the studio cum club, and finally seemed to have turned a corner.

'Daybreak', the only Roses song ever credited to all four members, was started here as an improvised instrumental jam. It was more the direction that Brown imagined the band going in, capturing the funk he knew the band had in them. It was also a powerful reminder of Squire and Reni's musical rapport, forged now over nine long years. There was a playful spirit to the song, as the two fought one another for the same space. Footage from these sessions was captured by Squire on a Super-8 camera, and would be used in the video for 'Love Spreads'. Squire and Reni were captured walking down the street towards the studio, both looking like heavy rock gods: Reni with a beard and mirror shades, and John, tall with his hair immaculately scruffy. They oozed a supreme confidence, and that's what 'Daybreak' sounded like.

Tolle and Al 'Bongo' Shaw were credited with the initial recordings of 'Daybreak', 'Tightrope' and 'Tears' on *Second Coming*. 'They didn't have to do that,' said Tolle, but it was a mark of how much the band had enjoyed their time in this obscure backwater club. The demos were sent to Leckie, but as usual the band cut it fine. 'I got the demos on the Saturday morning, and we were due in Rockfield the following Tuesday,' he said. On Monday he was in Rockfield, listening to the demos, waiting for the band, and on the Tuesday he resigned. 'When it came time for the proper recording Leckie said he didn't think we had the songs,' said Brown. 'We'd given him three of the best tracks on the album. I thought "Daybreak" was fantastic as it was. All the songs were in shape. He told us we weren't ready to record but we knew we were.'

The Roses were booked in for an initial period of two weeks. In fact, they would spend the next fourteen months, from July 1993 until September 1994, at Rockfield at the cost of approximately a quarter of a million pounds and their own sanity. Nine of the tracks on the album were already in shape: 'Tightrope', 'Tears', 'Breaking into Heaven', 'Driving South', 'Ten Storey Love Song', 'How Do You Sleep', 'Daybreak', 'Love Spreads' and 'Begging You'. 'I thought we would go in the studio and just bang it out in a month,' said Brown.

Based just outside the village of Monmouth, Rockfield Studios was where they had recorded parts of their first album. It was in a converted farmhouse, with the Roses in the Coach House studio where someone had scrawled a drawing of the devil on the door. The Roses called on Paul Schroeder, the dance engineer/producer they had worked closely with on their 1989 album and 'Fools Gold', to replace Leckie. 'I listened to the songs, the demos,' said Schroeder. 'I thought it was a good protest record, almost in a Dylan style.' 'Daybreak' name-checked Rosa Lee Parks, who'd helped galvanize the American civil rights movement in the Montgomery bus boycott. Brown played Schroeder a vinyl recording of a stirring Martin Luther King address in the studio. But he could tell it wasn't a happy camp. 'They were feeling the pressure. It was obvious that John had written pretty much everything, and the other three members were almost not a part of it. They were there for John, obviously, but because they hadn't done it themselves, it was difficult for them to put everything into it.'

There were signs, though, that the Roses were readying themselves for action, having decided on a new manager, their PR man Philip Hall. As well as running the industry's leading independent PR company, Hall Or Nothing, Hall was also now managing The Manic Street Preachers. While their lawyer, Kennedy, continued to look after the Roses' business, and had been running their affairs for the past three years, he had hundreds of other clients to consider. Hall would provide ideas, plus the good humour and common sense the band had been missing.

In the studio Schroeder quickly disabused the band of the idea that they had to record everything from scratch. 'We had a chat and they asked me if I wanted to redo "Tightrope",' he said. 'They'd done that, just fucking about [at Manor Park Studios] and it sounded great. There'd be no point in redoing it because it had that feeling of exactly what the record needed. We could have done a studio version and it would have come out like "Stairway to Heaven" or something. Why do that when you've got this fantastic backing track?' As early as September 1993, Schroeder had the basis of the record, the drums and bass, down on tape. The vocals couldn't go down until Squire had finished his guitar parts. 'We had all the rhythm tracks done so we were waiting for John to come out of his room and do it. It took a month and a half, two months, so we weren't doing anything.'

In this period, frustration, boredom – and drug use – grew exponentially. Brown even quit the group but was persuaded to stay. 'I kept on suggesting, Let's just go home,' said Schroeder. 'When they had the guitar parts we could resume. But John always said, If we leave, we won't come back. John knew that if he didn't pull something amazing out of the bag then the album would fall flat, so he was very probably scared of what he could put on the record and what he couldn't and, maybe, that's why he got into his coke. Nothing makes you feel good like good cocaine.'

The increasingly insecure Squire had started to use cocaine to bolster his confidence, and to give him the energy required for the long hours he spent concentrating on improving his guitar parts and the songs, but now he was addicted. With his personal life in chaos, Squire retreated to his room at Rockfield and locked the door, lost in his own private world. Reni tried to reach him, but Squire wouldn't let anyone in. 'Charlie [cocaine] is the devil, simple as that,' said Brown. When Squire did periodically emerge from his room, his drug-induced delusions and paranoia could translate into arrogance – alienating his band and destroying any sense of camaraderie – and even megalomania. He discussed the idea of sacking an under-performing Mani, who was self-medicating for depression caused by the death of his father. 'I'd go away for a week, come back and no one's talking,' said Brown. 'He's not talking to him – he thinks he's a dick and he thinks he's a dick, and I'm trying to be the daddy of them all. I'm walking in each room and getting big hugs, but he won't work with him.'

Cocaine was not the only drug problem in the band. As Brown, Mani, Reni and Schroeder waited for Squire to finalize his guitar parts, a heavy fug of cannabis hung over the studio, the weeks turning into months with nothing much else to do. Reni was now a father of three, and often excused himself to attend to his family in Manchester. In the studio Brown was smoking weed 'all day and all night'. It often became difficult to understand what he was saying. Cannabis turned his head to 'mush', he admitted. 'You get a false idea of what you're doing. You get hyper-critical and you never get to the end of it.'

15.

Reni II

Even at their weakest, the Roses remained a formidable beast. One of the highlights for Schroeder was a new song that emerged from Squire's bedroom, called 'Good Times'. Again, with Reni and Squire fighting each other for supremacy, the track had a real potency, a great feel, and a lyric that Brown delivered at the very limit of his comfort zone. Brown had taken Schroeder aside to say he wanted to do all the vocals in one take, and as a result the effect was noticeably different from the honeyed sound on the band's 1989 album.

'On the first album there's a lot of drop-ins, his voice is triple-tracked, a lot of jiggery-pokery,' said Schroeder. For *Second Coming* Schroeder, who was unsure that Brown could pull it off, attempted to double-track his voice while recording live by simultaneously putting it through a guitar amp. Ultimately these effects would be dropped, and hearing Brown sing with no trickery, laid bare and often sounding uncomfortable would give a purity and emotional impact to many of the tracks.

If Squire's lyrics were at times overwhelmingly dark, personal and laboured, then Brown's delivery suggested there was more to them. In exquisitely expressing his own disquiet, it took *Second Coming* to levels their 1989 album could never touch. It was a truly remarkable performance: 'Good Times' Brown disliked, as he did 'How Do You Sleep', but on 'Tears' you got down to the bone. ' "Tears" was a difficult song to sing, that's for sure,' said Schroeder. 'Even if you're an accomplished singer it would be difficult. And it was out of Ian's key. I quite liked the band taking it on because it's almost like a ballad.'

'Ian said to John, You'd have to wake me up, put a gun against my head and walk me down to the vocal booth for me to sing that again,' said Mani. 'He didn't like the song, and we didn't have a gun.'

Geffen A&R man Tom Zutaut visited Rockfield to check on the label's investment. Zutaut had handled A&R for Guns N' Roses since their 28-million-selling breakthrough album *Appetite for Destruction* in 1987. That group had a famously volatile inter-band dynamic, with rampant ego and drug problems. For Zutaut the unrest within the Roses would barely register. He was a Los Angeles classic rock man with long blond hair and deep knowledge of 1960s and 1970s guitar music. The Roses were cautious of his presence but he seemed to score with Squire over a shared appreciation of blues acts that had influenced the likes of Led Zeppelin, the Stones and Neil Young, particularly Mississippi Fred McDowell. Zutaut confidently announced to the press that The Stone Roses' album would be released in spring 1994 and that a single, 'Love Spreads', was being considered for a Valentine's Day release.

'The new guitar-orientated direction of The Stone Roses will establish them on a higher international level,' said Zutaut. 'It is a sign of one of the world's great rock bands reaching maturity.' His approach to the record did not chime with the 'dry, funky, Stevie Wonder sound' Schroeder was attempting to exert on *Second Coming*. 'Zutaut didn't want me there,' said Schroeder. 'I got the impression he was trying to get the band to work with someone else. The American company wanted some big record producer.'

In December 1993, genuine tragedy struck the Roses when their new manager Philip Hall, who had been receiving treatment for cancer, lost his life to the disease. 'That really took the wind out of everyone's sails,' said Schroeder. The Roses would dedicate *Second Coming* to Hall, whom Brown called 'one diamond man'. In February 1994, after two more maddening months, Schroeder retired from the project to finish the record he had abandoned to produce the Roses – an album by his sister. He felt that *Second Coming* was all but finished, but Squire had now decided he didn't like it. 'John felt it was going in a completely different direction to what he had in mind.' What was in Squire's mind now was becoming increasingly difficult to tease out. If he'd been unhappy with the direction Leckie had been taking the band, then Schroeder seemed an odd choice of replacement. The 'dry' and 'funky' sound the producer had spent seven months working on would now be drenched in reverb and guitar overdubs.

Simon Dawson, Rockfield's 33-year-old in-house engineer, took over as producer. He seemed more suited to Squire's tastes. A life-long Monmouth resident, Dawson had worked at Rockfield since 1988 and with the Roses in a junior capacity when they had recorded 'One Love' there in 1990.

With Dawson at the desk the band would spend a further six months working on the album, adding two further tracks but essentially reworking what they already had down. 'After such a whacking delay we thought, Why rush it?' Squire said. 'We were going to be criticized anyway, so we thought we might as well make a good album.' Zutaut claimed the album's 'best work' came in these final months and that the material had the 'potential to put English rock 'n' roll back on the map'.

The Roses knew the album recording had gone on for far too long, and the pressure to complete it was intensified by the worry another band might steal their thunder with a variation of their new sound. They thought that band would be Primal Scream, who released their long-anticipated follow-up to *Screamadelica* in March 1994. *Give Out But Don't Give Up* had seen the Scream radically alter their course and pursue a similar 1970s-influenced blues-rock over-load to the Roses. The album reached number 2 in the UK charts, but received mixed reviews – with the *NME* calling the band 'dance traitors'.

Squire's endless drive and determination to carry on working the record towards the sound he wanted was becoming even more obsessive and oppressive. His decision not to attend Hall's funeral compounded the feeling that he wasn't concerned about his band mates' personal lives, and he picked up the nickname 'Ice Cold Cube'. Reni was tired of re-recording parts he'd put down in some cases almost three years ago, expressing his frustration by playing in his dressing gown. His absences from the studio grew longer and would mean he had little input on the direction the album was now taking. 'Bitterness crept in,' said Brown. 'But in a way Reni got enjoyment because he thought that John would have to come round.' He never did. Instead, Squire grew increasingly resolute and consumed with picking apart the multitude of versions of the songs they'd already recorded, choosing which parts to use (and loop) from a bewildering array of recorded material. The fluency and texture of Reni's contributions would be noticeably absent from the finished record.

Mani, suffering deeply from the loss of his father throughout the recording of *Second Coming*, allowed himself to be steamrolled by Squire's single-mindedness. The album's title was chosen by Squire, and leaked to the press, as another Geffen deadline was missed and sessions on the album continued into the summer of 1994. Brown admitted the band's morale had hit new lows as Squire continued experimenting with the key the songs were written in, and indulging in adding guitar overdubs. With Dawson the band recorded, from scratch, a rockier version of 'Love Spreads', plus a new Squire song, the acoustic 'Your Star Will Shine'. Squire was captured on tape exasperatedly teaching Brown the vocal melody to the song.

Brown too was now a father, and these final long months in the studio, 'having to listen to twenty guitar tracks', were a drain. Reni had bought him an acoustic guitar and Bob Marley songbook, so he could be more self-reliant, and in these final few months of recording, Brown came up with his own song, 'Straight to the Man'. It was his attempt to rebalance the increasingly rock-orientated album and the last little bit of funk to be squeezed out of the band. Lyrically, also, it was a sharp reminder of what Squire was missing by cutting Brown out of the work he was doing.

In June the Roses gathered around a TV at Rockfield to watch Oasis make their debut appearance on *Top of the Pops*, with their second single 'Shakermaker'. Oasis had recorded their debut album, *Definitely Maybe*, virtually next door to the Roses at nearby Monnow Valley Studio, a former Rockfield rehearsal space. Oasis issued proud proclamations that they were the Roses' spiritual offspring, and *Definitely Maybe* would go to number 1 in the UK charts in

August. Squire was impressed and continued to pursue more guitar overdubs on *Second Coming*, determined to prove who was boss.

In preparation for the Roses' imminent comeback, Geffen suggested the band should try to secure new management to replace Hall. They put forward Peter Leake, the US-based English manager of The Waterboys' Mike Scott and 10,000 Maniacs. He travelled to Rockfield. 'I'd heard a little background that maybe there was strife within the band,' he said. Arriving at the studio, he was surprised to discover all the band members had their own living areas, and found it difficult getting them all together. 'But then when I mentioned it was actually my birthday, they all lit up and said, Let's go down the pub,' he said. 'We had a great night.' But he left the next day, citing other commitments. 'I could also see it was going to be hard to break them in the US. There was tremendous expectation on behalf of the record company because they'd paid a huge amount of money.'

They had now been on Geffen for over three years. To an extent the label could afford to write off the Roses as the other acts on the label such as Beck, Counting Crows and Nirvana (despite the death of Kurt Cobain in April) dominated the American charts, and Geffen would post record gross profits of $505 million in 1994. Eddie Rosenblatt had become CEO and chairman after David Geffen left, and he remained eager to see some money back on his investment in the Roses. Zutaut had convinced him *Second Coming* could be a huge hit in America.

The Roses handed over the all-important final mix of the album to Bill Price, who had worked with Zutaut on the mix for the Guns N' Roses' albums *Use Your Illusion I* and *II*. Price had also produced albums for The Clash and The Jesus and Mary Chain, as well as co-producing the Sex Pistols' *Never Mind the Bollocks, Here's the Sex Pistols*. He was given a free hand on the mix of *Second Coming*, and loaded up the reverb, making the album sound bigger and rockier, more suited to American radio.

It may have been the most difficult second album of all time to record, but it was finished. Although Oasis could be seen as rivals to the Roses, the band had sparked a revival in the fortunes of guitar rock in the UK and made no secret of the debt they owed to their Mancunian forebears. Their rise to the top had also coincided with the 1994 Criminal Justice Act, which handed the police new powers to stop illegal raves, signalling a return to the underground for innovative dance music. The Roses had sat out grunge, and were coming back with a new sound that was as timely as it was mature and supreme.

Promoting *Second Coming* would be as fraught as recording it. Brown and Reni didn't want to do any photographs or videos to promote the band's comeback. Squire would use various clips from the footage he'd taken on his Super-8 camera over the years to make a video for the scheduled first single, 'Love Spreads'. It featured Brown, Squire and Mani in death, chicken and devil costumes respectively and was the band's best video to date, but deemed so low-fi as to be unfit for purpose by Geffen after it was refused by MTV.

Terri Hall, Philip's widow, had honoured his wishes and taken on her husband's PR business. The band failed to show for their first meeting with her, and she was tasked with managing the considerable flak that came her way as the Roses declared their intention to provide their first exclusive interview to the *Big Issue*, a magazine sold on the street by the homeless. It was a philanthropic move but one which upset the music press.

The band were keen to use the same radio and TV pluggers they had always used, the trusted Beer Davies team of Gareth Davies and his business partner James Chapple Gill. The company came up with some novel promotion ideas. BBC1's Saturday football preview programme, *Football Focus*, agreed that they would film a five-a-side match of The Stone Roses v. Manchester United. 'I remember hearing that [Ryan] Giggs was in the Man United team,' said Davies. 'I thought we could put a short press release out saying: The Stone Roses – play live on BBC1 at 12.15.' In the final stages Squire said he didn't want to do it, for fear the band would look stupid.

MCA Records, who owned Geffen and handled their product in the UK, insisted their own in-house TV and radio promotion team handle the record, however, to the disgruntlement of the band. MCA and the Roses was not a good fit. The major label made a show of delivering 'Love Spreads' to Radio 1 in a security van on 7 November 1994. The release of the single, however, was quickly and disconcertingly delayed until December. The band were unhappy with MCA's campaign. The Roses wanted Beer Davies reinstated, and MCA backed down, but only to allow the independent company to do TV promotion.

As 'Love Spreads' picked up radio play, the date of former manager Gareth Evans's wrongful dismissal claim was confirmed. It would take place at London High Court on 15 March 1995. Evans had employed a powerful lawyer from media and entertainment giants Harbottle & Lewis, and was portraying the band as serial contract breakers. The thought of going back to the High Court would hang over the band in the coming months.

There were no promotional copies of 'Love Spreads' available for review, but on 19 November the *NME* took the opportunity to put the Roses on their cover, using the 1989 Kevin Cummins shot of Brown taken in Paris, under the headline 'Resurrection Kerfuffle! Where the hell have The Stone Roses been?' There was no interview, no new photos, just fifteen *NME* writers offering their opinions on 'Love Spreads'. It was a mixed response, with 'pub Zeppelin' and 'anticlimax' among the many negative comments. On 21 November the Roses did their 'comeback' interview with the *Big Issue*. Reni was notable by his absence, said to be 'back in Manchester sorting something for his mum'.

'Somebody's going to make money off us coming back, so it was the best thing to do,' Brown told the *Big Issue*. 'The last time the *NME* had us on the cover it was one of the biggest selling issues of the year. We'd rather the money went to helping the homeless than into the coffers of a big organization like IPC [who owned *NME* and *Melody Maker*].' Asked about the *Second Coming* album, Brown was typically bullish. 'This is how we wanted it to sound,' he said.

'It's much stronger and we sound like a proper live band. We like it, so there's going to be plenty of other people who do. Whatever response it gets is irrelevant to us.'

The band's long-time photographer Pennie Smith had taken the 'comeback' photo that accompanied the *Big Issue* piece. It was shot in Monnow Valley and featured the band up against a wall. They all looked healthy, not much different from how they had last appeared, except Brown, whose gaunt face was partly obscured beneath a baseball cap and behind cupped hands as he lit a cigarette. 'The band dynamic was different,' said Smith. 'It felt wrong. The band got on because they didn't really talk, and then they didn't get on because they didn't really talk. That's the story.'

'Love Spreads' was released on 28 November and entered the UK charts at number 2. There was no further UK promotion. The band turned down *Top of the Pops*, and a week after entering the charts the single dropped to number 8. The album was released on 5 December. Other bands would have released the album in the New Year, when the charts were traditionally at their softest – and a number 1 slot virtually guaranteed. 'We just thought the idea of timing it to have a number 1 was cynical music-biz bollocks,' said Squire. 'As for downplaying our return, we probably forgot how to present ourselves after five years away. We didn't know how to appear cool and accomplished. And we probably didn't care.'

On vinyl *Second Coming* came as a magnificent double album. The cover, by Squire, was an impenetrable collage of painted-over images, pasted on sewn-together rectangles of cloth. 'A nightmare,' he said. 'It was not supposed to be that dark.' The sleeve was rescued by the cheeky conceit of photographing the back of the artwork and the wire to hang it, and using that as the back cover. Again, there were no promotional copies of the album for review. *Second Coming* sold 100,000 in the UK in its first week, peaking at number 4, and quickly going on to sell 300,000 copies. There was high praise from the *Guardian*, *Melody Maker*, *Select* and *The Face*, but a smarting *NME* gave the album a mixed reception and it was panned in *Time Out* and *Q*. *Melody Maker* had the band on their cover on 17 December. There was no interview and the magazine was so desperate for copy they interviewed the *Big Issue* journalist who had interviewed the band.

In early January 1995 the Roses mixed and finished recording new B-sides for a second single from the album, which was scheduled for release at the end of February. They included a new Brown song, the sensual 'Ride On', plus a track attributed to Mani and Reni called 'Moses', a studio piece from Paul Schroeder's time producing the band. For the A-side it was reported that the band were considering 'Breaking into Heaven' or 'How Do You Sleep', the latter having already been play-listed on Radio 1. 'Ten Storey Love Song' was, however, finally selected as the second single. In America, 'Love Spreads' was picking up radio support and slowly climbing the Billboard charts, and the album was scheduled for release on 16 January.

Geffen A&R man Tom Zutaut told the press he wanted an 'organic, word of mouth' promotional campaign in America. But Zutaut knew it would take more than that, and had introduced the Roses to a powerful manager, Doug Goldstein, who had managed Guns N' Roses since 1991. It was Zutaut's last act for the Roses, as he then left Geffen after almost fourteen years. Goldstein travelled to Manchester to woo the band, and was holed up in the Midland Hotel for days before the band finally agreed to meet him. When they did, he told them they were a 'beautiful ocean liner without a captain'. He said he was their perfect manager because any problems they had he'd seen before with Guns N' Roses. Goldstein was sharp, and thought the Roses were on to something with *Second Coming*. He found Reni 'charismatic', and Brown 'intelligent, acerbic and hilarious'. 'Their personalities got to me. I wanted to work hard for them because I liked who they were.' He even laughed when Brown told him he thought Guns N' Roses were the worst band in the world.

Goldstein didn't pick up on any negative vibe among the band, except with Reni. 'Reni wasn't certain that he wanted to take it on: a year and a half of being away from home and touring and promoting the record, having to do the interviews. He just seemed to be content with the way his life was running.' But the Roses were determined to make it in America. 'That was the goal,' said Goldstein. 'I felt like doing a festival tour across the UK and Europe would have been the best way to go, but that seemed to fall on deaf ears. The band wanted to come to LA and promote the record.'

Chaperoned by Goldstein, the band finally arrived in America for their first visit, unprepared and falling apart. They were interviewed on radio stations in LA, San Francisco, New York and Toronto. In the LA interview Brown made controversial remarks about the US army killing babies. In Toronto Brown and Squire made life awkward for DJ Kim at the CFNY station with their usual yes/no answers. The interview was open to the public, and the studio was jammed with fans lapping up Squire and Brown's nonchalance. At Kits Live 105, in San Francisco, Reni took centre stage, cracking jokes, putting on accents and livening things up. Asked what he thought of America, he replied, 'Very small, cramped.'

'When we did the radio interviews they displayed this love-hate attitude towards America,' said Goldstein. 'We'd love to be accepted here but fuck you if we're not. They had this don't-give-a-shit attitude.' Reni, said Goldstein, didn't make himself nearly as available for promotional work as the rest of the band. 'He just seemed to not want to be there. I felt like replacing Reni was the only way the band was going to be able to travel on.'

In LA the Roses re-shot the video for 'Love Spreads' with director Steve Hanft, who had directed 'Loser' – the breakthrough US Top 10 single for the Roses' Geffen label mate Beck. The band performed as if live in the studio in front of oil-well pumpjacks, Brown now looking healthy, sporting a becoming plaid deerstalker hat. Reni looked less enthusiastic, Beck had a small cameo, and Squire memorably was shown playing his guitar while riding on a donkey. 'Love Spreads' would peak at number 55 in the Billboard charts.

Goldstein was not involved in the video shoot, as the Roses had decided against making him their permanent manager. 'I wanted to stay with them,' he said. 'My understanding is that John had said if

we want to make it in America we have to pay an American manager, and Ian just said, I'm not going to pay the gross dollar
figures – so they had a falling out.'

Second Coming performed well in America, reaching number 47
on the Billboard charts, but *Rolling Stone* awarded it only two of a
possible five stars, dismissing it as 'tuneless retro-psychedelic grooves
bloated to six-plus minutes in length'. In the *LA Times*, on 5 February, long-time fan Robert Hilburn countered, 'The critical furore is
reminiscent of the stir caused in the early 1970s by the Rolling
Stones' *Exile on Main St.*, another work that required repeated listening before the sprawl turned from chaotic to absorbing. Look for
Second Coming to eventually stand as one of the most important
albums of 1995.'

'The reason why no British band has taken the US in the last ten
years is that none of them have been any good,' Brown, now thirty-
one, told *Entertainment Weekly*. 'America's there for us if we want it.
It's ours.' The band's most controversial interview was with Robert
Hilburn, at the *LA Times*. 'I made the mistake of using cocaine for a
while, thinking that it would make me more productive but it made
me unsure, more paranoid,' Squire, now thirty-two, told Hilburn.
'One thing it gives you is endurance. A lot of what I do comes from
spending time on a guitar, just getting locked into a private world
and turning things around, and something will grow from that.'

This quote was duly reported back in the UK, where starved of
any real Roses news it was blown out of all proportion. 'People
were asking us why it took so long to come up with the second
album,' Squire said. 'We'd done other interviews and the same
excuses about the court cases and having children were getting recy-
cled. I thought the guy deserved something more.'

Aside from Hilburn, the Roses had treated the US media in the
same way they dealt with the UK media, with a mixture of disdain
and disinterest. There had been a particularly awkward interview
with MTV. Geffen's head of PR, Bryn Bridenthal, could not understand the band's stance: 'You can't just expect success in the UK to
translate over to the States without any churning of the waters.

The business was ruled by promotion and those people wanted to think you cared or they would move on to another band that did care.'

The Face had travelled to LA to interview the band during this promotional push in America. Squire was sick, confined to bed with pleurisy – a serious inflammation of the linings of the lungs and chest. The band were described as 'shambolic, lethargic, utterly wayward' and 'promotional duties were rearranged, missed or attended by half of the band'. The Roses were interviewed separately for the story that would appear in March 1995, with just Brown on the cover, and the headline 'Stone Roses to Hell and Back'.

'The Stone Roses were never as great as everyone said,' Squire said. 'I've got another album almost written, I made a list of songs up yesterday actually.' He was asked how he felt the other band members viewed him. 'Miserable, capricious and inscrutable,' he said. Reni was asked if the group were ultimately destined to underachieve. 'I get that vibe sometimes,' he said. 'But I'm sick of underachieving now.' Reni also talked, unusually for him, about his personal life. 'These things don't change the way you look, but you grow up so much inside.' Asked about his attitude towards the band, he appeared optimistic: 'There really is nothing I'd rather do, you know, than be in this band right now.'

Pennie Smith was again travelling with the band, documenting this American promotional trip. With Squire holed up in his hotel room, it was near impossible to shoot the band together. She memorably photographed them in LA, in the rain in a gas station, where Reni spent most of the shoot on a payphone and, inexplicably, wore a hat made to look like a chicken. 'Things felt odd with Reni,' Smith said. 'They were all on good form individually, but you didn't often see them together. Maybe they knew the game was up.'

The Roses returned to the UK in February 1995 to shoot a video for 'Ten Storey Love Song'. They were due back in America for live dates in mid-May, with a world tour planned to start, in Europe, on 19 April. There had been talk of UK dates in March, but they'd been cancelled due to Squire's pleurisy. A further batch of secret UK gigs intended for April was also cancelled, after, the band claimed, the dates were leaked. The real reason was the Roses weren't ready to play live. They did announce they would be headlining the Glastonbury Festival in June, their first UK date in over five years.

In Manchester, rehearsals for the tour were not running smoothly. Reni's erratic timekeeping and no-shows were causing problems, and he also failed to make it to the video shoot for 'Ten Storey Love Song'. Pennie Smith was asked to blow up a photograph of his head, and that was stuck on a stick and used in the background for the video. Geffen had hooked the band up with video director Sophie Muller, best known for her work with The Eurythmics, and had allowed her a big budget. She had met the band in New York and discussed ideas with Squire.

Muller hired a sixty-man crew and built an elaborate set in a studio in London's East End. As well as no Reni, Brown also missed the first day of the two-day shoot. The manager-less band was in organizational disarray, and the first day of the shoot clashed with Brown's son's birthday. He phoned Muller to tell her he'd be 'down later'. She was astounded. When he did show, Muller offered him a shooting script. The storyline focused on Brown lying ill on a bed with a fever, hallucinating, but it was the first he had heard about it. Brown didn't want to be perceived as being ill, and although he eventually acquiesced to the demands of the script, it was another unsatisfactory, unsettling episode.

'Ten Storey Love Song' was released on 6 March, and to promote it the band finally granted the *NME* an interview. Under the headline 'We're Still Arrogant Sods! The Stone Roses Take on the World' only three of the Roses appeared on the cover – Reni again absent. 'We hope we will be together this time next year but we can't say,' said Squire. 'It's a random universe. I can really see us drifting apart if the band didn't exist.' The cover shot was poorly choreographed and the band's look was not strong. Squire wore a cycling top, Brown's hair was still growing out from when he had shaved his long locks during the final stages of recording the album, and Mani looked ill in an oversized felt hat.

On the same day 'Ten Storey Love Song' entered the UK charts, at number 11, the Roses settled out of court with Evans. They simply could not face the ordeal of the High Court again, and it was reputed they paid off their former manager, who was now forty-five, with around a quarter of a million pounds. It left a huge hole in the band's finances, and the settlement was not publicized.

The Roses, minus Squire, who was still recovering from his illness – which had developed into pneumonia – appeared on Jo Whiley and Steve Lamacq's Radio 1 *Evening Session*. They were there to play some favourite records and talk up the comeback. Brown displayed a deep and impressive knowledge of rap and reggae, but it was Reni who dominated, cracking jokes (Squire was suffering from 'old-moania', he said), putting on accents and generally lightening the mood. His style clashed with Brown's more serious tone. For Reni the band had already broken up. Squire, he sussed, had his own agenda for the Roses, and Reni could see the guitarist was growing more dictatorial. The idea of the band as a unit – it was laughable.

Brown was wound up by all manner of irritations as the band headed to the wall: Squire, Evans, MCA, Geffen, Reni . . . the list went on. His personal life was in disarray, and every setback the band encountered eroded a little more of their once-indomitable status. Reni's attitude rankled him – quitting one minute, buoyant and bubbling the next – and as well as love there was hurt in Brown's heart. The two had already clashed over Goldstein, and Brown now attacked Reni over his catalogue of recent no-shows – venting his many frustrations. It was a big row, but the Roses had always argued, and perhaps a show of passion would be invigorating.

The malaise was, however, too firmly entrenched and could not be shifted so easily. Reni was caught in two minds. He faced problems over committing to the demands of a world tour, but he had given over ten years of his life to the Roses and making the decision to walk away was pulling him apart. There were suggestions that the songwriting income could be shared more equally, because otherwise the band would essentially be working for the benefit of main songwriter Squire – who would go on collecting his publishing royalties as the band toured to pay off the financial debt incurred from settling with Evans. It was an issue that had destroyed many bands, and Brown was open to suggestions of a more equal division.

In different ways, though, and for different reasons, all four Roses were sapped of their inner strength, and behind the famed Manc lip the band's belief in what they were and who they were had never been more vulnerable. The world tour was now less than three weeks away. The Roses were booked into New Order's rehearsal space in Cheetham Hill, Manchester, to prepare for what would be their first shows in almost five years. Reni's attitude was haphazard, and although that had always been part of his charm – an important part of what made them so unique – Mani and Squire were getting bored with it. Brown felt the noose around his neck tightening. Two weeks away from the world tour, Brown was fed up and frustrated. Reni needed reassurance, and his attitude only mirrored Brown's own doubt and disappointment with the band. The two had another row, turning on one another over the tension in rehearsals. Brown wanted to see more commitment. The argument escalated. Reni told Brown to get another drummer.

The next day at rehearsals, a still-smarting Brown relayed the news to Squire and Mani that Reni had quit – and it was the final straw this time. 'We said, Hang on a minute, we've got a tour starting in ten or twelve days,' said Squire. Brown was spitting feathers. 'Ian said he'd never work with him again, and that he wanted to see him in the gutter,' said Squire. 'I could see in Ian's eyes that there was no turning back and that was the last nail in the coffin.' Squire was annoyed, and a little ashamed, at two grown men – make that four – behaving like kids.

The next day Reni phoned Brown: 'I need to get down to rehearsal early so that me and Mani can rehearse, and you and John can come down later.' Brown replied, 'I've done what you told me to do last night.' 'What do you mean?' asked Reni. 'You told me to get another drummer, so I have,' said Brown. 'I'll make sure you get your quarter of the money.' It was sad. There was no fight left in either of them. 'What are you going to do now?' asked Brown. 'Sign on, I suppose,' was Reni's answer.

The band's PR, Terri Hall, was told to prepare a statement to announce that Reni had quit 'after a series of rows with the other three members'. She was shocked and immediately called the band's plugger, Gareth Davies. 'I pointed out to her that if ever there was a band that relied on the chemistry brought to it by its four members, that band was The Stone Roses,' he said. 'I said, If Reni goes, that's the end of it. Terri paused and said that I must not mention that to anyone because it was what Philip [Hall] always used to say.' On 5 April 1995 the statement was published in the *NME*. 'It had died for me,' Reni said. 'I was happy to have gone.'

16.

Robbie

With Reni gone, the Roses were over. Squire and Mani packed away their instruments. Brown did not, despite his claims, have another drummer ready to replace Reni instantly. But the Roses *had* approached another drummer. During the latter stages of recording *Second Coming*, when Reni's absences from Rockfield had been a cause for concern, tour manager Steve Adge had asked Robbie Maddix if he would be interested in 'helping out' in the studio. Maddix had declined, fearing that Reni would find out.

Adge didn't want the Roses to end like this, and returned to the idea of approaching Maddix, who had first been noticed by the Roses in the late 1980s when he drummed with the well-respected Manchester rock-funk collective Gina Gina. Brown was aware of Maddix's potential. His girlfriend Mitch had since taken him to see Rebel MC, the proto-jungle/pop rapper whom Maddix had drummed for at the time of his 1991 'Street Tuff' breakthrough.

More recently, Maddix had moved to London and enjoyed success as part of a production and songwriting team called New Underground. He had put a series of lucrative deals together for the team, such as work with the UK soul-scene connoisseurs' favourite, Vivienne Mckone. In London, Maddix enjoyed the good life, recording in top studios, wearing designer threads and indulging his passion for flash cars. But the lackadaisical approach of the other key members of New Underground had left him disillusioned, and, as Adge set about the frantic search for him, he was actually close at hand – back in Manchester, having agreed to form a new band called Pleasure with former Happy Mondays singer Rowetta Satchell. Pleasure were rehearsing for the first time when, via a series of phone calls with associates, Maddix was finally tracked down and told of the offer he couldn't refuse: the Roses drum stool.

Adge, who knew the Roses as well as anyone, believed Maddix had the personality and energy to uplift the band and bring them back together. 'He said, Remember when I was asking you before, and you said no, because Reni was still there?' said Maddix. 'Well, he's left now. It's official. It's Reni's choice. They haven't kicked him out. The news is going to break on Tuesday.'

Despite his experience and impressive presence, Maddix was just twenty-five, seven years younger than the rest of the Roses. Although he had played in an indie band as a teenager, indie music was not really his thing, and the only Roses song he knew was 'Fools Gold'. 'Adge just said, They don't think they can carry on without Reni. They are my friends. I don't want this thing to end,' Maddix said. 'It was put to me that the band was in a bit of a mess, so it wasn't just a drumming job – it was for me to try and galvanize the group.'

Maddix knew nothing of the Roses' impending world tour when he agreed to meet the band in New Order's Cheetham Hill rehearsal space. He borrowed a basic drum kit and set it up in the otherwise empty room. The Roses failed to show that day, and again the next. Maybe it was over. On the third day Squire walked in. 'It was very much, I can't get to know you because I don't think this is real,' said Maddix. 'It's a waste of time even being here. That's the body language: really down.' Next came Mani. 'Mani's more upbeat,' said Maddix. 'John picked out his guitar, tuned up – he only had a little amp and was just twiddling around. I couldn't get an angle. It was just chaos.' Squire started the 'Breaking into Heaven' riff, and Mani joined in. 'I could just hear hip-hop,' said Maddix. 'I didn't know the song. I just thought, That's what it sounds like, so I'll just put that beat there. John hooked on to it and it started to gel quickly. The levels started coming up and up, and it just became heavier. I saw Stevie Adge clicking his fingers as if to say, They're back.' Brown was the last to enter the room, carrying his microphone and a small Peavey PA system. 'He walked in with his hand in the air, like, Oh my God, this is sounding good,' said Maddix. 'He came straight over to me and said, You cannot leave this room.' It was 1 April 1995.

After three days of chaotic, feedback-disrupted jamming, which left Maddix wondering why the band had such poor amps, Brown levelled with him. They had a world tour booked to start in twelve days. 'I was like, What?' said Maddix. 'Where's the backline, where's the monitor engineer, where's the crew? There was none of that.' The band were ready to admit defeat. 'They were saying, We're going to have to cancel it. I said, No, we can do it.'

Motivated by Maddix, production details, personnel and equipment were all hastily assembled. As the sound and lighting requirements were broadly being put in shape, Maddix also needed to learn the set. 'We tried "Fools Gold" and it didn't work,' he said. There were fourteen other songs to negotiate, most from *Second Coming* but also studded with Roses' classics such as 'She Bangs the Drums' and 'I Am the Resurrection'. Maddix took his lead from Mani or Squire, who would both make characteristic physical moves while playing to indicate a change in the momentum or direction of the songs. 'It was tricky. Sometimes I'd get lost: where am I, what song is this? I would just carry it on.'

It was never going to be the same, especially as Maddix had only been in the band for ten days, rather than Reni's ten years. But there were encouraging signs, and the Roses decided they could make the first date of the world tour, in Oslo, on 19 April 1995. It was in that city that Maddix first realized the significance of what he had taken on, as a forty-strong press pack chased the band into the 1,350-capacity Rockefeller venue, cameras clicking non-stop. Maddix looked to the band for guidance, but they appeared to be as unprepared as he was. *Melody Maker* interviewed the band, and the departure of Reni was the obvious topic. 'You ain't getting shit out of us,' said Mani. All further European press interviews were cancelled. The gig, the Roses' first live date since June 1991, did not go well. After twenty minutes, frustrated with how the band were sounding, Squire smashed his guitar and walked off stage. Mani smashed his bass.

'I thought it was an act,' said Maddix. 'Then I thought, They never told me about this bit, what do I do here? I looked at their faces and realized John was serious – he was ramming the head of the guitar into his speaker. And Mani's face was contorted. Ian dropped the mic and that started feeding back.' It was chaos, and backstage was not a pleasant place to be. Maddix had never seen anything like it: the crowd had been responding well until the tantrums. He threatened to quit.

The European leg of the tour continued to be peppered by fractious on-stage moments as the band played in Sweden, Germany, Holland, Belgium, Switzerland, Italy and Denmark. 'Something Rotten in the State of Denmark,' ran the *NME* headline above a review of a show in Copenhagen, at the 1,000-capacity Pakhus 11 club, during which Squire smashed up another guitar. The review said the gig was 'tedious and an utter disappointment'. Brown's 'weak' vocals were singled out for criticism. Brown had not found anything like his old form, and often didn't even attempt to sing for a succession of songs – standing proud, shaking a tambourine. 'Every gig was a minefield,' said Maddix. Squire was smashing up thousands of pounds' worth of guitars.

The band's peculiar on-stage chemistry was not the only eye-opener. For this huge world tour the band had surrounded themselves with a familiar crew of roadies. Many were old mates who had never handled events on this scale. Adge was in charge as tour manager, Chris 'The Piss' acted as production manager and *Second Coming* producer Simon Dawson looked after the live sound. One-time Baldrick, and close friend of Squire, Al Smith was designated to look after Maddix's drum requirements. As the European tour continued through France and Spain, Maddix began to wonder if this cosy set-up was actually working to the band's benefit. The crew appeared to be suffering from the same sense of malfunction as the band. Maddix had asked Smith to organize replacement cymbals, and a frame to hold his kit in place, and waited – and waited. 'No one was listening,' he said. 'Our support, technically, was poor – no one really knew their shit except for John's guitar guy, Martin, who had worked with vintage guitars. Mani went round the world from the day he smashed his bass amp with gaffer tape on the speaker.'

With all-important American dates imminent, Geffen sent A&R representative Susanne Filkins to check out the new line-up. She had been Tom Zutaut's assistant, and now took his position as the key link between the label and the band. The Roses had never been close to Zutaut, but they warmed to the young, likeable and offbeat Filkins. Squire, in particular, struck up a close relationship with her.

The band's finances were in a perilous state. The profits from the tour would largely go towards paying off the debt caused by the settlement with Evans. Maddix had a keen interest in the business side of the band, having turned down an offer of £50,000, up front, for the tour, in favour of sharing equally in all future band revenues as a member of the Roses' limited company, Pierstone. He quickly realized the importance of impressing Filkins. 'The only time we're going to get any money is if we finish the tour and then, maybe, Geffen are gonna give us more money to record the next album,' he said. 'And that's only if Geffen want us to carry on.'

Filkins needed to deliver good news back to Geffen, but it was difficult to see how there would be any, given the band's unpredictable performances and attitude. Brown was in a tempestuous mood off stage. He pulled the band out of a promotional appearance on a TV show in Rome after overhearing a member of the show's crew making a racist comment. Yet there was still a remarkable demand for the Roses. Jive/Zomba continued to make purchase on the band's back catalogue, releasing a compilation album in May 1995, *The Complete Stone Roses*, which hit number 4 in the UK and went platinum with sales of over 300,000. 'Fools Gold 95' was also released as a single, peaking at number 25.

The American leg of the tour did not start well. In Atlanta, Georgia, on 14 May, in front of a festival crowd of over 20,000, Maddix's drum kit fell off a raised part of the stage as he was playing. His repeated request for a frame to hold it in place had gone unheeded. He kicked over his drums and walked off stage. Mani smashed up another guitar. It was the start of an increasing period of tension, revolving around issues with the road crew. Maddix, for instance, wanted to book rehearsal rooms in America, so the band could practise on days off: 'The crew never wanted to do more work, so it was like I was seen as a troublemaker.' The problems escalated over the issues of wages, made all the more contentious because of the friendships between Squire and many of the crew – and exacerbated by the lack of a manager. 'If you asked John he'd say, What does Ian think? And Ian would say, I don't want to talk about it today,' said Maddix. 'So nothing gets done.'

After the disaster in Atlanta, a gig in Washington was cancelled because the venue was seated and would prevent the Roses creating 'the right vibe'. This was followed by a more promising show in Toronto, where the band broke box-office records, selling out the 3,500-capacity venue in five minutes. Next came the band's crucial New York show, playing to 2,500 people at the Manhattan Ballroom. Geffen boss Eddie Rosenblatt, and Eric Eisner, the label's business manager, would be present to check out their investment – and decide whether or not to give the band the $4 million advance for their next album. Before the show the Roses were not confident. They came together in a familiar huddle backstage, just the four of them, and Maddix began pumping up the positive vibes to elevate the mood. They were due a good show, and this was their best yet.

'The fans, after so many years, were thrilled that somebody came to play that music,' said Rosenblatt. He saw enough to decide that the band was worth persevering with – but was not entirely convinced. 'We wouldn't have laid down our bodies because reviews were not great. We just hoped to give them a good feeling, create some kind of a relationship and go after the next record. How else do you handle it? It became a verb. The A&R guy brings in a band, and you say, Well, is this going to be another Stone Roses?'

The Manhattan gig was reviewed by *Melody Maker*, who commented on how Squire dominated proceedings to such an extent the band 'may as well be rechristened "The John Squire Blues Explosion", suggesting that the Roses' new sound required a singer as histrionic as Robert Plant. *Melody Maker* was not the only publication to notice how Brown struggled on stage with his vocals. The relative success of the New York show was only a brief respite from the ever-present tensions among the crew and band, with fractious shows following in Boston, a second New York date in the smaller Webster Hall club, Philadelphia, St Louis and Chicago. American reviews of the band were often negative, criticizing them for what seemed like an indifferent stage attitude, particularly from Brown.

The Roses' talisman had a vocal tone that made the band unique, but many of the *Second Coming* songs were in the wrong key for his voice. Squire also seemed determined to undermine him by turning the guitars up to deafening volume, and during his long guitar solos would leave Brown hopelessly exposed. From the start of the tour he had been missing notes on stage, and his confidence had never recovered. 'It was suggested Ian could do better, but nobody would dare tell him,' said Maddix.

Brown was growing increasingly frustrated by the myriad faults within the band, his own poor performances and the often luke-warm reaction the Roses generated among the audience. In Philadelphia his legendary temper exploded. The small scale of the venue meant that only half of the band's normal sound system was required, but Brown did not see it that way. 'Ian wanted to rip their heads off with sound, and he's seen a small rig – and some other things were pissing him off – so he literally started kicking the rig down,' said Maddix. An armed officer was policing the venue and, unsure who Brown was, as in his fury the singer pushed over the tower of speakers, the cop ran forward threateningly with his gun. 'It was chaos: Ian's shouting, You're taking the piss, we warned you,' said Maddix. 'The gig wasn't very good.'

Behind his back, a vocal coach had been hired for Brown and casually introduced into the touring set-up. The band and crew were worried how Brown would react, but he was pleased by the offers of honey-and-lemon drinks to soothe his throat and by – for him – the novel idea of doing a vocal warm-up before going on stage. Brown was led to believe the coach was just a friend of a friend who liked the band, but it didn't take long before the whole charade was revealed.

The Roses were readying to soundcheck in Los Angeles at the 5,000-capacity Palladium when Brown kicked open the dressing room and confronted Squire. 'I saw the fear in John – not that he was going to get assaulted, but that he'd let Ian down, a bit of a no-no,' said Maddix. Squire told Brown it was Maddix who had hired the vocal coach. Brown was furious, kicking out at doors and swearing – why had Robbie gone behind his back? 'I'm stood there, like, What do I say?' said Maddix. 'Do I say, Look, John did it? I looked at John, he looked at me, I looked at Ian and didn't say anything. Ian said, He's got to go.'

The Palladium was another major showcase for the band, in the city of Geffen's HQ and attended by hip acts such as Beck and The Beastie Boys. The mood among the Roses had never been worse. Before the argument over the vocal coach, Brown and Mani had been upset that Squire had taken it upon himself to visit Geffen on his own, for what should have been a band meeting. Brown's mood was further aggravated by the discovery that the set-up on stage at the Palladium was noticeably different, with Squire placed in a more pronounced position.

'Deep down I knew there was something not right,' said Maddix. It was a feeling shared by Brown and Mani. The Palladium show did not go well. 'It was shit,' said Maddix. 'We had some bad ones, but this was really bad.' Afterwards a disgruntled punter came backstage and openly stole an ounce bag of weed from Brown, claiming it was the least he was owed after such a poor performance. Mani waded in and punched the guy on the back of his head, seriously damaging his own hand. A trip to hospital resulted in a finger on his left hand being put in a metal splint and his arm rested in a sling.

The following night, on 31 May, the band were in San Francisco for the final night of the American tour. 'I'm sure Mani was crying in pain through some of the gig,' said Maddix. 'I couldn't believe he managed to play.' After all the arguments of the past two weeks, and despite Mani's broken finger and the unspoken suspicions about Squire's true intentions, the show in San Francisco was the highlight of the tour. The band played the set list backwards and rediscovered the idea that they were supposed to be having fun. The next day Squire and Al Smith went mountain-biking in San Francisco. Squire crashed, breaking his collarbone in four places, and the ten Japanese dates due to start on 5 June were immediately cancelled.

It was another classic case of one step forward, two steps back for the Roses, who had all been keenly looking forward to the visit to Japan, where they were guaranteed an ecstatic reception. The cumulative effect of the negative live reviews that had featured in the UK press, and persistent rumours of the band's lack of together-ness, led to suggestions that Squire's injury was a ruse to avoid the headline slot at Glastonbury scheduled for the end of June. In the respected US magazines *Billboard* and *Cashbox* it was reported that the band had actually split up.

The Roses held out some hope of making Glastonbury, but when it became apparent Squire would not recover in time a bizarre advert was placed in the *NME*, featuring an X-ray of Squire's broken collarbone. 'People don't believe the Roses any more,' said an *NME* report. Slash, the Guns N' Roses guitarist, also signed to Geffen, offered his services as Squire's replacement for the gig, but the Roses refused.

At the start of July, quietly, tentatively, they began rehearsing again in Rockfield Studios in Wales. Geffen was putting pressure on them to record a new album, but an extended spell in the studio was not an idea that appealed to the band, who had just spent the better part of three gruelling years on *Second Coming*. The Roses wanted to continue touring. The cancelled Japanese gigs were rescheduled, dates in Australia added, and a UK tour was being finalized.

Initially the rehearsals featured just Mani and Maddix, both now living near Rockfield in Monmouth, and keyboard player Nigel Ipinson-Fleming, who had come to several gigs on the Roses tour and had worked with Maddix for many years as part of Android Productions. Brown was the next to arrive, driving down from Lymm, a picturesque village in the Warrington borough of Cheshire, where he had a house.

When the recuperated Squire arrived in Wales, Brown, who had been impressed with the sound cooked up by bass, drums and keyboards, suggested to Squire he should check out Ipinson-Fleming, who played Squire's 'Ten Storey Love Song' as a piano piece. 'John liked it and started to play along,' said Maddix. It was suggested to Squire that with Ipinson-Fleming riffing along, it would fill out the band's sound and be easier for all to hear where they were during the guitar solos. Squire agreed it was a good idea.

At the end of July, after a two-month enforced break, the Roses were back on the road – with the upbeat and enthusiastic Ipinson-Fleming. They played the Lollipop Festival, Stockholm, followed by three dates in Finland. Next, on 5 August, the Roses played the Feile Festival in Cork, a headline gig shared with Shaun Ryder's new band Black Grape. 'It was the most enjoyable gig we've done,' Brown said. The *NME* called the Cork gig 'ecstatic' and 'exhilarating'. The set, with Ipinson-Fleming's keyboards adding a new texture, was recorded live – as Geffen eyed the option of releasing a stop-gap live album. Four tracks from this gig, 'Daybreak', 'Breaking into Heaven', 'Driving South' and 'Tightrope', would surface on a live EP, *Crimson Tonight*, released in Australia and Japan in February 1996. It was heartening to hear Brown talking up the band again. 'I never feel we've been overtaken by anyone else. Things have gone backward not forward. There's been a lull and we're here to bring things forward – we do what we want. All these bands who want to sound like Ray Davies or Paul McCartney, that's just retro shit.'

In August, Mani became a father and the Roses did venture back to the studio, albeit for one day, to cut a new version of 'Love Spreads' to be included on the charity album *Help*. Oasis, Paul McCartney and Paul Weller also contributed tracks to the album, which raised over £1 million for the thousands of families caught up in the Balkans war. Brown and Maddix were pictured on the *NME* front cover to promote the album, while Squire contributed the cover art.

On 1 September, before heading off for twelve dates in Japan, the Roses played at the annual Pilton village party in Somerset. The event was organized by Glastonbury boss Michael Eavis, and all profits went to the local villagers who suffered the disruption of his nearby festival every year. The Roses felt they owed Eavis for pulling out of Glastonbury, and their appearance guaranteed a sell-out of the 1,000 tickets. The *NME* reviewed the show, again heaping praise on the band, saying they had 'recaptured their magic'. Much of the praise was directed at Squire, with further doubt cast over Brown's vocals.

The Roses smashed Japan. *Second Coming* had sold over 250,000 copies in the country, and *Vox* magazine travelled to Japan to witness the hysteria, reporting that Brown and Squire were writing new songs about 'positivity' and 'injustice'. In a club in Tokyo, on the band's final night in Japan, despite the presence of his minder, Noel Walters, Brown was grabbed behind the head and punched in the mouth by a burly Australian. The next morning when they were boarding flights for Australia, Brown's face was a mess.

Squire had already got his own personal security man, whom the others referred to as the guitarist's 'valet'. Maddix was angry that Walters had not stopped the attack on Brown. 'I said to Ian, This is not the first time, look at all the people who have wanted to have a fight with you on the tour,' said Maddix. He arranged for his cousin, Martell Prince, to join the crew to prevent any such further incidents.

Although the gigs were getting better, organization continued to be a problem. In Australia the band members were forced to share twin rooms – the same as the crew. The dates in Brisbane, Sydney, Melbourne and Perth, in theatre venues that held around 2,500 people, were well received, and demand for the band high. The Roses could easily have sold out four or five nights at the 2,500-capacity Metro club in Melbourne alone.

In November, with the much-anticipated UK tour starting at the end of the month, 'Begging You' was pulled off *Second Coming* and released as a single. It was the first Roses release in eight months, but featured no new songs. Instead, the added tracks on the various formats were all remixes of the original – six in total. While Brown,

Maddix and Mani had all enjoyed the process of the remix work, Squire was not impressed or prepared to take part. The single peaked at number 15 in the UK charts. The video for the single, put together by Geffen, intercut live footage from the tour with four gyrating, kinky-booted, bikini-clad women – each wearing a mask of one of the band members – and indigenous dancing from around the world.

The UK tour had already sold out, with 53,000 tickets snapped up in twenty-four hours. On the opening date in Bridlington, on 28 November, the band were interviewed by *Q*. 'We just plug away,' Squire said. 'If we do cross paths with popular culture, it's by accident. That's what happened last time.' *Melody Maker* slammed the Bridlington show, but after waiting for five long years to see the band play live, every night was magical for the band's fans. The ecstatic audience reaction filled the band with confidence. There were moments on the UK tour when the Roses reached the heights of their power, when it all came together and there could surely be no better band in the world. Brown said some of these UK shows were the best ever, singling out the second night at the Brixton Academy – where Reni saw the band and said that although it wasn't the same, he could see the good in Maddix's playing. The live reviews would pick up too; with headlines such as 'The Unforgettable Squire' (*NME*) and 'Squired for Sound' (*Melody Maker*) it was self-evident where much of the praise was being directed.

For classicists, the uneasy gel between Squire's explosive, foot-on-the-monitor, guitar histrionics and Brown's almost atonal vocals was obvious, especially on the rockier *Second Coming* material. Brown had the room and the quiet to shine during the acoustic section of the show, coming across as a modern-day Jim Morrison, while Maddix added a relentless power to the old classics that Squire appended with excessive guitar. It was now, however, all just a show; an altogether different experience from being at Blackpool in 1989 or Spike Island in 1990, when it was a happening, and the band had the power to cleanse. Now you felt dirty believing that had ever happened. The Roses had to accept they were now just another band. The treadmill of album, tour, album, tour ad infinitum lay ahead.

Off stage the divisions between Squire and Brown were as pronounced as on stage. Squire now largely travelled on the crew bus, where his pop-star pretensions attracted those comfortable with preen and sheen. On the band's bus Brown, often sullen, defensive and hard to reach, defiantly played hardcore hip-hop, gangster rap and reggae. The potent, aggressive lyrics were a turn-off; not just for Squire's crowd, but also for the man he had relied on throughout the tour for support, Maddix – who went between UK venues in an XJS Jaguar.

Brown, despite his apparent isolation from Squire, still cared. He had made it clear he didn't want to see anyone giving cocaine to Squire, whose episode with pneumonia had been more serious than had been reported in the media. But the communication channels between the two men had disintegrated slowly over three years and now were all but irreparable. It was, again, sad. 'Sometimes John would come down in the morning, and as opposed to coming over, he'd go stand with the crew,' said Maddix. 'I did say to Ian, You should at least say hello in the morning to one other. Mani would say, John's strange, it makes you feel as if you've done something wrong, so you don't know what to say to him for half the day. Then you realize there's nothing wrong, it's just a lack of people skills.'

At Wembley Arena, the UK tour's final show on 29 December, the Roses, supported by The Manic Street Preachers, played to 12,500 fans in an atmosphere of triumph. The band had never truly delivered a big gig in London, until now.

Backstage, after the show, celebrating with family and friends, the band were euphoric, imagining where they would go next and looking forward to recording new material. The high of the show made the possibilities seem endless. Squire did not share in the celebrations, and had quickly disappeared back to his hotel, in Brixton. 'John's then missus said, I don't know what's the matter with him, because as soon as we got in the hotel he was jumping on the bed like a baby, saying, We've smashed it, we've smashed it!' said Maddix. 'She asked John, Why didn't you tell them that? Why have you come all the way back to the hotel to do that? Why aren't you with your mates? If you've got this feeling, why are you not there?'

Geffen were anxious that the Roses capitalize on the momentum, and wanted the band to start recording a new album as soon as possible. In January 1996 they began this process. Maddix had moved to Lymm to be close to Brown, and, with Ipinson-Fleming, they began to loosely outline a handful of songs in a basement studio at Maddix's new home. Mani was on holiday in Jamaica and Squire was being non-committal. The world tour had generated £1.2 million but the band's debt, and the touring costs, had eaten up almost all of that – and the Roses made only a few thousand pounds each for their efforts. The $4 million advance due from Geffen couldn't come soon enough.

Unable to contact Squire, Brown, Maddix and Ipinson-Fleming invited accomplished Mancunian session guitarist Aziz Ibrahim to help them flesh out the new songs. Like Ipinson-Fleming, Ibrahim was a pal of Maddix, and the pair had worked together many times in the past. 'Robbie told me that they'd had problems getting hold of John but they wanted to complete the songs they were writing, so would I come in and help with guitars?' said Ibrahim. Work continued through February, on four tracks – 'Ice Cold Cube', 'Nah Nah', 'Black Sheep' and 'High Times' – intended for the new Roses album.

Brown and Maddix already harboured concerns that Squire's private meetings with Geffen, pronounced role with the band on stage and non-communication were signs he planned to get a new project off the ground. They hoped the progress being made on the new songs would convince him of the life left in the Roses. It seemed foolish now, after ten months of hard struggle to get the band working again without Reni, to throw it all away.

But that was exactly what Squire was about to do. For him the disintegration of his relationship with Brown had been frightening. He could not see it being fixed easily, and the prospect of working together under a bad atmosphere was not appealing. The news that the band were recording demos of new songs without him, *with a new guitarist*, further led him towards the decision that the time had come. He saw his control of band, particularly the songwriting, being wrestled away.

'John took it the wrong way,' said Maddix, 'but we'd be asking him to come down.' They had no intention of replacing Squire, quite the opposite: they were trying to re-engage him. It became apparent, however, that Squire was actively avoiding contact. Mani, back from Jamaica, Brown and Maddix made visits to Squire's Manchester home, but he never answered the door. Finally, Squire called Brown. 'I don't believe in the band any more,' he said. He felt 'like a fraud'. The conversation was surprisingly convivial. Squire said he wanted to quit, but the two men shared twenty years of history. Surely they could work something out? 'There was a chink of light,' Squire said. And there was $4 million on offer to record the new album. Brown told Mani and Maddix that Squire was thinking about leaving the band. 'It came as a massive shock,' said Maddix. 'We were just about on top of the world, just about to do a new album. Geffen were just about to send the money.'

On 21 March 1996 the Roses – Squire, Brown, Mani and Maddix – met to try to thrash out a future at John Kennedy's London office. No definite decision had been reached, and there remained hope that Squire could be talked around. It was the first time since the end of the tour they had all come face to face. 'We're in the meeting and there's silence,' said Maddix. 'Kennedy doesn't say a word. John's facing us, and Mani tried to say, Come on, John, and plead to his better nature.'

'It's us,' said Mani. 'You know what Reni did to us, you're doing the same thing, whatever it is, just make it known and we'll fix it.' Squire snapped back, 'I'm not your keeper.' Mani was hurt by the remark, angry. Brown saw red, accusing Squire of 'taking the absolute piss'. Squire seemed relaxed, unconcerned that his leaving the band would put the $4 million advance from Geffen in jeopardy. When the rights to the band's name came up, he even made a joke.

'You can have the vowels and I'll have the consonants,' he said. It only cranked up the hostility.

'Ian now wanted to murder John,' said Maddix. 'I knew it was finished.' Maddix tried to defuse the situation, saying, 'John is free to do what he wants. I don't want John to leave, but the fact is you cannot make someone do something they don't want to do. We just have to accept it.' A nervous Kennedy seized on this comment. 'Listen to Robbie,' he told the band. 'What about the bills?' Brown asked Kennedy. The band's lawyer was owed £75,000 in legal fees. 'Wipe that off,' said Kennedy. 'No,' said Brown. Kennedy insisted. 'My gift to you guys.'

On 1 April 1996 Squire released a statement to confirm he had quit the group. 'After lengthy deliberation, it is with great regret that I feel compelled to announce my decision to leave The Stone Roses,' he said. 'I believe all concerned will benefit from a parting of the ways and I see this as the inevitable conclusion to the gradual social and musical separation we have undergone in the last few years. I wish them every success and hope they go on to greater things. My intentions are to continue writing while looking for partners in a new band and to begin working again as soon as possible. Thanks for everything.' A statement from The Stone Roses, jointly signed by Brown, Mani, Maddix and Ipinson-Fleming, read: 'We feel as cheated as everyone else who has heard the news. We are in the middle of recording the next LP. We're disgusted yet feeling stronger and more optimistic than ever.'

The news put the Roses back on the *NME* front cover, on 6 April, under the headline 'The Stone Roses Split! John Squire Quits'. Two weeks later, Squire was on the *NME* front cover to talk about his future, having already found a bassist for his new band. Described as 'the musical genius behind the most important rock band since the Sex Pistols', Squire said that playing with Maddix had liberated him. 'Musically, it became apparent I existed as a separate entity and that you can play with different people and have "the experience" in a different way. It helped me decide I could be in a different group.' He didn't want to 'compromise' and 'fight' to make the music he wanted to make. He made a point of denying that his leaving the Roses had anything to do with Brown's voice, and said that he didn't feel as if he was the 'gifted one [who] dragged the rest of the band behind'. He couldn't understand the hostile statement from the Roses. 'I thought it was an honourable time to go. Reni seemed to get a pat on the back when he left.'

It appeared, from the outside, as if the Roses *would* continue, although the *NME* suggested Squire had taken away their dignity, the band was now a 'debacle' and Brown was 'fatally flawed'. 'There is no reason the Stone Roses cannot continue and remain on Geffen,' said the band's publicist, Terri Hall. There was much media speculation about who would replace Squire, rumours of a new Roses album in the autumn, and confirmation the band would play the Reading Festival on 25 August. The Roses, however, knew there was no replacing Squire, and that it was over. The band's agent, Nigel Kerr, had a few deposits for gigs that had been pencilled in before Squire had left, and the band intended to honour these responsibilities. They could also do with the money, as no more would be coming from Geffen now.

'It was never going to carry on, from the day we had the meeting in London and John left,' said Maddix. 'We spoke about it. We said, It's not going on, it can't go on. I said to Ian, I told you it was going to end like this because you guys weren't talking properly. That's it. He said, I know. There was none of this, Who can you get on guitar? We had no intention of replacing John – it was never going to work. It was over.' The band was not short of offers. They were approached by Slash, who was on the verge of leaving Guns N' Roses, and former Smiths guitarist Johnny Marr, who both felt they were up to the job. 'It's not like we couldn't have replaced John,' said Maddix. 'But the whole point was who [would leave] next? Ian? It was done.'

Brown, Mani and Maddix stewed for the next two months, upset and angry – the bright and brilliant future they had imagined for the Roses had been snatched away by Squire, for reasons they did not completely understand. Geffen were now aware of the band's decision to break up, and made no effort to dissuade them from doing so, believing Squire had been the main creative force in the Roses.

In July the Roses began rehearsing at a nightclub in Southport, close to Maddix's new home in Birkdale, for a small clutch of European festival dates that would be a prelude to the Reading Festival. They had seriously considered using Kelly Johnson, former lead guitarist and singer with all-girl heavy metal band Girlschool, as guitarist for the dates. The idea had a perverse charm. Instead, however, they turned back to Aziz Ibrahim, who was given two weeks to learn Squire's guitar parts. 'I told him, All we're interested in is doing these gigs the way people remember [the band] and that's it,' said Maddix. 'There is no more.'

Brown was 'obviously hurting a lot', said Ibrahim. 'There was a lot of bitterness. They all knew how great a thing it had been, and saw other bands pick up the baton where they'd dropped it, knowing they could absolutely squash them.' The band were flushed out of the Southport nightclub after a day, when news that the Roses were rehearsing there leaked and fans mobbed the place. Rehearsals concluded at the Renaissance Gym in Manchester.

The idea of a happy ending was doomed from the start. For the first festival show, in Spain on 2 August, none of the Roses' equipment showed up, and they were forced to beg and borrow what they could. They made a brave attempt to play 'Fools Gold', but 'it was a disaster,' said Ibrahim. 'Mani was the first to kick off on stage, and he started having a go at Robbie, then Ian was having a go at him. It ended up in a big fight.' The three other European festival dates, in Portugal, Denmark and Hungary, saw a gradual improvement in performance, but the prospect of bringing this new version of the band before 60,000 fans at Reading Festival (the band's biggest ever audience) was daunting.

Mani had already been approached by Primal Scream and asked about the possibility of joining them, but there was a loose idea that he, Brown, Maddix and Ipinson-Fleming might carry on playing together under a new name, with a new musical identity. On 24 August, the eve of the Reading show, Mani told Brown and Maddix he had made the decision to go with Primal Scream. 'It really created a bad stink,' Mani said. Before the Roses took to the stage there was an ill-tempered press conference. The band had planned to bow out with good grace, claim that no one had fallen out, and announce that this was the last Roses show, a final chance to enjoy the music. But Brown and Mani became agitated with questions about Squire, particularly when asked whether there was any virtue in carrying on without him. Their pride got the better of them; both had been upset to see Squire take to the stage earlier in the month, as a guest, with Oasis, at their zenith – playing two massive Knebworth shows to a crowd of 250,000. Squire was a 'regular, coked-up, spoilt brat guitarist', 'pathetic and weak' and on a 'power trip', said Brown. 'You're all dumb, complete wankers, the lot of you,' Mani said.

'They were hurting, they were very raw,' said Maddix. 'We're only human, we all say things,' said Ibrahim. 'Frustrations sometimes get the better of people. I called John a joker. I've no idea why I said it. If anybody was a joker it was myself, thinking I belonged in this band.'

The band's posturing gave a contrary impression to the one they had intended, many now believing the Roses saga would continue, and that this was the unveiling of a new line-up. Their behaviour at the press conference had destroyed any sense of goodwill towards them among the media. The knives were out. Brown said he wanted to use the Reading Festival show to 'smash the myth, and destroy the mystique of the Roses', allowing for this band of musicians to continue without those shackles. Instead, it was *his* reputation now on the line.

He had stayed up the night before, drinking and smoking, and never even began to get to grips with the show. The short eleven-song set was shorn of most *Second Coming* tracks, save for 'Daybreak', 'Ten Storey Love Song' and 'Breaking into Heaven', and packed with classics such as 'I Wanna Be Adored', 'She Bangs the Drums', 'Waterfall', 'I Am the Resurrection' and 'Made of Stone'. The band included two new songs: 'High Times' and 'Ice Cold Cube'. The response from the crowd, despite press reports that suggested people were in tears and leaving the scene in thousands, was over-whelmingly positive. 'I saw arms in the air and smiling faces,' said Brown. 'But when I heard the tape a couple of days later, I thought, Oh, the singing is appalling. The band was smoking but the singer let them down, definitely.'

It seemed predetermined that reviews would be uniformly negative – and they were, although this did not stop the *NME* from putting Brown on the cover, on 21 August, to help sell their Reading issue. Variously, the gig was described as a 'nightmare', an 'embar-rassment', a 'tragedy', a 'farce' and 'unlistenable' – with particular scorn reserved for Brown's off-key singing and the girl dancing on stage with the band.

Even those who hoped it wasn't over – and there had remained a part of Brown that couldn't let go of the name and the dream – were now resigned to the fact. The festival dates, including Reading, had generated around £200,000 for the band kitty, but there were many debts still outstanding. 'Even at the end, we owed,' said Maddix.

Some of the festival money was channelled into buying the old Square One studio in Bury, where the Roses had rehearsed and attempted to record *Second Coming* tracks in 1993, and they renamed it Rose Garden. 'The idea was we could record there on whatever we were going to do next, and other people could record there and pay us,' said Maddix. 'But we had problems with one of the partners involved in the deal, and everything started falling apart. Everything was so raw – no one was thinking business, even me.'

Brown wanted to carry on playing with Maddix, Ibrahim and Ipinson-Fleming, but Maddix told him it would be a mistake, and would only continue to fuel the idea that they were trying to keep the Roses alive. He wrote a song called 'What Happened to Ya', 'specifically about John and Ian', and gave it to Brown, advising him to use it as a start to build a solo career. Brown was skint and often slept on Maddix's couch, his personal life as broken as his dreams and self-belief. A solo career, he felt, was beyond him. 'He was look-ing at me with tears in his eyes, saying, Are you selling me out as well?' said Maddix. 'I was trying to say to him, I'm doing the complete opposite, my friend. Here's a song, why don't you write an album about what you're going through, what we've all been through, here's your start.'

It was the beginning of something new, but also the sad end. On 29 October 1996 Brown released the following statement to the press: 'Having spent the last ten years in the filthiest business in the universe, it's a pleasure to announce the end of The Stone Roses. May God bless all who gave us their love and supported us throughout this time. Special thanks to the people of Manchester who sent us on our way, peace be upon you.'

17.

Fifteen Years

A new Roses album was released in November 1996. There had always been rumours that, in the period between their 1989 eponymous album and *Second Coming*, the band had recorded and abandoned an album of lost material: a glorious batch of golden 'Fools Gold'-style workouts. It was a haunting thought of what could and should have been. Instead there were more arguments, as the *Garage Flower* album finally saw the light of day.

Brown thought he had bought back, and owned, the Roses' 1985 album recorded with Martin Hannett. 'He didn't,' said Howard Jones. 'He bought the multi-tracks, not the mix. The album is the final agreed production mix, which is what I had.' Jive/Zomba approached Jones, who had managed the band between 1984 and 1986, about the album, with a view to releasing it. Jones had kept Squire's original artwork, intended for the record sleeves of the planned 1985 singles 'I Wanna Be Adored' and 'This Is the One' – and the art was included in the package.

'The next thing I know is I get a call off Ian saying, I want to see you,' said Jones. 'He told me, I'm not happy about this.' Four of the five Roses who had recorded the album – Brown, Reni, Pete Garner and Andy Couzens – showed up at Jones's house in Manchester, and a protracted argument took place. Brown was keen to find out how much Jones was making on the album – the band had, after all, never signed a proper deal with him or Thin Line. Brown, still hurting from the Roses' disintegration and financially stretched, was clearly agitated. 'Ian was slowly but surely losing his rag and a fight was going to break out, and I was going to be the recipient of any violence,' said Jones. He asked them all to leave his house. 'They weren't having it. So I said, Oh right, well, I've run out of cigarettes, I'm just going out to get some. I went out and rang the police and got them to come and throw them out. Obviously that didn't go down very well.'

Legal bills subsequently ate up much of the profit there was to be had from the release of the *Garage Flower* album, which included the eleven original songs recorded for the album in 1985, plus the stand-alone Thin Line single, 'So Young'/'Tell Me'. The band's former guitarist, Andy Couzens, came to an arrangement that saw him credited as co-writer of all the tracks on the album, with Squire and Brown, apart from 'I Wanna Be Adored', 'Here It Comes', 'This Is the One', 'Tell Me' and 'So Young', which remained Squire/Brown compositions. The album reached number 58 in the UK charts. 'In a way I wish I'd never done it,' said Jones, whose relationship with Brown never recovered. 'But I didn't put it out as a bootleg. It was an official release, and it was an important part of their history. People who are interested in Martin Hannett's work and career should have a copy of it.'

Since leaving the Roses, Reni, now sporting a big bushy beard and long hair, had kept a low profile. He'd had plenty of offers of work. Paul Ryder, the former bassist with the Happy Mondays, had wanted to get a new project going, but despite Reni being a fan of Ryder's work, he was determined that his next band would be *his* band. He also turned down offers to drum for emerging British reggae star Finley Quaye, whom he knew and liked – uninterested in session work. Rough Trade boss Geoff Travis tried to get him hooked up with ex-Suede guitarist Bernard Butler, but he wasn't interested in playing with refugees from other name bands. The management of hit Scottish band Texas were keen for him to work with the band on an album. He liked the demos they sent, but wanted to concentrate on his own material. Reni retreated to the attic of his Manchester home with former Roses bassist Pete Garner to work on his own band, in which he would not drum but sing and play guitar. A great deal of intrigue surrounded his plans for the band, which had a great name, Hunkpapa.

Squire's new band also now had a name, The Seahorses. The Roses' tour manager, Steve Adge, who had quit the group with

Squire, was co-managing them. It was quickly pointed out by the *NME* that The Seahorses was an anagram of 'he hates Roses'. Squire, now thirty-four, continued to associate himself with Oasis, who were, he said, 'an inspiration', and had co-written a song with Liam Gallagher for The Seahorses' upcoming album. Squire's new lead singer in The Seahorses was a former busker, Chris Helme, who bore more than a passing resemblance to Brown. He had a similar northern inflection, but his vocals were more melodic and strident, in the vein of Roger Daltrey or Robert Plant. When Squire quit the Roses, Geffen had picked up their option to sign him, and The Seahorses recorded an album in thirty days in Los Angeles with producer Tony Visconti, famed for his work with T Rex and David Bowie.

In April 1997 The Seahorses toured the UK, in small, sold-out venues, to hundreds rather than thousands, with a *Second Coming*-lite first single, 'Love Is the Law', charting at number 2. The Roses had recorded a version of the Squire song in 1994, during the *Second Coming* sessions. Squire was back on *Top of the Pops* promoting the single, and his new band received heavy media coverage, although, invariably, many of the questions were related to The Stone Roses' break-up. He talked of Reni's departure as the moment the band truly ended – when their unique chemistry evaporated.

Squire was also asked about the bitterness Mani and Brown had recently expressed towards him. Mani had said his ambition for 1997 was to 'piss all over Squire'. He wasn't surprised. 'I knew there was no love lost, so I didn't expect fond wishes.' He had 'no regrets' about leaving the Roses. Already the question was put to him: ten years down the line, someone offers you $10 million to re-form the Roses, would you do it? No, he said. 'No chance.' There were no ego wars in The Seahorses, and he had experienced a better feeling playing with them than he'd ever had in the Roses. His personal life was still chaotic, however, and, despite his apparent confidence, there was a brittleness and emptiness to such proclamations.

The same could be said of the band's debut album, *Do It Yourself*, released in June 1997. The title came from the last three words

Brown had said to him. It went to number 2 in the UK, selling over 300,000 copies, and gave Squire his first major hit in the US, peaking at number 8 on the Billboard charts. Despite an appealing goofiness to some of the lyrics, the band's middle-of-the-road radio pop-rock appeal was deeply soulless. Any echoes of the Roses – and Squire's guitar work was often, heartbreakingly, a reminder of what could have been – were distinctly hollow. Helme had written the best new tune on the album, 'Blinded by the Sun', and it became The Seahorses' second single, reaching number 7 in the UK. Disruptive behaviour saw Squire sack The Seahorses' drummer, Andy Watts, before the year was out – following the release of a third single from the album, the one co-written with Liam Gallagher, 'Love Me and Leave Me', which peaked at 16.

The Seahorses' musical nadir came via a stand-alone single, released in December 1997, written by Squire/Helme, a rock-by-numbers Oasis-a-like tune called 'You Can Talk to Me'. It reached number 15 in the UK and did well in America, but it was truly a death knell for anyone who had thought Squire would walk from the Roses wreckage unscathed. The Seahorses remained a viable commercial proposition, however, despite looking increasingly like a charade, and the single was supposed to be the start of a second album. Geffen put much effort into promoting the band with slick videos, and in the coming year The Seahorses continued to spread their name, playing Glastonbury and supporting U2, The Rolling Stones and Oasis.

Squire and Mani had quickly and easily patched up their relationship. But he did piss all over Squire in 1997, as Primal Scream resurfaced with a wildly original, experimental and challenging new sound. The Scream's career since the early 1980s had paralleled the Roses' in many ways, and the arrival of Mani revitalized the group, who had been considering splitting up following the poor critical response to their retro-rock 1994 album, *Give Out But Don't Give Up*. A single, 'Kowalski', co-written by Mani, reached number 8 in the UK in May 1997 (thanks in part to a video featuring Kate Moss), as a prelude to the album, *Vanishing Point*, released in July.

With its deep dub bass, aggressive electronic edge and irregular song structures, it was a huge critical hit. The album, although uncompromising, was also a great commercial success, hitting number 2 in the UK.

The Scream had not just found a future – they were the future, and Mani's funk was an elemental part. Mani said his talent had often gone unrecognized in the Roses, and he was 'happy as Larry' to play a lead role in the Scream. Like Squire, he could not avoid questions about the Roses. 'Ian's been unfairly savaged, I know he will have the biggest and loudest laugh some day,' he said. The Roses, he made clear, had refused to 'flog a dead horse. People will remember that.'

In September 1997 it was reported that Brown had signed a solo deal with Polydor and was finishing his first solo album. Brown had asked Reni to drum with him again, but Reni didn't want to revisit the Roses and had not taken up the offer. Reni also showed disinterest when Mani tried to get him to join Primal Scream in late 1997. In September 1997 Reni made headlines during a brief appearance in Manchester Magistrates' Court on charges of driving with no insurance. It should have been a perfunctory matter, but the 33-year-old was up before a judge well known for his eccentricities. When the judge misread a letter of mitigation, Reni launched a verbal assault on him, accusing him of behaving 'like a five-year-old'. Warned he could be in contempt of court, Reni replied, 'Big deal, so what?' He was sentenced to seven days in prison and served three.

From Squire's announcement to leave the band to the Roses' ignoble ending, Brown had been on the receiving end of nothing but bad press. He had talked of giving up music to pursue a 'purer' career, as a gardener or flower seller. Maddix, however, had given him a great gift with the song 'What Happened to Ya', planting the seed for a solo album that had slowly blossomed. Aided by guitarist Aziz Ibrahim, and with encouragement from old friends and fans, he self-financed the deliberately lo-fi record. Much of it was written and recorded in his ex-council house in Lymm, and he played many of the instruments himself. When he was happy with the songs, he shaved off his beard and took them to the Roses' former lawyer, John Kennedy, who was now the chairman of Polygram Records. Kennedy loved the work, and it resulted in Brown signing a deal with one of the company's labels, Polydor. 'It became clear he was a stronger songwriter than he was first given credit for,' said Kennedy.

Brown released his first solo single in January 1998, 'My Star', a seductive mix of snaking guitar lines, military beats and lyrics that explored the politics of American space exploration. The single entered the UK charts at number 5, and he appeared on *Top of the Pops*, causing a stir by having someone 'play' a tray of eggs, and then by tossing the eggs at the backdrop. In interviews he said he didn't want another band: 'I feel I've done that.' He had started to get his personal life in order. He had two children to provide for, and a new girlfriend who lived in New York.

Invariably he was asked about the Roses. It was the band's 'tightness' as a gang that had made them unique, but that had dissipated during the recording of *Second Coming*, when in the 300 days of studio work they had sat down for a meal together only once. He was asked about his relationship with Squire. 'I don't have one,' he replied. He was also asked about The Seahorses. 'They sound like what they are,' he said, 'a quarter of one band. They do sound poor.' He could not hide his bitterness towards Squire. 'That fucker,' he said, had left him 'high and dry' and then 'magically' discovered a new band, got management, and a deal, in the blink of an eye. Squire was 'a grown man who turned into a pure baby', he said. 'He's just empty.'

Produced and mixed by Brown, his first solo album, *Unfinished Monkey Business*, released in February 1998, was a surprise and a joy. 'My Star', while clever and catchy, had been fairly predictable. The album was anything but, and the obvious comparison was Syd Barrett's eccentric solo work following his departure from Pink Floyd. Rudimentary, doused in reggae rawness, deeply idiosyncratic, *Unfinished Monkey Business* bowed to no prevailing fashion or trend. It was warm, alive, childish, profound and full of soul: the singer who critics had said couldn't sing was now doing it all himself. Tracks such as 'Ice Cold Cube', 'Can't See Me' and 'Deep Pile Dreams' addressed Squire, and eviscerated him. Although Brown hoped his new songs would stand on their own, a good deal of intrigue came from the damnation Brown brought down on his former Roses band mates.

The album made number 2 in the UK, selling 300,000 copies. Brown was still smoking weed, and deeply into reggae and rap, and when asked didn't hold back his criticisms of the crop of bands who idolized the Roses, such as Oasis ('babies pretending to be The Beatles'), The Charlatans ('laughable') and The Verve ('miserable'). 'First is first, and second's nothing,' he said. Brown also appeared at Glastonbury in 1998, and two further singles from the album, 'Corpses in Their Mouths', peaking at number 14 in April, and 'Can't See Me', number 21 in June, kept the momentum rolling. His cocksure persona and forthright views attracted controversy. He threatened to sue *Melody Maker* over impenetrable comments he'd made about homosexuals and Western power structures (while talking about a Divine Comedy single), which had been shaped to portray him as homophobic. He was badly beaten up twice in unprovoked attacks in Warrington. And in October 1998 he was jailed for four months following an arrest for threatening behaviour on an aircraft.

The incident had happened in February when he had been arrested on a return flight from Paris to Manchester. He had over-reacted to a dismissive gesture by an air stewardess, and told her he would 'chop her hands off'. The heavy sentence handed down at Manchester Magistrates' Court on 23 October came at a time of growing concern about 'air rage' incidents, and Brown was made an example of. He was forced to cancel tours of the UK and Japan. While he was in prison, Reni sent him a letter every three days. Squire sent him a gift of a box of Maltesers, the present they had always exchanged at Christmas, plus a message that read, 'I still love you'. Brown was released on 22 December 1998. He sent thanks to Squire via a third party, his reputation as an outlaw figure now entrenched.

In January 1999 The Seahorses, having recorded much of their second album, split up. Singer Chris Helme called Squire's new songs 'muso wank' and criticized both the lyrics and tunes. The break-up coincided with Jive/Zomba releasing a remix of 'Fools Gold' that reached number 23 in the UK in February, and with Mani associating himself, as DJ, with Roses tribute band The Complete Stone Roses. Jive/Zomba also released a tenth-anniversary edition of the Roses' eponymous album, and it made its highest showing on the UK charts yet, hitting number 9. With Squire now unattached, Mani apparently up for it and the Roses' music more popular than ever, there was the first serious talk of a band reunion, and they were offered £1.25 million for two gigs.

Brown's spokesman issued a firm denial. After being released from prison, Brown was soon back in the Top 10, having collaborated with the innovative DJ Shadow of the London collective U.N.K.L.E. on a new single, 'Be There'. 'There's something different, more than just music, about Ian,' said Mo' Wax Records and U.N.K.L.E. founder James Lavelle. In November 1999, Brown's second solo album, *Golden Greats*, was released, peaking at number 14. It had critics frothing at the mouth, and was variously called a 'leftfield masterpiece' and a 'magisterial comeback'. It had a heavy electronic sound and the lyrics were less concerned with Squire, many written while he had been in prison. It was seen as mature, brave work, and the singles from it – 'Love Like a Fountain' (UK no. 23), 'Dolphins Were Monkeys' (UK no. 5, featuring a cover of Michael Jackson's 'Billie Jean' as a B-side) and 'Golden Gaze' (UK no. 29) – firmly established Brown as a solo artist of stature.

Squire, meanwhile, was reduced to advertising in the music press for applications to join his new 'Skunk Works Project'. He briefly hooked up with a former member of The Verve and a former male fashion model, but it was destined to come to nothing, as he now admitted it was 'impossible to create the chemistry' the Roses had once had.

In early 2000 there were rumours of a single, 'Selective Indignation', from Reni's new band, now called The Rub. He had auditioned many players for The Rub, a name taken from Shakespeare's *Hamlet* soliloquy 'To be or not to be'. A short UK tour was arranged to test the waters. He played six gigs in small venues but, despite the West Coast rock sound and attractive harmonies, there was no getting away from the fact that the audiences wanted to see him play drums, not the guitar. After the tour he got back into painting, forsaking music for art for long periods.

Mani and Primal Scream maintained their momentum with a new album, *XTRMNTR*, which reached number 3 in the UK in 2000, recording a swift follow-up, *Evil Heat*, which reached number 9 in 2002. Both albums were unconventional, experimental and confrontational, and the way the Scream worked was almost as an anti-group, an egoless conglomerate of moveable parts. The process, although artistically rewarding, often left Mani pining for the more traditional rock-band set-up – the Roses. 'I want to put our differences aside and get together for one summer,' he said. 'We'd just do a tour and show all the kids who never saw us what we were about. I think the Roses deserve another shot.'

In October 2001 Brown released his third solo album, *Music of the Spheres* (UK no. 3), which included his most accomplished single to date, 'F.E.A.R' (UK no. 13). The album's lyrics had a hippyish, quasi-visionary aspect; the music was minimal and sensual. It was another step forward, and in 2002 he was rewarded with an *NME* award for 'best solo artist' and a Brit Awards nomination for 'best male solo artist'. He was treated to glowing profiles and serious reappraisals of his talent, and was asked to make a cameo appearance in a Harry Potter film. Questioned about the possibility of re-forming the Roses – there were rumours of a coming together to play the opening ceremony of the Commonwealth Games, which came to Manchester in the summer of 2002 – he remained unoptimistic. 'I can't see the day. We're all too far apart.' He attributed his prodigious output as a solo artist to the wasted years recording *Second Coming*. When he was asked more specifically about his relationship with Squire, he said, 'John's a great guitar player, one of the greatest. I don't want John playing dull or flat songs. I don't associate him with those feelings. I'd like him to come out with a great record again.'

Squire released his first solo album, *Time Changes Everything*, in September 2002, on his own North Country label. It was recorded in his farmhouse in the Peak District, close to Macclesfield. He was settled with a new partner, had two children from previous relationships, and the music was rustic, reflective, acoustic and homely, with shots of subdued electric guitar. It was a shock to hear Squire sing, and it was almost impossible to get over that. His voice was nasal and unappealing, but he poured his heart into the tracks, which bore many echoes of former glories. Unlike Brown, who had damned Squire on his debut solo album, Squire was more forgiving in his ruminations on Brown – particularly on the emotional 'I Miss You'. He even included a song about the Roses, '15 Days'. Co-produced by Simon Dawson, who had worked on *Second Coming*, the album reached number 17 in the UK charts, but a single, 'Joe Louis', failed to break the Top 40.

While Squire promoted the solo album, a new Roses compilation album, *The Very Best of The Stone Roses*, was released in November 2002, making number 19 in the UK. This had followed an album of Roses remixes, *The Remixes*, which had reached number 41. Squire had not hidden his feelings for Brown, or the Roses, on his album, and the songs were easy to interpret as a gesture towards ending their long-running feud, and perhaps as a sign that a Roses reunion might yet happen. Squire was friendly with Mani, but had not spoken to Brown for seven years, nor to Reni since he'd quit the band. He admitted to being hurt the deepest by his falling out with Brown, and said reconciliation was long overdue. 'I do not accept I was responsible for the break-up [of the Roses], if Ian is willing to stop saying that and accept that wasn't the case, then I'm sure we can talk again.'

To promote his solo album Squire took to the road and surprised fans by including a handful of Roses songs, including 'She Bangs the Drums', 'Waterfall' and 'Fools Gold', in the set. Squire recorded a second solo album, *Marshall's House*, with each song inspired by and sharing a title with a painting by American realist Edward Hopper.

The album failed to chart. He enjoyed more success as an artist with his first solo exhibition at the ICA in London in 2004, including his work which had adorned the Roses' record covers. He also played live at the exhibition launch, his set featuring many Roses songs.

The *Observer Music Monthly* magazine placed the Roses' eponymous 1989 album at number 1 in their 100 Greatest Albums of All Time in 2004, and this, plus a best-selling double DVD, featuring the Roses' 1989 Blackpool Empress Ballroom show and a compilation of all their video and TV performances, reinvigorated the rumours that the Roses would re-form. It was no secret that Squire's manager, Simon Moran, now one of the UK's leading concert promoters, held a torch for the band he'd promoted as a young man in Blackpool, and had an appetite to see the Roses reunite. The figure now being put on such a happening was £5 million.

Hope that this might happen was soon to be blown away by Brown, however, when in the summer of 2004 he astonished a crowd of 5,000 at a National Trust benefit gig in Surrey by playing an entire set comprised of Roses songs: 'I Wanna Be Adored', 'Sally Cinnamon', 'Sugar Spun Sister', 'Waterfall', 'Mersey Paradise', 'Made of Stone', 'She Bangs the Drums', 'Where Angels Play' and 'I Am the Resurrection'. He used members of a Roses tribute act, Fools Gold, to recreate the songs. Brown had never previously played Roses songs during any of his solo shows; the decision to do so, he said, was because of Squire's playing of the Roses songs during his own shows, which he said Squire did out of 'self-interest . . . He's got no respect. He's butchering them. I did it for the people. It felt great – they really are the people's songs.'

Brown was asked about the huge figures being offered to re-form the Roses. 'It was never about money. It was about changing the world,' he replied. So much love had been poured into the band that he couldn't fathom why Squire had not called him in eight years. It was unlikely that Squire would now, after such an attack. 'There's a misconception I developed a monstrous cocaine habit and that destroyed the band, and Ian is responsible for that,' said Squire. 'So under those conditions, I can't entertain working with him.' Squire said he would 'rather remove my liver with a teaspoon' than re-form the Roses. He was tired of Brown blaming him, and hit back. 'Ian blew it,' he said, saying that it was Brown's marijuana habit that had ruined the band, turning him into a 'tuneless knob' and a 'paranoid mess'.

In September 2004 Brown, now forty-two, released his most accomplished solo album to date, *Solarized*, which reached number 7 in the UK charts. A single, 'Keep What Ya Got', co-written with Noel Gallagher, went to number 18. He responded to questions about Squire aggressively. 'He split up the best band in the country for what? He went on to do nothing, he must be bitter, seeing me steaming ahead. I announce shows and they're [the tickets are] gone in a day. It must be killing the kid. He was the best guitarist of his generation. All I know is when he stood next to me he had pure success; since then, nothing. How can I be the villain when I was the last man standing?'

But now Brown overstepped the mark, recording the Roses song 'Where Angels Play' as a B-side to 'Time Is My Everything', and his band butchered it on the BBC2 TV show *Later with Jools Holland*. *Solarized* was Brown's first album to interest America, but dates there ended badly when in March 2005 he was arrested, following an on-stage fight in San Francisco. He was released without charge but his American career had failed to ignite. Back in the UK, his standing was at its peak. He played Blackpool Empress Ballroom, fifteen years after his triumph there with the Roses, and the set was studded with Roses classics. He was joined on stage by Mani to play 'I Wanna Be Adored'. 'The songs have bled into English culture,' Brown told the *NME*, 'like no other band but The Beatles.'

In 2005, Squire, recently a father to twins, patched things up with Reni. The two of them met at an Arthur Lee show in Manchester, where Lee was recreating the Love album that the Roses had so loved, *Forever Changes*. Mani was also at the show and took Squire over to Reni. Squire now talked about making 'a ferocious guitar record' and then getting the Roses back together, suggesting they might play Glastonbury that summer as a replacement for headline act Kylie Minogue, who had pulled out due to illness. Mani told the

Guardian that Squire wanted to make up with Brown, 'hopefully have a natter and see what comes of it . . . It's getting undignified,' he said. 'I'm determined to orchestrate the two of them being in the same room. I'd like to close the book properly.' 'Never say never,' said Reni, but he didn't think it would be this year. He was right.

Brown dismissed the talk, despite the offer of $1.8 million for each member should they re-form. It annoyed him. 'John bangs on about putting the group back together,' he said, 'why doesn't he call me?' Brown said they were too far apart musically. 'We were like brothers once,' he said, 'and that spirit is what made us. Now the spirit simply isn't there. I don't see how we could recreate what we had. It would spoil everything by trying.' Brown played Glastonbury solo that year, and Mani played with the Scream. The two briefly came together during Brown's set when Mani joined him to play 'I Wanna Be Adored'.

The Greatest, a greatest hits selection of the finest moments from Brown's solo career, was released in September 2005, selling over 100,000 and peaking at number 5. His attitude towards any idea of a Roses reunion remained aggressive, however. Squire had 'stabbed me in the back', he said. 'Do you think if he was sat here now with his greatest hits, he would be talking about putting the band together? I don't think he would. Fuck what he wants, I don't care what he wants, he didn't care what I wanted.'

Brown signed a new deal with Polydor for two more solo albums. Upon accepting a 'Godlike Genius' award from the *NME* (who had recently voted the Roses' 1989 album as the best British album of all time) in 2006, he said, 'If I was in the gutter and my kids lived on the kerb, I'd go and get a job at B&Q before I'd re-form the Roses.' Almost every British guitar band that had emerged of note in the decade, in particular The Libertines and Arctic Monkeys, made no secret of the fact the Roses were a core influence. Mani was now back attending to business with Primal Scream, as well as DJing and playing with Freebass, which featured three bass guitarists – himself, New Order's Peter Hook and The Smiths' Andy Rourke – and even he could now see no reconciliation.

Mani took out his frustrations on the band's infamous manager Evans. Having failed to ignite Oldham-based band The Ya Ya's, Evans, with business partner Matthew Cummins, had realized a dream of building a golf course, near Warrington, called High Legh Country Park and Golf Club. He had also starred in a 2004 BBC3 documentary about the band, *Blood on the Turntable*. Brown had expected the show to make his blood boil, but still found that he had a soft spot for Evans, whose chutzpah was distilled in his pronouncement, 'I am the Stone Roses.' Mani did not share Brown's evaluation, and assaulted Evans at the annual Manchester-based In The City music business conference, organized by Tony Wilson. Paul Birch, the boss of FM Revolver, with whom the Roses had clashed in 1990 over the re-release of 'Sally Cinnamon', was also at the conference, and had told Mani about the £5,000 he had handed Evans just before the controversial paint incident.

Now living in Wales, Evans was involved with a band called The Lizzies, and in 2006 he was attacked again at his home (where he kept a room packed with Roses ephemera, including guitars, photographs and T-shirts) in a brutal late-night assault. The 56-year-old was reportedly hit in the head several times with a blunt weapon and required twenty-eight stitches. 'I could have died because of the blood I lost,' he said. No arrests were made over the incident, which was said to concern issues unconnected with the Roses. Evans then fell out with Cummins over the sale of their Cheshire golf club. In September 2007 Cummins was found dead with a broken neck on the floor by an industrial bin at the club. The coroner returned a verdict of accidental death: Cummins had climbed into the bin, attempting to compact rubbish by jumping up and down on it, when the bin had started to roll, smashing into a wall.

In 2007, Squire held two exhibitions of new artworks in prestigious London galleries, to much acclaim. He said he had given up on music: 'I'm enjoying this far too much to go back to music.' Brown had his fifth solo album out, *The World Is Yours*. It peaked in the UK at number 4 and featured former Sex Pistols Paul Cook and Steve Jones. On the album's lead single, the strident anti-war protest song

'Illegal Attacks' (UK no. 16), he shared vocals with Sinéad O'Connor. The whole album was overtly political, and heavy on strings and hip-hop beats. Still the questions about the feud with Squire continued. 'I'd have a Starbucks with him if he was buying,' Brown said. 'He better have some pretty good tunes, after this long, they'd want to be pretty great.'

Mani was back with Primal Scream in 2008, with an album *Beautiful Future*, but had one eye on the upcoming lavish twentieth-anniversary edition of the Roses' 1989 album, and was again hoping for a reunion. 'Me, John and Reni are up for doing it and Ian just needs some working on,' he said. 'Next year is the ideal time.' The rumour had been given some credence by a comment Squire had made after witnessing the 2008 Led Zeppelin reunion show: 'It would be good to do something like that one day.'

The twentieth-anniversary edition of the band's eponymous album, released in 2009, came in many beguiling formats. Clive Calder had sold Jive/Zomba to BMG in 2002 for $2.7 billion, after success with Britney Spears, N'Sync and The Backstreet Boys. In 2004 BMG merged with Sony. This new release of the album was being sold on more favourable percentage terms for the band members. It had been a bitter pill that for twenty years the band's most popular work was attached to a contract that had been described as the worst in history.

The album made its highest chart position in the UK yet, at number 5, proving that the band's popularity had not just sustained but grown in the thirteen years since they had split up. The album now featured in the 'greatest ever' lists of publications such as *Time*, *Rolling Stone*, the *Guardian* and *Q*, and had sold several million copies worldwide. The *Daily Mirror* reported that the Roses *had* re-formed – for a twenty-one-date tour. Squire, this time, stamped on the idea, and produced a metallic artwork on which he had scratched the words 'I have no desire whatsoever to desecrate the grave of seminal Manchester pop group The Stone Roses.'

Brown had a new album out, *My Way*, in 2009. It was his sixth. The title said it all, and he had little left to prove. Above all, he was still believable, empowering and bedevilling in equal parts. Tracks such as 'Always Remember Me' – on which Brown returned to sermonize on Squire and the Roses – 'So High' and 'By All Means Necessary' were profoundly emotional, quivering with defiance. After a decade of solo work, he was undefeated. *My Way* was pure gospel. The singer who couldn't sing was all soul. The album was recorded at Battery Studios, where the Roses had made album tracks in 1989, with long-time collaborator Dave McCracken. Squire had sent Brown a song that he had considered including on the album. 'It was pretty good, sounded nice,' said Brown. But his son had said, 'Dad, you can't work on that, he sold you out, didn't he? He left you for dead.' Even Simon Moran – who as well as managing Squire also promoted shows for Brown, and had been the catalyst for the 2009 Take That reunion tour, the UK's biggest tour to date – failed to tempt Brown with his calculations of the fortunes the Roses could earn if they re-formed. 'It's getting very boring now,' said Mani. 'I don't know why they don't kiss and make up'.

Squire held a further art exhibition in 2010, and designed a series of book covers for the publisher Penguin. Brown took his solo act on the road, peppering his set with Roses tracks and playing in over eighteen countries. His relationship with his wife had broken down, and he returned, after almost a decade in London, to live in Manchester. He was writing songs for his seventh solo album, but admitted that, aged forty-seven, it was getting hard. 'Life's about ideas,' he said, and wondered how many he had left; as an indication of that, he was considering writing his memoirs. Returning to Manchester had felt like 'coming home', and he and Mani enjoyed nights out on the town.

Primal Scream were also looking backward in 2010, celebrating the twentieth anniversary of *Screamadelica* by performing the album in its entirety at two wildly successful shows in London. Mani talked about plans to take the album on the road in 2011, and also ended his association with Freebass, a band he described as 'something to keep me match fit while the Scream were doing nothing', after arguing with fellow band member Peter Hook on Twitter. Mani had accused Hook of getting fat off Ian Curtis's blood money after Hook took to touring Joy Division songs, but quickly apologized. 'I'm from Manchester and we're a bunch of gobby bastards, so whatever I said that was just me being me,' he said. 'That's what comes from spending time with the likes of Ian Brown and Liam Gallagher in the pub.'

Reni remained a mystery. The man rated as the drummer of his generation, and one of the best of all time, had not released a note since quitting the Roses. In those almost fifteen years of silence, he had assumed the mantle of one of rock's greatest recluses. He had contributed an intriguing, oblique poem to the band's twentieth-anniversary release of the album that defined a generation, but had never publicly spoken about his time in the Roses, maintaining his dignity and privacy. Reni also had a stable and fulfilling private life, with no apparent craving to return to the limelight. He trusted few people, and although he had created an impressive body of artwork over the years, was uncertain about the prospect of exhibiting it. His own musical ambitions seemed abandoned. Offers continued to come his way, but 'No' had become his de facto position. Ironically, by doing and saying nothing, it was Reni who kept aflame much of the Roses' mystique – and magic. His silence said that there was them, or there was nothing. And he would rather have nothing.

18.

Reunion

On 11 March 2011, Squire and Brown came face to face for the first time in fifteen years. It was a bittersweet moment, for what had brought them together was the death of Mani's mother. At the wake in the Nelson Tavern in Failsworth, north Manchester, they spent a couple of hours chatting. They were both forty-eight. They did not talk about re-forming the Roses, but it was the start of a chain of events.

'They got on great, all very relaxed,' said one of Mani's old pals, Clint Boon, XFM DJ and Inspiral Carpets' main man. 'It was amazing,' said Mani. 'And somewhat bizarre. I've always wanted them to do it – even if the band never re-formed, I always wanted them to re-make the friendship.'

Three days later, Mani was back with Primal Scream as the band took *Screamadelica* around sold-out arenas for the rest of March. On 7 April the *Sun* printed a story under the headline 'Stone Roses Resurrected'. It claimed the Roses 'are getting back together' after Squire and Brown had 'buried the hatchet on one of the most bitter feuds in rock 'n' roll history'. A source said, 'Ian has been mulling over reaching out to John for a while now. A lot of water has gone under the bridge and everyone has grown up. It was an emotional reunion. There were no harsh words. It was a heartwarming breaking of bread. They had a lot to catch up on and have been in regular contact since.' The only stumbling block, the *Sun* reported, was the 'pinning down' of Reni, 'which is about as easy as trapping mercury'.

Reni immediately and flatly denied the story. Although the *Sun* had not mentioned where Squire and Brown had established contact, Mani was fuming. 'I'm disgusted that my personal grief has been invaded and hijacked by these nonsensical stories,' he said. 'Two old friends meeting up after fifteen years to pay their respects to my mother does not constitute the reformation of the Stone Roses. Please fuck off and leave it alone. It isn't true and isn't happening.'

A week later, on 14 April, the *Sun* had more details about the whereabouts of the Squire and Brown meeting, and published a camera phone shot, taken by bar staff at the funeral wake, of Mani with his arms draped over Squire and Brown – the 'picture every music fan wanted to see'.

Squire, who was preparing paintings for a major art exhibition due to start in June, said, 'They're just rumours. I can't see it. As you get older, you realize you are on the downward slope of your life in terms of time and there are only so many things you can do. There was a time when I tried to do both things [art and music] side by side and I don't think either of them got a fair shot as a result. I'm happy where I am.'

Squire was a father of five, with a sixth on the way. He was busy at his workshop at his farmhouse in Macclesfield, and the new art show meant a lot to him. The London show was entitled 'Celebrity', and was 'anti-idolatory' in sentiment. The twenty-one abstract works were named after figures such as serial killer Harold Shipman and footballer David Beckham. 'It's an indictment of our celebrity-obsessed culture because I think celebrity is the new opiate of the masses,' he said. But serious art critics still did not take him seriously, and only five of the twenty-one paintings sold.

Brown had a new track out in May, having contributed vocals to an electro house single, 'Open Your Eyes', by respected DJs and remixers Alex Metric and Steve Angello. Ever since his collaboration with U.N.K.L.E. in 1999 and his hook-up with the Mo' Wax label, Brown had been feted by a fashionable collective, loosely revolving around Mo' Wax founder James Lavelle and Japanese fashion impresario Nigo, famed for his A Bathing Ape label. Brown had spoken of wanting to design clothes. In March he had collaborated with Adidas on a pair of trainers. They were launched with an elaborate exhibition of Brown memorabilia at the Adidas store in Soho, London. Despite 'Open Your Eyes' failing to make the Top 40, as Brown contemplated recording his seventh solo album (his final one on his current contract with Polydor) it was clear he was still open to new ideas and considered a force in the worlds of rock, dance and fashion.

In Manchester he was a folk hero. 'I've only ever had love here,' he said. 'I've never had a bad word shouted at me in twenty years.' Brown said he thought he was one of the 'last working-class musicians'. He sang in front of a crowd of 42,000 at Manchester United's Old Trafford stadium in May, leading out the team for Gary Neville's testimonial match against Juventus. His team had long played 'This Is the One' when they walked out onto the pitch on match days, and Brown sang accompanied by only the crowd. There were also many friendly faces to catch up with. The old Roses rehearsal rooms, Spirit, had closed in 2009 when owner John Breakell reinvented his business as the School of Sound Recording (SSR). After establishing the Manchester facility, Breakell opened a similar operation in London, and Brown agreed to supply prospective students with a £10,000 bursary, advertised as the Ian Brown Scholarship.

Reni was busy in the summer of 2011, having sold his house in Whalley Range, and was in the process of buying a new home in Manchester that needed serious renovation. There was a loose plan to exhibit his art in 2012, but family life dominated. 'He would fill the Manchester Apollo if he just set up his drum kit in there and played,' said Brown. But Mani knew Reni wouldn't consider doing anything that wasn't better than before. And the drumming on The Stones Roses' 1989 album, all agreed, was unbeatable.

Brown sat down for a meal with Reni in early August 2011, the first time the two had met for many years. Brown and Squire had been in regular contact since Mani's mum's funeral, and had 'gone from laughing and crying about the old days to writing songs in a heartbeat', said Squire. They sometimes collaborated over Skype. Brown was free and easy – single again. Reni had the stresses and strains of moving home. He was forty-seven, healthy and remarkably fresh-faced, unlike the weather-beaten Brown. He was still eccentric, but with a mature perspective on what Brown was now loosely discussing: a Roses reunion. He thought he was 'too old' to drum again. 'As far as drummers are concerned you should really quit at thirty-five,' he would say later, but he was still thinking about music, and the challenge interested him, even if he had serious doubts about the musical worth of re-forming.

Mani, who had been a guest at Kate Moss's wedding in July, was often back in Manchester for a few days between Scream gigs. He was godfather to three of Squire's children, and Squire took the kids for a visit. Squire's outlook had changed since his chance meeting with Brown. It had made him think a reunion was possible, 'even enjoyable', he said. Mani was happy to hear of Squire and Brown's ongoing rekindling of their friendship, of the progress being made in the songwriting, and also of the news that Brown and Reni had met up. The heavy touring schedule of the Scream was tiring. He would soon be forty-nine, had sworn off booze and drugs, and was trying to kick the fags. Before he set off again for another two months of globe-trotting on the *Screamadelica* tour, in principle it was agreed the Roses were all broadly in favour of re-forming.

There could be no band rehearsals until Mani returned from his tour with the Scream at the end of September. Brown wanted the band to play before announcing any plans for a reunion. 'Just in case someone said, When you play together, how do you know it's not going to be shit?' It gave him and Squire further time to work on songs, and Reni the time to finalize the purchase of his new home. There were also other issues that needed thinking through. Brown, for instance, managed himself, Squire was managed by Simon Moran, Reni had his own manager, and Primal Scream were talking about recording a new album, having been reinvigorated by the reception of the *Screamadelica* tour. It was a given that Simon Moran, as managing director of SJM, the country's leading concert promoter, would organize the dates, but myriad other business decisions needed addressing. It was also inevitable that, given the volatile and unpredictable mix of the four Roses' personalities, there would be arguments. Nothing but that was certain.

Mani told the Scream he was leaving the band to join the Roses in a bar in Buenos Aires, at about two o'clock in the morning. It was 28 September and hard for Mani. He had 'mixed emotions', said the

Primal Scream guitarist Andrew Innes. Mani had been in the Scream for longer now than he had the Roses, and they were family to him. He was back in England at the beginning of October, however, and the Roses played together for the first time. Squire and Reni were rusty, Mani was recovering from the Scream tour, but Brown was on sparkling form. Reni had 'never heard him sing better'.

The first song they played was 'Shoot You Down'. 'It's just something magical when us four are in a room together,' said Mani. 'And you can't put your finger on it, and it's just so beautiful to catch back hold of it again.' There were arguments, quite serious arguments, but they worked through them.

Next, all four were down in London to meet with Moran and finalize arrangements. Again, tempers frayed. Tensions that had been fifteen years in the making had to be aired. The band were photographed by their favourite, Pennie Smith, for shots to be used to promote the comeback.

On Friday 14 October, PR Murray Chalmers, who now had his own company after spending twenty-four years as Director of Publicity for EMI Records, sent out invites to a press conference on 18 October where a 'very special announcement' would be made. The band had originally wanted the conference to take place at the Radisson Hotel in Manchester, but it had been switched to Soho House in London. The 'special announcement' was quickly linked to the Roses and their re-formation, initially by *Clash* magazine on their website, and the news immediately trended on Twitter and spread across the Internet. It was still touch and go, and there was no guarantee all four would show up. Squire's wife was due to give birth, and on the Friday evening Reni's manager texted a message, on behalf of Reni, that read, 'Not before 9T will I wear the hat 4 the Roses again.' Although the *Sun* confirmed the conference was for the Roses, who were definitely re-forming, there remained intrigue about Reni's statement – a deliberate hoax – and fans and the media spent the next three days discussing whether they would re-form without Reni, and whether the reunion would really happen. It was headline news around the world.

On 18 October, at 2 p.m., filmed by Shane Meadows, famed for his film *This Is England* (2006), and with Liam Gallagher in attendance, the four Roses took their seats on stage at the press conference. Brown, his hair flecked with grey, said they planned to 'shake up the world', and announced two dates in Manchester at Heaton Park, on 29 and 30 June 2012, which would be a prelude to a world tour. They would be doing new songs. Squire said very little, just that the friendship he and Brown shared defined them both, and it 'needed fixing'. Brown confirmed they had met for the first time in fifteen years at Mani's mum's funeral. 'A beautiful thing has come out of a really sad situation.' Reni remained cautious: 'We'll see how beautiful it is when it's on record and on stage,' he said. When Mani thanked Primal Scream for 'saving his arse' after the Roses split, Reni said, 'They might be saving your arse again in a couple of weeks.'

'We've got a long way to go,' Reni said. 'I've never seen anyone our age do what we're attempting to do.' He said he was probably too old to drum again, was rusty, but had the eight months ahead to prepare. 'You've got to understand that we've not played much yet,' he said. 'We've been circling around each other for a while and it's just like joining a new band . . . with ghostly kind of presences. It's a strange phenomenon.' Brown described the process of remoulding the band as 'like a language we all used to speak that we've not spoken for a while'. 'In some ways it seems like fifteen years ago was yesterday,' said Squire.

There were thorny questions too. Were they getting back together for the money? 'The money's always been there,' said Brown. A recent Shaun Ryder quote was put to him – Ryder had suggested Brown's recent divorce had stripped him financially. 'There's always truth in Shaun's comments,' Brown replied. What about the hurtful things they had said about one another over the years, and the acrimonious nature of their original break-up? 'Life's full of hurt,' said Reni. 'You're never going to get away from the hurt, but what happens is you grow away.'

'I think we've still got it and I think we've still got something to give to people, and I think that at times like this we can uplift people,' said Brown. 'We're doing it for ourselves, I'm not going to lie, but . . . it sounds magic.'

The next day the Roses had an official website and the tickets for the two Manchester dates went on sale on 21 October. Demand was such that a third date in Manchester was added, and all 210,000 tickets sold out in sixty-eight minutes, the fastest-selling events in UK rock history. That evening Reni was in a state of disbelief. He had not expected this. The band were overjoyed. The press quickly calculated the concerts would gross £12 million.

In November, as the band continued their rehearsals on a farm in Cheshire, further live dates were added at festivals over the summer of 2012, in Spain, Japan and Scotland. There was also an array of new T-shirts for sale on the official website. The four of them could not, however, simply walk in a room and immediately recreate their magic, and rehearsals were frustrating and hard work. It was not just a question of new material, of which they had plenty, especially as Reni had brought some of his own material to the table; they needed to breathe new life into the old songs. Even those closest to the band admitted, despite everything, the comeback was not guaranteed.

The Roses were exactly the type of band, the only band in fact, who were capable of raising expectations to this level and suddenly walking away from it if they didn't feel it was right. It could still fall apart, and nearly did when a tyre on Reni's car blew out when he was driving back from rehearsals one night. He escaped unscathed. 'We'll ride it till the wheels fall off, like we did last time,' Brown had said at the press conference. Brown also faced a distraction when he twice appeared in court on charges of speeding while driving, and was banned for three months.

In December, more summer 2012 festival dates were added, in Denmark, Sweden and Norway, and Squire and Brown made a surprise appearance to play a Roses song, 'Elizabeth My Dear', and The Clash's 'Bankrobber' with Mick Jones of The Clash and members of The Farm, for the Justice Tonight: A Concert in Aid of The Hillsborough Justice Campaign and the Don't Buy the *Sun* Campaign at Manchester's Ritz club.

This was followed, on 10 December, by news that the Roses had concluded negotiations on a record deal for the new material. Simon Moran was now the band's official manager, and the Roses had signed to Universal in the UK and Columbia in America. More dates were added for summer 2012, with festival shows in Portugal, Hungary, Germany, Ireland and South Korea. There would also be a gig in Dublin at Phoenix Park, for which all 45,000 tickets immediately sold out. The band had a Lollapalooza Festival-shaped hole in their schedule for August 2012, as the Roses planned a second assault on America, but were wondering if they should delay it until 2013.

The band stopped rehearsing during Christmas, with Mani playing three final *Screamadelica* shows that climaxed in a Hogmanay gig in Edinburgh, and in January 2012, rehearsals picked up again. Shane Meadows told the press the band were not just in it for the money. 'It goes way beyond that, because they're all fucking intelligent and very proud and they wouldn't go out there to the slaughter,' he said. 'I saw them rehearsing one verse of "Bye Bye Badman" for an hour yesterday. I looked at that and thought, They are taking this fucking seriously.' The explosive arguments – particularly between Brown and Reni – had cleared the air, and all four were enjoying themselves. The *Sun* ran an entirely false story in February 2012 that quoted Mani saying he had been amazed to find £2 million deposited into his bank account. The others had to be scraped off the roof, having all agreed to stick to a media blackout until June 2012. In mid-February, however, Reni said that the band had finally gelled and once again become the band that they used to be. Brown, sounding happy and relaxed, said much the same.

There was now no doubt the Roses would deliver, on stage and on record. They had never had a number 1 up to now, nor had Brown as a solo act, The Seahorses, or Mani with the Scream. And being number 1 was everything. It always had been. A new album would now surely and finally give them that satisfaction. The last great rock 'n' roll band deserves nothing less.

Afterword

I had started chasing Reni in 2008, forewarned with the knowledge that he usually said no to all requests. He seemed intrigued, however, by my work with Andrew Loog Oldham on the books *Stoned* and *2Stoned*. I sent him copies and he liked them. Loog Oldham had been a recluse in Colombia for twenty years when I brought him to book, and that took ten years. Reni hadn't spoken to the press in fifteen years, and I was told he was a great storyteller when in the mood. He was tantalizingly close, just across the city. Although it hadn't been a no, it didn't ultimately translate into a yes and he remained out of reach.

Towards the end of 2010 I made a fresh play. Any last flicker that the Roses would re-form had been extinguished. It was known, however, that all the other Roses had a great deal of esteem for Reni, as did almost all who had worked with the band.

Reni, true to form, wasn't particularly interested in talking about himself or his family, but now agreed a broader effort about the band could work. A list of over a hundred interviewees was drawn up with everybody on it, bar Gareth Evans. Reni's manager, John Nuttall, who had known all the Roses since the mid-1980s and was respected by them all for his level-headedness, was instrumental in securing many contacts. I had conducted over 300 interviews for *Stoned* and *2Stoned*, so was in it for the long haul and, this being the Roses, aware of the pitfalls. I'd been on the rack with Loog Oldham, but this was a new form of exquisite pain. Work started in March 2011.

Some names were given to me, some depended on the wind, and others were chased. When I tracked down Toxin Toy, who had played with them on their seminal 1985 tour of Sweden, it seemed to be a real positive. Reni added a batch of new names that seemed to illustrate just how little was really known about the band, and hinted at hidden treasure. The information that David Bowie had offered to produce the Roses around 1990 was new. As was the fact Paul McCartney had wanted to get to know the Roses in the same period, but that Evans had cut him off at the pass, thinking he was being clever by asking McCartney's secretary, 'What's in it for Paul?'

One disappointment was the Roses' road manager Steve Adge, who is involved in a similar capacity on their comeback. He was working on his own book and understandably preferred to keep his stories to himself. There were many more successes, and many spoke for the first time on record. Soon I had interviewed eighty people. I was pleased to have opened a window onto the Roses' American career, and had managed to separate fact from fiction, without relying on old press cuttings in the attempt. I'd spoken with six of The Stone Roses, and I only had the final four left to cover. We were weeks away. Reni was ready to answer a long set of questions, Mani was on board, Brown was said to be in markedly good spirits, with only Squire unfathomable. As his own father said of him, Squire seemed to 'live in a world of his own', but he is also a genuine friend and admirer of Reni.

Things began to change on 4 October 2011 when this book made national news, including a two-page spread in the *Independent*. This was only two weeks before the band's press conference, and the book was interpreted by many as a sign of an imminent 'third coming' of the Roses. Reni walked into an almighty row about the book at the band's first rehearsal. Brown was particularly unhappy with the book being described as 'authorized by the band'.

When Brown and Reni were dining, or Mani and Squire socializing, I took these as good signs. Reni said he had talked to Brown about the book, and he was okay with the idea. It was only when all four were down in London to talk to Moran that I began to suspect a reunion was definitely on the cards. After the press conference, the book continued to be a source of argument between the band members, and any idea of using the word 'official' or 'authorized' was repudiated. Brown telephoned to call me a 'parasite', and would hear no defence. Mani now didn't want to get involved in the spat, having previously been amenable, even open to DJing at the launch of the book.

Although all the band had warmed to the suggestion that Toxin Toy should support them in Sweden in 2012, the members themselves remained elusive, focused on rekindling the magic that makes them so unique. The V Festival was added to the list of comeback gigs in late February, with surely more to follow. Reni suggested we wait a year before working on the book. Squire wasn't bothered. To the end, the Roses remained endearingly themselves – truly one of a kind. This is the truth. And this book is their true story.

Gigography/Discography

1984

23 October: The Moonlight Club, London
21 November: Labour Club, Exeter
22 November: Ad-Lib Club, London

1985

4 January: Fulham Greyhound, London
12 January: Piccadilly Radio, live session
19 January: The Marquee, London
8 February: Dingwalls, London
20 February: The Maze, Nottingham
29 March: Clouds, Preston
6 April: Oddys, Oldham (cancelled)
10 April: Bing Bang Club, Linköping, Sweden
11 April: Olympia, Norrköping, Sweden
12 April: Rockborgen, Borås, Sweden
19 April: Lilla Marquee, Stockholm, Sweden
21 April: Kolingsborg, Stockholm, Sweden
24 April: Studion, Stockholm, Sweden
26 April: Kulan, Lindigö, Stockholm, Sweden
27 April: Ultra, Stockholm, Sweden
30 April: Lindigö Stadium, Stockholm, Sweden
10 May: The International, Manchester
24 May: Gallery, Manchester
4 July: Fulham Greyhound, London
20 July: Flower Show 1, Manchester
10 August: The Marquee, London

15 August: The Haçienda, Manchester

19 August: 'So Young' / 'Tell Me' – UK indie charts no. 2 (Thin Line, 12-inch only)

24 August: The Marquee, London

27 August–1 September: *Garage Flower* album (Thin Line Records, unreleased)

11 September: Embassy Club, London

September: 'I Wanna Be Adored' single (Thin Line Records, unreleased)

October: 'This Is the One' single (Thin Line Records, unreleased)

26 October: Riverside, London

2 November: Manchester University

30 November: Warehouse 3 . . . Take Two, Manchester

1986

5 March: King George's Hall, Blackburn

25 March: Warwick University

10 May: Manchester University

24 May: Warwick University

31 May: McGonagle's, Dublin, Ireland

6 June: Warehouse, Leeds

5 July: Three Crowns Club, London

7 July: The Ritz, Manchester

13 August: Bluebird Club, Barrow

22 August: Mardi Gras Club, Liverpool

1987

30 January: The International, Manchester

18 May: 'Sally Cinnamon' – UK indie charts no. 38; B-sides 'All Across the Sands' and 'Here It Comes' (FM Revolver Records, 12-inch only)

30 May: The International, Manchester

26 June: The International, Manchester

3 July: Take Two Club, Sheffield

17 July: Planet X, Liverpool

16 August: Earthbeat Festival, Sefton Park, Liverpool
12 November: Hummingbird, Birmingham
13 November: The International, Manchester

1988

23 January: Dingwalls, London
15 February: 'Elephant Stone'; B-sides 'Full Fathom Five', 'The Hardest
   Thing in the World' (Rough Trade Records, 7-inch, unreleased)
26 February: The International II, Manchester
11 March: The International, Manchester
30 May: The International II, Manchester
13 June: The International II, Manchester
17 October: 'Elephant Stone' – UK indie charts no. 27; B-sides 'Full Fathom
   Five', 'The Hardest Thing in the World', 'Elephant Stone' 12-inch mix
   (Silvertone Records, 7-inch and 12-inch)
18 November: Legends, Warrington
19 November: The International II, Manchester
26 November: Citadel, St Helens
28 November: London Polytechnic
29 November: Olivers, Chester
2 December: London School of Economics
7 December: Belfast University, Northern Ireland
11 December: Venue, Edinburgh, Scotland

1989

17 February: Legends, Warrington
20 February: Sheffield University
23 February: Middlesex Polytechnic
27 February: The Haçienda, Manchester
27 February: 'Made of Stone' – UK indie charts no. 4; B-sides 'Going
   Down', 'Guernica' (Silvertone Records, 7-inch and 12-inch)
28 February: Escape Club, Brighton
1 March: Club Rio, Bradford

2 March: Coal Exchange, Cardiff

3 March: Legends, Warrington

5 April: Liverpool Polytechnic

17 April: *The Stone Roses* album – UK charts no. 32, peaking at UK no. 19 in February 1990: 'I Wanna Be Adored', 'She Bangs the Drums', 'Waterfall', 'Don't Stop', 'Bye Bye Badman', 'Elizabeth My Dear', '(Song for My) Sugar Spun Sister', 'Made of Stone', 'Shoot You Down', 'This Is the One', 'I Am the Resurrection' (Silvertone Records, vinyl, CD and cassette)

28 April: South Parade Pier, Portsmouth

29 April: Brunel University, Uxbridge

4 May: Liverpool Polytechnic

5 May: Queen's Hall, Widnes

6 May: The International II, Manchester

7 May: Sheffield University

8 May: Warehouse, Leeds

11 May: Trent Polytechnic, Nottingham

12 May: JBs, Dudley

13 May: Angel Centre, Tonbridge, Kent

15 May: ICA, London

17 May: Edwards No. 8, Birmingham

19 May: Aberystwyth University

22 May: Dingwalls, London

24 May: Oxford Polytechnic

25 May: Shrewsbury, Park Lane

26 May: Elektra, Milton Keynes (cancelled)

27 May: Citadel, St Helens (cancelled)

30 May: Guildhall Foyer, Preston

3 June: Junction 10, Walsall

6 June: Majestic, Reading

7 June: Leicester University

8 June: Lancaster University

20 June: Riverside, Newcastle

21 June: Venue, Edinburgh

22 June: Rooftops, Glasgow

23 June: Town Hall, Middlesbrough

24 June: Roadmenders, Northampton

25 June: Arts Centre, Norwich

26 June: Bierkeller, Bristol

27 June: Civic Hall, Stratford-on-Avon

28 June: Irish Centre, Birmingham

30 June: Leeds Polytechnic

10 July: La Cigale, Paris, France

17 July: 'She Bangs the Drums' – UK charts no. 36/Billboard Modern Rock US charts no. 9; B-sides 'Standing Here', 'Mersey Paradise', 'Simone' (Silvertone Records, 7-inch, 12-inch, CD and cassette)

27 July: Riverside, Newcastle

12 August: Empress Ballroom, Blackpool

18 September: 'I Wanna Be Adored' – Billboard Modern Rock US charts no. 18 (US single only; Jive/Zomba 12-inch)

23 September: Barraca, Valencia, Spain

28 September: Rolling Stone Festival, Milan, Italy

1 October: Futurama, Dienze, Belgium

3 October: Club Logo, Hamburg, Germany

4 October: Luxor Club, Cologne, Germany

10 October: Melkweg, Amsterdam, the Netherlands

12 October: Les Inrockuptibles Festival, Paris, France

23 October: Club Citta, Kawasaki, Japan

24 October: Kan-i Hoken Hall, Tokyo, Japan

25 October: Mainichi Hall, Osaka, Japan

27 October: Nihon Seinenkan, Tokyo, Japan

13 November: 'Fools Gold' – UK charts no. 8/Billboard Modern Rock US charts no. 5; B-sides 'What the World Is Waiting For', 'Fools Gold' extended mix (Silvertone Records, 7-inch, 12-inch, CD and cassette)

18 November: Alexandra Palace, London

4 December: *The Stone Roses* album – Billboard US charts no. 86 (US release, with extra track 'Fools Gold', Jive/Zomba, vinyl, CD and cassette)

11 December: 'Sally Cinnamon' – UK charts no. 46 (reissue, FM Revolver, 7-inch, 12-inch CD and cassette)

1990

12 February: 'Elephant Stone' – UK charts no. 8 (reissue, Silvertone Records, 7-inch, 12-inch, CD and cassette)

26 February: 'Made of Stone' – UK charts no. 20 (reissue, Silvertone Records, 7-inch, 12-inch, CD and cassette)

5 March: 'She Bangs the Drums' – UK charts no. 34 (reissue, Silvertone Records, 7-inch, 12-inch, CD and cassette)

15 May: Patrol, Copenhagen, Denmark

16 May: Mejeriet, Lund, Sweden

17 May: Fryshuset, Stockholm, Sweden

19 May: The Voice, Oslo, Norway

27 May: Spike Island, Widnes

3 June: Féria de Nîmes Festival, Spain (cancelled)

3 June: Provinssirock Festival, Seinäjoki, Finland

7 June: Maysfield Leisure Centre, Belfast, Northern Ireland

9 June: Glasgow Green, Scotland

21 June: Chicago, USA (cancelled)

22 June: New York, USA (cancelled)

24 June: Detroit, USA (cancelled)

29 June: Hollywood High School Gymnasium, USA (cancelled)

30 June: San Francisco, USA (cancelled)

2 July: 'One Love' – UK charts no. 4/Billboard Modern Rock US charts no. 5; B-sides 'Something's Burning', 'One Love' extended mix (Silvertone Records, 7-inch, 12-inch, CD and cassette)

1991

June: Madison Square Garden, New York (cancelled)

June: Forum, Los Angeles (cancelled)

June: San Francisco (cancelled)

2 September: 'Elephant Stone' (reissue, Silvertone Records, 7-inch, 12-inch, CD and cassette)

9 September: 'Waterfall' – UK charts no. 27 (Silvertone Records, 7-inch, 12-inch, CD and cassette)

7 October: 'I Wanna Be Adored' – UK charts no. 33 (Silvertone Records, 7-inch, 12-inch, CD and cassette)

14 October: *The Stone Roses* album (reissue, Silvertone Records, double vinyl, CD and cassette)

2 December: *Blackpool Live* (Silvertone Records, video of Empress Ballroom gig)

1992

9 March: 'I Am the Resurrection' – UK charts no. 33 (Silvertone Records, 7-inch, 12-inch, CD and cassette)

4 May: 'Fools Gold' remix (Silvertone Records, 7-inch, 12-inch, CD and cassette)

6 July: *Turns into Stone* album – UK charts no. 32; compilation of A-sides and B-sides: 'Elephant Stone', 'The Hardest Thing in the World', 'Going Down', 'Mersey Paradise', 'Standing Here', 'Where Angels Play', 'Simone', 'Fools Gold', 'What the World Is Waiting For', 'One Love', 'Something's Burning' (Silvertone Records, CD and cassette)

13 July: *The Singles Collection* (Silvertone Records, 8CD box set)

13 July: 'So Young' (Silvertone Records, CD)

1994

28 November: 'Love Spreads' – UK charts no. 2/Billboard US charts no. 55; B-sides 'Your Star Will Shine', 'Breakout', 'Groove Harder' (Geffen Records, 7-inch, 12-inch, CD and cassette)

5 December: *Second Coming* album – UK charts no. 4/Billboard US charts no. 47; 'Breaking into Heaven', 'Driving South', 'Ten Storey Love Song', 'Daybreak', 'Your Star Will Shine', 'Straight to the Man', 'Begging You', 'Tightrope', 'Good Times', 'Tears', 'How Do You Sleep',

'Love Spreads', secret track (Geffen Records, double vinyl, CD and cassette)

1995

6 March: 'Ten Storey Love Song' – UK charts no. 11; B-sides 'Ride-On', 'Moses' (Geffen Records, 7-inch, 12-inch, CD and cassette)

10 April: 'Fools Gold 95' – UK charts no. 25 (Silvertone Records, 12-inch, CD and cassette)

19 April: Rockefeller Music Hall, Oslo, Norway

20 April: Palladium, Stockholm, Sweden

24 April: Docks, Hamburg, Germany

25 April: Metropol, Berlin, Germany

26 April: Paradiso, Amsterdam

27 April: La Luna, Brussels, Belgium

29 April: E-Werk, Cologne, Germany

1 May: *The Complete Stone Roses* album – UK charts no. 4; compilation of A-sides and B-sides: 'So Young', 'Tell Me', 'Sally Cinnamon', 'Here It Comes', 'All Across the Sands', 'Elephant Stone', 'Full Fathom Five', 'The Hardest Thing in the World', 'Made of Stone', 'Going Down', 'She Bangs the Drums', 'Mersey Paradise', 'Standing Here', 'I Wanna Be Adored', 'Waterfall', 'I Am the Resurrection', 'Where Angels Play', 'Fools Gold', 'What the World Is Waiting For', 'Something's Burning', 'One Love' (Silvertone Records, vinyl, CD and cassette)

1 May: Zurich, Switzerland

3 May: Art Palladium, Rome, Italy

5 May: Pakhus 11, Copenhagen, Denmark

7 May: Aqualung, Madrid, Spain

9 May: Le Transbordeur, Lyon, France

11 May: Elysée Montmartre, Paris, France

14 May: Midtown Music Festival, Atlanta, USA

16 May: Gaston Hall, Washington DC, USA (cancelled)

18 May: Marine Terminals, Toronto, Canada

20 May: Manhattan Ballroom, New York, USA

21 May: Avalon Club, Boston, USA

22 May: Webster Hall, New York, USA

24 May: The Trocadero, Philadelphia, USA

26 May: Riverport Amphitheater, St Louis, USA

27 May: World Music Theater, Chicago, USA

29 May: Palladium, Los Angeles, USA

31 May: Fillmore Club, San Francisco, USA

5 June: Factory Hall, Sapporo, Japan (cancelled)

7 June: Club Citta, Kawasaki, Japan (cancelled)

8 June: Club Citta, Kawasaki, Japan (cancelled)

10 June: Century Hall, Nagoya, Japan (cancelled)

12 June: Nippon Budokan, Tokyo, Japan (cancelled)

13 June: Nippon Budokan, Tokyo, Japan (cancelled)

14 June: Kousei Nenkin Kaikan, Osaka, Japan (cancelled)

16 June: Yuubin Chokin, Hiroshima, Japan (cancelled)

17 June: Sun Palace, Fukuoka, Japan (cancelled)

19 June: Festival Hall, Osaka, Japan (cancelled)

24 June: Glastonbury Festival, Somerset (cancelled)

30 July: Lollipop Festival, Stockholm, Sweden

31 July: Tullikamari Club, Tampere, Finland

1 August: Tavastia Club, Helsinki, Finland

2 August: Tavastia Club, Helsinki, Finland

5 August: Feile Festival, Cork, Ireland

1 September: Pilton Party, Somerset

11 September: Club Citta, Kawasaki, Japan

12 September: Nippon Budokan, Tokyo, Japan

13 September: Nippon Budokan, Tokyo, Japan

15 September: Convention Hall, Okinawa, Japan

17 September: IMP Hall, Osaka, Japan

18 September: Century Hall, Nagoya, Japan

20 September: Yuubin Chokin, Hiroshima, Japan

21 September: Sun Palace, Fukuoka, Japan

24 September: IMP Hall, Osaka, Japan

25 September: IMP Hall, Osaka, Japan

27 September: Factory Hall, Sapporo, Japan

28 September: Club Citta, Kawasaki, Japan

1 October: Festival Hall, Brisbane, Australia

2 October: Enmore Theatre, Sydney, Australia

3 October: Enmore Theatre, Sydney, Australia

5 October: Metro, Melbourne, Australia

7 October: Thebarton, Adelaide, Australia

8 October: Metropolis, Perth, Australia

9 October: Metropolis, Perth, Australia

13 November: 'Begging You' – UK charts no. 15; B-side remixes (Geffen Records, 7-inch, 12-inch, CD and cassette)

28 November: The Royal Hall, Bridlington Spa

30 November: Civic Hall, Wolverhampton

1 December: Corn Exchange, Cambridge

2 December: Brighton Centre

4 December: Newport Centre, Wales

5 December: Exeter University

7 December: De Montford Hall, Leicester

8 December: Brixton Academy, London

9 December: Brixton Academy, London

11 December: Rivermead, Reading

12 December: Norwich University of East Anglia

13 December: Town and Country Club, Leeds

15 December: Royal Court Theatre, Liverpool

16 December: Whitley Bay Ice Rink

17 December: Music Hall, Aberdeen

19 December: Barrowlands, Glasgow

20 December: Barrowlands, Glasgow

22 December: Apollo, Manchester

23 December: Apollo, Manchester

28 December: Sheffield Arena

29 December: Wembley Arena, London

1996

February: *Crimson Tonight* live EP; 'Daybreak', 'Breaking into Heaven', 'Driving South', 'Tightrope' (Geffen Records, Australia and Japan only)

2 August: Festival Internacional, Benicàssim, Spain

10 August: Festival Vilar de Mouros, Portugal

11 August: Skanderborg Festival, Denmark

12 August: Budapest, Hungary

23 August: Lowlands Festival, Holland (cancelled)

25 August: Reading Festival

25 November: *Garage Flower* album – UK charts no. 58; 'Getting Plenty', 'Here It Comes', 'Trust a Fox', 'Tradjic Roundabout', 'All I Want', 'Heart on the Staves', 'I Wanna Be Adored', 'This Is the One', 'Fall', 'So Young', 'Tell Me', 'Haddock', 'Just a Little Bit', 'Mission Impossible' (Silvertone Records, vinyl, CD and cassette)

1999

February 22: 'Fools Gold 99' – UK charts no. 25 (Silvertone Records, 12-inch, CD and cassette)

October 11: *The Stone Roses* album – UK charts no. 19; tenth-anniversary edition (Silvertone Records, double CD)

2000

9 October: *The Stone Roses: The Remixes* album – UK charts no. 41 (Silvertone Records, double vinyl, CD)

2002

4 November: *The Very Best of the Stone Roses* album – UK charts no. 19; compilation: 'I Wanna Be Adored', 'She Bangs the Drums', 'Ten Storey Love Song', 'Waterfall', 'Made of Stone', 'Love Spreads', 'What the World Is Waiting For', 'Sally Cinnamon', 'Fools Gold', 'Begging You', 'Elephant Stone', 'Breaking into Heaven', 'One Love', 'This Is the One', 'I Am the Resurrection' (Silvertone Records, double vinyl, CD)

2004

28 June: *The Stone Roses: The DVD*; Blackpool live, music videos and TV performances (Silvertone Records, double DVD)

2009

10 August: *The Stone Roses* album – UK charts no. 5; twentieth-anniversary edition (Silvertone Records, Special Edition, Legacy Edition, Collector's Edition, double/triple CD, DVD, triple vinyl)

Notes

It was not my intention, and has never been my style, to have to rely on press cuttings. However, as events overtook the writing of this book, it became a necessity to pull some quotes from cuttings. I have tried, wherever possible, to avoid the old quotes other Roses books are based on. So, while the majority of material in this book is original and based on interviews I conducted in 2011 and 2012, the following quotes are from previously published interviews.

Prologue

2 *'We wanted to do a gig . . . it was perfect'*: Ian Brown, *The Face*, July 1990, interview with author.

4 *'bored, lazy, snotty twat'*: Ian Brown, *Q*, July 1990.

5 *'We're getting nish'*: Ian Brown, Spike Island press conference, May 1990.

9 *'Then suddenly I realized I didn't have any weed . . . Spike Island'*: Mani, *Scootering*, January 2004.

9 *'We had lots of rows . . . It was horrible'*: John Squire, *Q*, November 2002.

12 *'I didn't say anything . . . Frankie Bones playing house'*: Paul Oakenfold, *The Face*, July 1990, interview with author.

12 *'I was 100 per cent relaxed . . . been nervous?'* Ian Brown, *The Face*, July 1990, interview with author.

13 *'It was like a massive pilgrimage . . . a statement'*: Roddy McKenna, *Clash*, April 2009.

13 *'We were just a very small part . . . what we do'*: Ian Brown, *Number One*, July 1990.

14 *'proof rock music had become showbusiness'*: John Squire, *Melody Maker*, December 1990.

15 *'We were a bit disappointed . . . laws will let us'*: Ian Brown, *The Face*, July 1990, interview with author.

Notes

1. The Patrol

17 Never Mind the Bollocks, Here's the Sex Pistols *'was going to change the world'*: Ian Brown, *Record Collector*, February 1998.

17 *'rebellious streak'*: Ian Brown, *Guardian*, February 2002.

18 *'I think he was the first kid . . . by himself'*: Ian Brown, *Uncut*, February 1998.

19 *'Poor, down to earth'*: Ian Brown, *Clash*, April 2009.

19 *'a bit to the left of Arthur Scargill'*: Ian Brown, *Independent*, October 2011.

19 *'I didn't hear a bad song until I left home'*: John Squire, *NME*, April 1989.

20 *'We became friendly at thirteen, fourteen . . . he was the loner'*: Ian Brown, *Uncut*, February 1995.

20 *'Virtually everything we did . . . how long it would take'*: John Squire, *XFM*, July 2007.

21 *'the most exciting thing I'd ever experienced . . .'*: John Squire, *Guardian*, September 2002.

24 *'That stuff came easy . . . the sound'*: John Squire, *XFM*, July 2007.

25 *'I was always on the move . . . kids everywhere'*: Ian Brown, *Record Collector*, February 1998.

28 *'The first thing I did was scrub pots'*: Ian Brown, *NME*, November 1989.

29 *'a barman at the local, a labourer . . . maintenance firm'*: John Squire, *Aesthetica*, July 2005.

29 *'The Scooterboys were not Mods'*: Ian Brown, *Melody Maker*, June 1990.

31 *'They'd try to . . . fight them every week'*: Ian Brown, *Record Collector*, February 1998.

32 *'We'd kick fuck . . . anything like that'*: Mani, *Scootering*, January 2004.

33 *'We always used to think the southern Manchester . . . good music'*: Mani, *Scootering*, January 2004.

33 *'We were having problems . . . all their lot'*: Mani, *Scootering*, January 2004.

33 *'We'd heard about this kid . . . He ain't no fighter'*: Ian Brown, *Record Collector*, February 1998.

34 *'We were joint singers . . . play his guitar'*: Ian Brown, *Record Collector*, February 1998.

2. *Reni*

37 *'It was my cousin who told me . . . I loved it'*: John Squire, *Mojo*, May 2002.

37 *'I had a friend who worked . . . brought him down'*: Ian Brown, *Record Collector*, February 1998.

39 *'Geno was like . . . it was, like, okay'*: Ian Brown, *Record Collector*, February 1998.

40 *'We started a few rehearsals . . . three weeks with her'*: Ian Brown, *Record Collector*, February 1998.

41 *'spent a lot of time with "Red House" '*: John Squire, *XFM*, July 2007.

42 *'proper rocker'*: Ian Brown, *Uncut*, February 1998.

42 *'When I went to the audition . . . I just had to join'*: Reni, *Melody Maker*, June 1990.

44 *'For an eight-track . . . definitely'*: Ian Brown, Swedish interview, 1985.

44 *'They had some kind of passion . . . a tune'*: Ian Brown, *Buzzin'*, May 1987.

44 *'Wild sounds with attractive melodies . . . the contradiction'*: John Squire, *Debris*, December 1988.

46 *'We came off stage . . . with Townshend'*: Ian Brown, *Record Collector*, February 1998.

46 *'We were told he'd said . . . nicking Reni'*: John Squire, *Mojo*, May 2002.

47 *'You didn't have to be Mystic Meg . . . a wild weekend'*: Garry Johnson, The Punk Poet blog, January 2010.

47 *'turned down by every single one . . . massive bender'*: Garry Johnson, The Punk Poet blog, January 2010.

48 *'leap around . . . and safe'*: Ian Brown, Swedish interview, 1985.

50 *'These were the things . . . meant something to us'*: Ian Brown, *Mojo*, May 2002.

3. *Sweden*

54 *'I was aggressive on stage . . . people remembered us'*: Ian Brown, *Uncut*, February 1998.

56 *'Too much enthusiasm . . . with the safer mix'*: Ian Brown, *Buzzin'*, May 1987.

56 'We don't want to be clothes horse puppets': John Squire, *City Life*, March 1985.

56 'We're five people who all want to be a front man': Ian Brown, *City Life*, March 1985.

57 'The respect and musical integrity . . . would be ideal': Reni, *Buzzin'*, May 1987.

59 'I told him we were a big group . . . eight or nine shows': Ian Brown, *Record Collector*, February 1998.

61 'It was great . . . We got in the daily papers': Ian Brown, *Record Collector*, February 1998.

61 'We all write all the music . . . we're just a 1980s band': Ian Brown, Swedish interview, 1985.

63 ' really could happen . . . I couldn't go back': John Squire, *Mojo*, May 2002.

4. So Young

68 'The situation got a little crazy . . . touch and go for a while': Ian Brown, *Melody Maker*, February 1987.

69 'It was where we got our following': Ian Brown, *Record Collector*, February 1998.

69 'I knew exactly how it should look . . . be complete': John Squire, *Spin*, May 1990.

70 'dreadful angst-ridden rock . . . day we heard it': Ian Brown, *Buzzin'*, May 1987.

70 'it was was alright at the time . . . powerful and raw': Reni, *Buzzin'*, May 1987.

71 'They were a big influence . . . loved about The Beach Boys': John Squire, *XFM*, July 2007.

5. Hannett

74 'We caught Martin at the wrong time . . . hard to work with': Ian Brown, *Record Collector*, February 1998.

76 'I walked into the control room . . . gone to the pub for a pint': Ian Brown, *Buzzin'*, May 1987.

78 'Martin taught us . . . pull our melodies out': Ian Brown, *Melody Maker*, June 1990.

78 'We weren't really in control . . . we shouldn't have': Ian Brown, *Buzzin'*, May 1987.

81 *progression comes from hate*: Ian Brown, *Buzzin'*, May 1987.

81 'We were terrible at the start . . . and sleeping bags': Ian Brown, *Record Collector*, February 1998.

83 'That's just stupid people . . . And we will be massive': Ian Brown, *Mancunion*, February 1987.

84 'Me and Reni decided . . . the copper couldn't see him!': Ian Brown, *Record Collector*, February 1998.

84 'That caused us . . . of all Manchester architecture': Ian Brown, *M62*, July 1988.

84 *As far as I'm concerned . . . rather dull and grey*: Reni, *Buzzin'*, May 1987.

85 'I think we'd been in the room . . . dealing in them': Ian Brown, *Uncut*, February 1998.

85 'He was trying to impress us . . . underpants he was wearing': John Squire, *NME*, November 1989.

85 'We thought he was crazy . . . clicked straight away': Ian Brown, *Uncut*, February 1998.

86 'He didn't have any fear . . . anyone was out of reach': Ian Brown, *Clash*, April 2009.

6. Gareth

90 'It solved a lot of problems . . . a bad move': John Squire, *Debris*, December 1988.

91 'John didn't want to . . . play with him any more': Ian Brown, *Clash*, April 2009.

92 'Took him to the cleaners . . . a lot of it was his fault': Ian Brown, *Record Collector*, February 1998.

95 'Me and John would plan . . . Wow this is it': Ian Brown, *Mojo*, May 2002.

95 'We got together with . . . original, commercial and inspirational': John Squire, *Cut*, September 1987.

96 *'I'm not going in fucking there with him'*: John Squire, indirect quote, interview with John Nuttall, June 2011.

98 *'A lot of people say . . . enough money to get out of it'*: Ian Brown, *Mancunion*, February 1987.

98 *'The angle on these photographs . . . all at once'*: Gareth Evans, *Buzzin'*, May 1987.

99 *'We blew it . . . a few thousand copies'*: Reni, *Buzzin'*, May 1987.

99 *'As far as I'm concerned, we put out "So Young" . . . two songs'*: Ian Brown, *Buzzin'*, May 1987.

99 *'It doesn't bother us at all'*: John Squire, *Buzzin'*, May 1987.

100 *'We learned how to write . . . hard as we always were'*: Ian Brown, *Buzzin'*, May 1987.

100 *'firebombs on the end of his tongue'*: *Buzzin'*, May 1987.

102 *'We thought they were wankers . . . the albatross'*: Ian Brown, *Record Collector*, February 1998.

7. Mani

105 *'in my bedroom pogo-ing about with my tennis racket'*: Mani, *Smash Hits*, July 1990.

105 *'I got hold of Squire's number . . . first, he said'*: Mani, *Mojo*, February 2001.

105 *'I always knew I was the main man'*: Mani, *Scootering*, January 2004.

106 *'was playing catch up when it came to John and Reni'*: Mani, *Mojo*, February 2001.

106 *'Andy Couzens had gone . . . around us knew it'*: Ian Brown, *Uncut*, February 1998.

106 *'We'd rearranged the songs . . . bass lines got funkier'*: Reni, *Mojo*, May 2002.

106 *'Northern Soul was doubly . . . hear it in the music'*: Mani, *Mojo*, May 2002.

106 *'You've got to look like proper scallies'*: Mani, *Mojo*, February 2001.

106 *'The next night . . . played to about five people'*: Mani, *Red Issue*, February 1996.

108 *'We had rated New Order's . . . hit on his name'*: Ian Brown, *Debris*, December 1987.

108 *'We wanted people to hear what he could do'*: Ian Brown, *M62*, July 1988.

110 *'Pennie Smith had made a comment . . . guitars early on'*: John Squire, *XFM*, July 2007.

111 *Evans turned on the charm . . . 'real blast' working with him*: Roddy McKenna, in *Breaking into Heaven* by Mick Middles (Omnibus, 1999).

111 *'A lot of bands in the city . . . we're of some value'*: Ian Brown, *Debris*, December 1987.

114 *'I wanted to sign to Rough Trade . . . as far as I was concerned'*: John Squire, *Mojo*, May 2002.

115 *'We all passed round this telephone directory . . . and signed it'*: John Squire, *Mojo*, May 2002.

115 *'We were musicians . . . had a good time with him'*: John Squire, *Guitar*, July 1995.

8. Leckie

117 *'to handle such a cool act'*: Roddy McKenna, in *Breaking into Heaven* by Mick Middles (Omnibus, 1999).

118 *Brown described the gig as 'perfect'*: M62, July 1988.

119 *'We want to be the first band . . . bigger than The Beatles'*: Ian Brown, *NME*, June 1988.

119 *'We've got to get in the middle . . . our own way'*: Ian Brown, *M62*, July 1988.

120 *'We wrote most of the first album . . . only had about eight'*: Ian Brown, *Uncut*, February 1988.

120 *' "I Am the Resurrection" started out . . . sounds really good'*: Reni, *Guitar*, July 1995.

121 *'Everything was worked out'*: Ian Brown, *Uncut*, February 1998.

124 *'Pop music was saved . . . done nothing for ten years'*: Ian Brown, *Spin*, October 1989.

124 *'We didn't play acid house but we did enjoy it'*: Ian Brown, *Mojo*, May 2002.

124 *'We saw some of the spirit . . . governments don't want that'*: Ian Brown, *Mojo*, May 2002.

125 *'Football hooliganism got finished overnight . . . look at us'*: Ian Brown, *Guardian*, February 2002.

125 *'You can make yourself everlasting by making records'*: Ian Brown, *Melody Maker*, November 1988.

126 *'If I thought we'd remain . . . going to be huge'*: Ian Brown, *NME*, November 1988.

126 *'Love and death. War and peace. Morecambe and Wise'*: John Squire, *Transmission*, October 1998.

127 *'There were only three or four . . . like everybody else'*: Cressa, 'This Is the Daybreak', May 2003.

9. Blackpool

129 *'When we started, Factory . . . things started to happen'*: Ian Brown, *Mojo*, May 2002.

131 *'It was me who coaxed them . . . with your fingers kind of thing'*: Ian Brown, *Mojo*, May 2002.

132 *'We were getting right down . . . didn't really know the part'*: John Squire, *Guitar*, August 1997.

132 *'And we just said, Yeah we know . . . we were good'*: Ian Brown, *Clash*, April 2009.

132 *'Even on songs we've got that . . . less exciting for us'*: Ian Brown, *Q*, July 1990.

133 *'We wanted the tune to be familiar . . . the lyrics clearly'*: Ian Brown, *Uncut*, February 1998.

133 *'A big thing was happening . . . real and beautiful'*: Ian Brown, *Uncut*, February 1998.

133 *'The E-scene is just going to explode . . . in the provinces'*: Mani, *NME*, June 1988.

134 *'Your eardrums sound like . . . as an A-side'*: Ian Brown, *Melody Maker*, March 1990.

136 *'Everyone I know has always liked rock music . . . there any more'*: Ian Brown, *Record Collector*, February 1998.

136 *'It takes effort to sound effortless'*: Ian Brown, *NME*, April 1989.

136 *'The lemons aren't part of the picture . . . tricolour is there'*: John Squire, *Select*, November 1997.

139 *'I'll be severely disappointed . . . end of 1989'*: Ian Brown, *Melody Maker*, June 1989.

139 *'I think I've got divine knowledge . . . about clothes'*: John Squire, *Melody Maker*, June 1989.

139 *'I'd like to shoot Prince Charles'*: Ian Brown, *Melody Maker*, June 1989.

141 *'I think Buckingham Palace . . . cardboard boxes'*: Ian Brown, *Melody Maker*, June 1989.

141 *'If you want to be as big . . . in that forum'*: John Squire, *Sounds*, August 1989.

141 *'After the first few interviews . . . we've resisted that'*: John Squire, *Sounds*, August 1989.

142 *'People around us, press officers, said . . . It's us'*: Ian Brown, *Sounds*, August 1989.

142 *'The Roses still had an awful lot . . . and good bye'*: Gareth Evans, in *Breaking into Heaven* by Mike Middles (Omnibus, 1999).

142 *'We wanted to give people . . . beyond just a concert'*: Ian Brown, *NME*, August 1989.

143 *'Having done a tour . . . vibe in the air here'*: Ian Brown, *NME*, August 1989.

143 *'We didn't know or expect that . . . had the hat on'*: Ian Brown, *Clash*, April 2009.

144 *'I don't usually think about anything . . . Labour Party conference'*: Ian Brown, *NME*, August 1989.

144 *'Proper dancing'*: Ian Brown, *Clash*, April 2009.

10. 'Fools Gold'

146 *'I wasn't familiar with the song . . . made it what it was'*: John Squire, *Mojo*, May 2002.

146 *Mani said clubbing was for research*: *Scootering*, January 2004.

146 *'Three geezers who are skint . . . end up dead'*: Ian Brown, *Independent*, November 2010.

152 *'Ally Pally was the best legal alternative'*: Ian Brown, *Q*, February 1990.

153 *'Anything is possible . . . not having it any more'*: Ian Brown, *Sounds*, August 1989.

155 *Mani, bluntly, said the gig was 'crap' and 'a disaster'*: *Scootering*, January 2004.

155 *'Ally Pally wasn't what it should have been'*: Ian Brown, *Uncut*, February 1998.

155 *Squire had aimed to put the 'human touch' back into acid house*: John Squire, *Spin*, October 1989.

155 *'We never intended to sound like a 1960s group'*: Ian Brown, *Spin*, October 1989.

155 *'We said a little prayer . . . and it did'*: Ian Brown, *Later with Jools Holland*, 2004.

157 *The show 'felt like a vindication for the city of Manchester'*: Mani, in *Stone Roses 'Talking'* by Brian Chapman (Omnibus, 2003).

11. Madchester

159 *'I'm not particularly keen . . . shit me out again'*: Ian Brown, *NME*, November 1989.

164 *'We want to keep moving . . . doesn't end at Manchester'*: Ian Brown, *The Face*, January 1990.

164 *'The next album will be . . . don't want to sound like a band'*: John Squire, *The Face*, January 1990.

164 *'We said no to the Stones . . . they're just patronizing'*: Ian Brown, *The Face*, January 1990.

164 *'We sat in the International . . . refuse to support'*: Gareth Evans, in *Breaking into Heaven* by Mike Middles (Omnibus, 1998).

164 *He had already called U2 'drivel', Lou Reed 'a miserable bastard'*: Ian Brown, in *Stone Roses 'Talking'* by Brian Chapman (Omnibus, 2003).

164 *Bruce Springsteen 'always sounds like he's having a shit'*: Ian Brown, *NME*, July 1990.

164 *'We were never strung out'*: John Squire, *Q*, February 2005.

164 *'A lot of the drug stuff . . . trying to make us notorious'*: Ian Brown, *Uncut*, February 1998.

165 *'Ecstasy wasn't the band's fuel . . . and create'*: John Squire, *Rolling Stone*, May 1990.

165 'We're the most important group . . . our potential yet': Ian Brown, *NME*, December 1989.

167 'We should have been negotiating . . . ahead of the band': Gareth Evans, in *Breaking into Heaven*.

169 'They answered the front door . . . called the police': John Squire, *Q*, November 2002.

169 'He thinks we're just puppets . . . to make an appointment': Ian Brown, *NME*, March 1990.

170 'The police woke me up . . . next to my bed': John Squire, *NME*, March 1990.

171 'I didn't know abstract expressionism was an offence': John Squire, *NME*, March 1990.

171 'Just the sweetest irony . . . wrote "Exhibit A" on it': Mani, *Mojo*, May 2002.

12. 'One Love'

172 'He kept telling us to slow down': John Squire, *Q*, February 2005.

173 'The Manchester scene . . . records or newspapers': John Squire, *Rolling Stone*, May 1990.

174 'We feel we're the only . . . the Sex Pistols, definitely': Ian Brown, *Rolling Stone*, May 1990.

174 'We don't want to be an English phenomenon': John Squire, *Rolling Stone*, May 1990.

174 'There's a lot of other British groups . . . as Manchester': Ian Brown, *Rolling Stone*, May 1990.

175 'big lad's court': Reni, *NME*, March 1990.

175 'We're going to get our bottoms smacked . . . in prison': John Squire, *NME*, March 1990.

177 'It needs more than . . . it needs loads of them': Ian Brown, *NME*, December 1990.

177 'We've never gone out of our way . . . it's where you're at': Ian Brown, *Rolling Stone*, May 1990.

177 'I felt like we were flogging something . . . An attitude': John Squire, *Smash Hits*, July 1990.

178 'The best ever': Ian Brown, *Number One*, July 1990.

178 'We all looked at each other . . . to another level': Mani, *Scootering*, January 2004.

179 'I came home from Glasgow Green . . . eighteen months': Cressa, 'This Is the Daybreak', May 2003.

179 'America doesn't deserve us yet': Ian Brown, in *Stone Roses 'Talking'* by Brian Chapman (Omnibus, 2003).

179 'We're just naturally stubbon . . . we'll turn it down': John Squire, in *Stone Roses 'Talking'*.

179 'defining gig of a generation . . . top record man in the industry': Gareth Evans, in *Breaking into Heaven* by Mike Middles (Omnibus, 1999).

180 'I liked the idea of sending them . . . rock star class': Gareth Evans, in *Breaking into Heaven*.

182 'We tried in vain . . . but it was a poor chorus': Ian Brown, *Record Collector*, February 1998.

183 'bigger than The Beatles . . . put together': Ian Brown, *Smash Hits*, July 1990.

183 'Some people say . . . But they say fuck all': Ian Brown, *Melody Maker*, December 1989.

13. Geffen

186 'We weren't confident of winning . . . to just tour': John Squire, *Red Issue*, February 1996.

187 'I'm just glad to stay out of the nick': John Squire, *NME*, October 1990.

188 'The first two weeks . . . five weeks in the studio': Mani, *Clash*, April 2009.

190 'At least I'm beginning to understand their double-speak': Ian Brown, *Melody Maker*, March 1991.

191 *Evans tried to dissuade him from testifying in court*: Roddy McKenna, in *Breaking into Heaven* by Mike Middles (Omnibus, 1999).

192 'It's probably a greater contribution . . . ever recorded': John Squire, *Melody Maker*, May 1995.

192 'The week after . . . attacking their whole industry': Ian Brown, *The Face*, March 1995.

192 'A massive surprise on the scale of Spike Island': Gareth Evans, *Select*, July 1991.

192 'the might of the American music industry . . . my demise in the other':
Gareth Evans, in *Breaking into Heaven*.

192 'The case had highlighted . . . the original contract': John Squire, *Mojo*,
September 2001.

194 'The Roses were tilting on the brink . . . in America': Gareth Evans, in
Breaking into Heaven.

194 'It's easy to say . . . those big American dates': John Squire, *Mojo*,
September 2001.

196 'If you are away from the action it's like over, really': Mani, *Scootering*,
January 2004.

196 'Ian was quite happy . . . help with the songwriting': John Squire, *Uncut*,
February 1998.

197 'I want £1 million . . . every day for them': Gareth Evans, *NME*, February
1992.

14. Second Coming

198 'Anything you didn't eat . . . melted cheese on it': Mani, *Red Issue*, February
1996.

199 'Too much like a science lesson': John Squire, *Select*, November 1997.

199 'in any form that it came . . . haircuts were like': John Squire, *Select*,
November 1997.

199 'Reni wasn't an elitist . . . would listen to': John Squire, *Select*, November
1997.

200 'When we started . . . Can't this be the album?': Ian Brown, *Clash*, April 2009.

201 'I'm watching them watching Led Zeppelin . . . really stupid': Ian Brown,
Uncut, February 1998.

203 'we had no one . . . just four chiefs and no Indians': Ian Brown, *Clash*, April
2009.

203 'big mistake': John Squire, *Mojo*, September 2001.

203 'We should have written . . . We lost momentum': John Squire, *Mojo*,
September 2001.

203 'He cut himself off . . . anyone else's stuff': Ian Brown, *Uncut*, February
1998.

205 *'He took my fun off me there . . . a bee in his bonnet'*: Ian Brown, *Clash*, April 2009.

205 *'the people who make decisions . . . into battle'*: John Squire, *Spin*, May 1995.

205 *'maybe that was something that Ian had a problem with'*: John Squire, *Q*, February 2005.

205 *'John was being the prolific one . . . get on with it'*: Mani, *Mojo*, September 2001.

206 The house *'was a loafer's paradise'*: Mani, *Mojo*, September 2001.

208 *'When it came time . . . but we knew we were'*: Ian Brown, *Guitar*, July 1995.

208 *'I thought we would go . . . bang it out in a month'*: Ian Brown, *Melody Maker*, October 1997.

210 *'Charlie [cocaine] is the devil, simple as that'*: Ian Brown, *Uncut*, February 1998.

210 *'I'd go away for a week . . . he won't work with him'*: Ian Brown, *Uncut*, February 1998.

211 *'You get a false idea . . . get to the end of it'*: Ian Brown, *Guardian*, September 2009.

15. Reni II

212 *'Ian said to John . . . didn't have a gun'*: Mani, *Q*, February 2005.

213 *'The new guitar-orientated . . . reaching maturity'*: Tom Zutaut, *NME*, July 1994.

213 *'one diamond man'*: Ian Brown, *Uncut*, February 1998.

214 *'After such a whacking delay . . . good album'*: John Squire, *Big Issue*, December 1994.

214 *'best work . . . back on the map'*: Tom Zutaut, *Vox*, February 1995.

215 *'Bitterness crept in . . . would have to come round'*: Ian Brown, *Uncut*, February 1998.

215 *'having to listen to twenty guitar tracks'*: Ian Brown, *Guardian*, February 2002.

218 *'back in Manchester sorting something for his mum'*: Ian Brown, *Big Issue*, December 1994.

219 'We just thought the idea . . . we probably didn't care': John Squire, *Select*, December 1995.

219 'A nightmare . . . It was not supposed to be that dark': John Squire, *NME*, April 1996.

220 'organic, word of mouth': Tom Zutaut, *Vox*, February 1995.

222 'The reason why no British band . . . It's ours': Ian Brown, *Entertainment Weekly*, March 1995.

222 'People were asking us . . . deserved something more': John Squire, *Guardian*, September 2002.

223 'The Stone Roses were never as great . . . capricious and inscrutable': John Squire, *The Face*, March 1995.

223 'I get that vibe . . . sick of underachieving now': Reni, *The Face*, March 1995.

226 'We said, Hang on a minute . . . in ten or twelve days': Squire, *Select*, December 1995.

226 'Ian said he'd never work . . . nail in the coffin': John Squire, *Guardian*, September 2002.

226 'I need to get down to rehearsal . . . John can come down later': Ian Brown, *Clash*, April 2009.

227 'It had died . . . happy to have gone': Reni, *NME*, April 1995.

16. Robbie

230 'You ain't getting shit out of us': Mani, *Melody Maker*, April 1995.

237 'It was the most enjoyable gig we've done': Ian Brown, *Select*, December 1995.

237 'I never feel we've been overtaken . . . just retro shit': Ian Brown, *NME*, August 1995.

242 'I don't believe in the band . . . a fraud': John Squire, *NME*, April 1996.

242 'There was a chink of light': John Squire, *Q*, February 2005.

243 'You can have the vowels and I'll have the consonants': John Squire, *Q*, February 2005.

244 'There is no reason . . . remain on Geffen': Terri Hall, *NME*, April 1995.

246 'It really created a bad stink': Mani, *Scootering*, January 2004.

246 *'smash the myth . . . of the Roses'*: Ian Brown, *Melody Maker*, October 1997.

247 *'I saw arms in the air . . . definitely'*: Ian Brown, *Melody Maker*, October 1997.

17. Fifteen Years

251 *'an inspiration'*: John Squire, *Melody Maker*, May 1997.

251 *'piss all over Squire'*: Mani, Reading Festival press conference, August 1996.

251 *'I knew there was no love lost . . . no regrets'*: John Squire, *Melody Maker*, October 1997.

251 *'No chance'*: Ian Brown, *Melody Maker*, October 1997.

253 *'Ian's been unfairly savaged . . . People will remember that'*: Mani, *Q*, January 1997.

253 *'Big deal, so what? . . . like a five-year-old'*: Reni, *NME*, September 1997.

254 *'I feel I've done that . . . They do sound poor'*: Ian Brown, *Melody Maker*, October 1997.

254 *'That fucker . . . He's just empty'*: Ian Brown, *Select*, February 1998.

255 *'babies pretending to be The Beatles . . . and second's nothing'*: Ian Brown, *Uncut*, February 1998.

256 *'muso wank'*: Chris Helme, *NME*, February 1999.

256 *'There's something different . . . about Ian'*: James Lavelle, *NME*, February 1999.

256 *'impossible to create the chemistry'*: John Squire, *NME*, September 2002.

257 *'I want to put our differences aside . . . another shot'*: Mani, *Manchester Evening News*, January 2001.

257 *'I can't see the day . . . a great record again'*: Ian Brown, *Guardian*, February 2002.

258 *'I do not accept I was responsible . . . can talk again'*: John Squire, *C4 Planet Sound*, September 2002.

259 *'self-interest . . . they really are the people's songs'*: Ian Brown, *XFM*, August 2004.

259 *'It was never about money . . . changing the world'*: Ian Brown, *XFM*, August 2004.

259 *'There's a misconception I developed . . . liver with a teaspoon'*: John Squire, Virgin Radio, February 2004.

260 *'Ian blew it . . . paranoid mess'*: John Squire, *Q*, December 2004.

260 *'He split up the best band . . . last man standing'*: Ian Brown, BBC6 Music, January 2005.

260 *'The songs have bled into English culture . . . The Beatles'*: Ian Brown, *NME*, March 2005.

260 *'a ferocious guitar record'*: John Squire, *Observer*, June 2004.

261 *'hopefully have a natter . . . close the book properly'*: Mani, *Guardian*, June 2005.

261 *'Never say never'*: Reni, BBC Manchester, June 2005.

261 *'John bangs on about . . . everything by trying'*: Ian Brown, *Mail on Sunday*, May 2005.

261 *'stabbed me in the back . . . care what I wanted'*: Ian Brown, *Clash*, September 2005.

261 *'If I was in the gutter . . . re-form the Roses'*: Ian Brown, *NME*, March 2006.

262 *'I could have died because of the blood I lost'*: Gareth Evans, *North Wales Daily Post*, April 2006.

262 *'I'm enjoying this . . . back to music'*: John Squire, *Manchester Evening News*, July 2007.

263 *'I'd have a Starbucks . . . pretty great'*: Ian Brown, *Manchester Evening News*, August 2007.

263 *'Me, John and Reni are up for doing . . . the ideal time'*: Mani, *NME*, December 2008.

263 *'It would be good to do something like that one day'*: John Squire, *NME*, March 2009.

264 *'It was pretty good . . . left you for dead'*: Ian Brown, *The Word*, October 2009.

264 *'It's getting very boring . . . kiss and make up'*: Mani, BBC6 Music, August 2009.

264 *'Life's about ideas . . . coming home'*: Ian Brown, *City Life*, June 2010.

264 *'something to keep me match fit . . . Liam Gallagher in the pub'*: Mani, 'Digging a Hole', http://guestlisted.blogspot.com, January 2011.

18. Reunion

266 *'They got on great, all very relaxed'*: Clint Boon, Twitter, April 2011.

266 *'I'm disgusted that my . . . isn't happening'*: Mani, *NME*, April 2011.

267 *'They're just rumours . . . happy where I am'*: John Squire, *Daily Record*, June 2011.

267 *'It's an indictment of . . . opiate of the masses'*: John Squire, *Daily Record*, June 2011.

268 *'I've only ever had love here . . . last working-class musicians'*: Ian Brown, *City Life*, June 2010.

268 *'He would fill the Manchester Apollo . . . and played'*: Ian Brown, sleeve notes to the twentieth-anniversary edition of *The Stone Roses* album.

268 *'As far as drummers . . . quit at thirty-five'*: Reni, reunion press conference, October 2011.

269 *'even enjoyable'*: John Squire, reunion press conference, October 2011.

269 *'Just in case someone said . . . to be shit'*: Ian Brown, reunion press conference, October 2011.

269 *'mixed emotions'*: Andrew Innes, *Hot Press*, December 2011.

270 *'It's just something magical . . . hold of it again'*: Mani, reunion press conference, October 2011.

272 *'We'll ride it till the wheels fall off . . . last time'*: Ian Brown, reunion press conference, October 2011.

273 *'It goes way beyond that . . . taking this fucking seriously'*: Shane Meadows, *NME*, December 2011.

Afterword

276 *'live in a world of his own'*: John Squire, *Daily Record*, June 2011.

Bibliography

'Don't Stop': www.stoneroses.eu
'This Is the Daybreak': www.pdmcauley.co.uk
Official site: www.thestoneroses.org

Benson, Richard (ed.), *Night Fever: Club Writing in The Face 1990–1997* (Boxtree, 1997)

Bez, *Freaky Dancin': Me and the Mondays* (Pan, 1998)

Cawthorne, Nigel, *Vinyl Frontier: The Making of The Stone Roses* (Unanimous, 2005)

Chapman, Brian, *Stone Roses 'Talking'* (Omnibus, 2003)

Coryn, Stan, with Paul Scanlon, *Exploding: The Highs, Hits, Hype, Heroes and Hustlers of the Warner Music Group* (Harper, 2002)

Davies, Hunter, *The Beatles: The Only Authorized Biography* (Arrow, 1992)

Einarson, John, *Forever Changes, Arthur Lee and the Book of Love* (Jawbone, 2010)

Green, Alex, *33⅓: The Stone Roses* (Continuum, 2006)

Hann, Dave, and Steve Tilzey, *No Retreat: The Secret War between Britain's Anti-Fascists and the Far Right* (Milo, 2003)

Haslam, Dave, *Manchester, England: The Story of the Pop Cult City* (Fourth Estate, 1999)

Hook, Peter, *The Haçienda: How Not to Run a Club* (Simon & Schuster, 2009)

Middles, Mick, *Breaking into Heaven: The Rise and Fall of The Stone Roses* (Omnibus, 1999)

Nice, James, *Shadowplayers: The Rise and Fall of Factory Records* (Aurum, 2010)

O'Connell, Michael, *Ian Brown: Already in Me* (Chrome Dreams, 2006)

Read, Lindsay, *Mr Manchester and the Factory Girl* (Plexus, 2010)

Bibliography

Robb, John, *The Stone Roses and the Resurrection of British Pop* (Ebury, 1997)

Sharp, Colin, *Who Killed Martin Hannett? The Story of the Factory Records' Musical Magician* (Aurum, 2007)

Simpson, Dave, *Stone Roses – The Illustrated Story* (Hamlyn, 1996)

Taylor, Neil, *Document and Eyewitness: An Intimate History of Rough Trade* (Orion, 2010)

Acknowledgements

This book is based on interviews conducted in 2011 and 2012, and would not have been possible without the following: Bushra Ahmed, Shami Ahmed, Paul Birch, Anthony Boggiano, Johnny Bolland, John Breakell, Bryn Bridenthal, Jon Brookes, Tim Chambers, Andy Couzens, Kevin Cummins, Gareth Davies, Sue Dean, Bob Dickinson, Anthony Donnelly, Christopher Donnelly, Bruce Flohr, Pete Garner, Gary Gersh, Doug Goldstein, Paula Greenwood, Dave Haslam, Peter Hook, Steven Howard, Aziz Ibrahim, Nigel Ipinson-Fleming, Clive Jackson, Dougie James, Keith Jobling, Phil Jones, John Kennedy, Lewis Kovac, Stephen Lea, Peter Leak, John Leckie, Greg Lewerke, Steve Lock, Robbie Maddix, Howard Marshall Jones, Mensi, Tony Michaelides, Bruce Mitchell, Dennis Morris, Eileen Mulligan, Micke Murhoff, John Nuttall, Mike Phoenix, Brian Pugsley, Lindsay Reade, Dave Roberts, Eddie Rosenblatt, Phil Saxe, Paul Schroeder, Harald Sickenga, Slim, Mike Smith, Pennie Smith, Robbie Snow, Lawrence Stewart, Joe Strong, Annette Svensson, Trevor Taylor, Michael Tedesco, Ian Tilton, Mark Tolle, Geoff Travis, Tim Vigon, Geno Washington, Si Wolstencroft and Geoff Wonfor. Apologies to those who gave considerable time that is not reflected in the finished work.

Reni's manager, John Nuttall, deserves much credit for corralling many of the above, and for assisting in the accuracy and authenticity of the book – from the beginning to the end, and particularly during the sticky bit in the middle.

Thanks to Reni for the inspiration and the start; Kevin Pocklington, at Jenny Brown Associates, for the deal and support; Joel Rickett, at Penguin, for riding out the bumps; Andrew Loog Oldham for taking me to the top of the mountain; and Shirley Spence for allowing me to see clearly from it.

Index